SHAKESPEARE'S LONDON

Archaeology, History

Published in July 2012 by Museum of London Archaeology

© Museum of London Archaeology 2012

A CIP catalogue record for this book is available from the British Library

ISBN 978-1-907586-12-5

Written, designed and photographed by
Museum of London Archaeology

Illustrations: Carlos Lemos, Hannah Faux, Judit Persztegi and Faith Vardy
Photography and reprographics: Andy Chopping, Maggie Cox
Editor: Sue Hirst with Susan M Wright
Index: Auriol Griffith-Jones
Design and production: Tracy Wellman

*The cover shows a well-dressed gentleman of the period (a detail from
a maiolica bowl of c 1575–1620, made in Montelupo, Italy), against a
background of the London playhouses on the south bank (a detail from*
London from Southwark, *Dutch school, 1626–55)*

*Right: a fragment of a serving jug in Surrey-Hampshire border whiteware,
featuring a typical Tudor bearded figure with ruff, reminiscent of portraits
of Shakespeare; the piece was excavated from the Theatre in Shoreditch
(built 1576) and may have been used to serve refreshments there*

SHAKESPEARE'S LONDON THEATRELAND

Archaeology, history and drama

Julian Bowsher

CONTENTS

PLAYERS, PLAYHOUSES AND PLAYGOERS

WALKS

*Decorated maiolica bowl of c 1575–1620
made in Montelupo in northern Italy showing
a well-dressed gentleman; the pottery, the first
of its kind to be excavated in London, was
found in the city ditch outside the city walls*

ACKNOWLEDGEMENTS

Most of the historical and archaeological research has been based on decades of work arising from our excavations on London's theatrical sites. Many colleagues within MOLA have helped greatly by providing information on historical and archaeological projects: Bob Cowie, Heather Knight, Tony Mackinder, Pat Miller, Taryn Nixon, Dave Sankey, Dave Saxby, Al Telfer and Bruce Watson. Nick Holder wrote the text on the Blackfriars and Whitefriars theatres from his own research.

The Shakespearean element of this book has benefited greatly from the advice and help of a number of literary scholars and historians, architects and actors: Susan Cerasano, Ralph Alan Cohen, Sarah Dustagheer, Gabriel Egan, Sarah Enloe, Reg Foakes, Eva Griffith, Andrew Gurr, Michael Holden, William Ingram, Grace Ioppolo, Farah Karim-Cooper, David Kathman, Kent Rawlinson, Leslie Thomson, Dora Thornton and Martin White. Numerous institutions have also been most helpful: American Shakespeare Center, British Library, British Museum, Dulwich College, Historic Royal Palaces, Shakespeare Birthplace Trust, The Shakespeare Globe Trust and Shakespeare Library Group, amongst others.

There has been fantastic support, advice and encouragement from the MOLA production team – David Bowsher, Amy Chambers, Andy Chopping, Maggie Cox, Hannah Faux, Sue Hirst, Carlos Lemos, Judit Peresztegi, Tracy Wellman and Susan M Wright – which reflects the excitement we feel at discovering Shakespeare archaeologically.

FOREWORD

Museum of London Archaeology has had the enormous privilege of excavating and researching the sites of six of the famous Elizabethan and Jacobean playhouses, as well as two of the contemporary bear-baiting rings. Through my involvement with Shakespeare's Globe and the Royal Shakespeare Company I know only too well what vital facts these archaeological excavations have yielded for the theatre world. The momentous discovery of the Rose and the Globe 20 years ago showed that the working life of Shakespeare and his contemporaries could be revealed and explained through archaeology. Since then we have been lucky enough to experience that same thrill with the further discovery of the Theatre, the Curtain and the Hope.

This book is written from a unique perspective: Museum of London Archaeology has brokered an incisive partnership between archaeology, theatre, literary scholarship and even engineering to shed remarkable light on the playing venues, on the meaning of the plays and acting styles, on the vibrancy of the audiences and the origins of London's theatreland itself.

A. Michael Hoffman
Chairman, Museum of London Archaeology (MOLA)
Former Director, Shakespeare Globe Theatre and Royal Shakespeare Company

INTRODUCTION

In the year of the World Shakespeare Festival, this book celebrates Shakespeare's London, the city where he worked and lived. The theatre was his life and London the centre of the dazzling new theatreland of Elizabethan England.

When the sites of the Rose and Globe playhouses on London's south bank were found 20 years ago, there was an explosion of academic and popular excitement across the world. Historical documents and maps existed, and above all the play texts themselves, but archaeologists had finally provided a physical link to the actual playhouses that Shakespeare and his contemporaries knew, wrote for and acted in. Further discoveries have provided (in varying detail) the location, size and shape of these buildings – often with evidence for rebuilding or alteration – and of the stages and auditoriums. There is also the exciting evidence left behind by the people who attended and worked in these venues – audience, management and actors – their clothes, money, personal items and so on.

Museum of London Archaeology has spent over 30 years uncovering a wealth of archaeological evidence for the whole history of London. For the Tudor period, we have excavated and examined numerous sites, from domestic and commercial to ecclesiastical and palatial, enabling us to look at this 'Shakespearean' period within a greater context. Uniquely, we now have a record in pioneering the excavation of the theatrical venues described in this book. No less than eight of the sites discussed have been subject to archaeological investigation: the Theatre, the Curtain, the Rose, the Boar's Head, the Globe and the Hope, as well as two of the Bankside animal-baiting arenas. Furthermore, traces of the Whitefriars theatre were found in excavations in the 1920s. The *Shakespeare: staging the world* exhibition at the British Museum, associated with the World Shakespeare Festival of 2012, included many of the objects excavated on the London sites described here.

Of the other venues, we have pinpointed their locations with research showing whether any buried remains associated with some of them are likely to have survived. Some are known to have disappeared under subsequent development, whilst others still survive under important buildings which are unlikely to be disturbed. But there is potential for further discoveries.

A programme of full academic publication of all this work is in progress, but this book presents a timely overview for a more general audience. It sets out to give a guide to the 'entertainment' world of London in the late 16th and early 17th centuries. The book is aimed at the general reader, but will also contain sufficient synthesis of new research to appeal to actors, students, archaeologists and historians. It will concentrate on the buildings: the playhouses, theatres and other playing venues, and the bear-baiting rings, with some mention of the various inns and taverns associated with them. It will describe what led to their development, where they were and why, how they prospered or not, their rivalry and their eventual demise. Nevertheless,

Detail from Wenceslaus Hollar's preliminary drawing of c 1644 for his Long view of London, *showing the second Globe (centre top)*

there is an important human component which includes the patrons, entrepreneurs, builders, actors and audiences. 'The play's the thing', of course, and we will see what was put on where, and the evidence for staging.

The 'Shakespearean' theatre period has been defined as that between 1567 and 1642, which might otherwise be defined as that of the 'early modern theatre' within the historical Elizabethan, Jacobean and Caroline ages. Although Shakespeare was only three years old at the start, it was the year when the first definable playhouse, the Red Lion, was built. Playhouses continued to be developed and, though Shakespeare died in 1616, at least two more were built after his death. With the onset of the Civil War, Parliament closed down all the theatres and other entertainment venues in 1642; this conclusively ended the 'Shakespearean period'. The theatre that re-emerged at the Restoration in 1660 was a very different one in terms of drama and buildings.

There were many other talented and well-known playwrights within this period, but Ben Jonson anticipated Shakespeare's future impact when he declared 'He was not of an age, but for all time'. Shakespeare's fame and reputation grew so much, particularly in the 18th century, that he may be taken as a representative for all the playwrights and actors who were his contemporaries. Today, he is revered throughout the world, wherever poetry, drama and literature are taught. The national curriculum for schools in Britain stresses the importance of Shakespeare as dramatist and thus the importance given to an understanding of the original physical environment wherein 'Shakespearean' drama was first played and performed.

Although we know Shakespeare primarily as a poet and playwright, we should not forget that in his own time he was also very much an actor. Like many others he will have toured the provinces, but his London playing record included at least seven of the venues described below, ranging across town from Shoreditch to the Elephant and as far outside from Greenwich to Hampton Court.

The 'golden age of English drama' was one of the greatest cultural achievements of our history, felt nowhere as much as in London. The iconic polygonal playhouses that sprang up to cater for this appetite were unique buildings – represented today by the 'new' Globe on the south bank (Walk 4, location 6).

The book opens with thematic discussions on the history of London and the theatre, with a list of key dates for the theatre and the period. The bulk of the book, however, comprises the history and description of the individual buildings – in various categories. This will include contemporary documentary and illustrative material, as well as archaeological information where available. After these descriptions there is another section on the development, form and function of the buildings and on the human – and dramatic – activity within them.

The second narrative exploration comprises a series of 'walks' divided geographically, so that each theatrical 'area' can be looked at individually – though there will of course be cross references between the two. It is envisaged that the book can be used as a guide to the various areas of London where the original venues stood. The basic street pattern and a few alleyways survive in many areas across London, though later development has changed the urban topography enormously. Many of the theatrical buildings described in this book survived into the Restoration period, though most in the City were lost in the Great Fire of London in 1666. Some of them even survived into the 19th century and two performance venues, albeit not purpose-built theatres, survive today – Middle Temple hall in the City and the great hall at Hampton Court, south-west of London along the river. Nevertheless, there are surviving contemporary buildings around the country with quite a few in London. To be sure, most of our sites are now marked by an office block, housing or even open spaces, though many carry plaques to commemorate the theatres that once stood there, and where there are not, there should be! Though some imagination is needed to envisage Elizabethan London and find Shakespeare 'in the alley with his pointed shoes and his bells', we hope that the descriptions, maps and illustrations here will help you to explore Shakespeare's London.

We have to imagine walking the streets of London. Unless you had the money for a horse or were really wealthy enough to have a carriage, your shoes were your only means of transport – there was no alternative for the bulk of the population. Although London in the 16th and 17th century was much smaller than now, it is almost inconceivable to us to today to get from one side of London to the other without any form of mechanised transport – the taxi, bus, tube or train. For the purposes of this book I have indeed walked throughout London and timed the duration – London is and certainly was small. From central London (the City) I have reached almost every site described here, including the once rural Mile End and Elephant and Castle, within an hour, most of them much less. This was an almost negligible time for most Elizabethans. The exceptions of course, were the court venues in Whitehall and in outer London.

These walks also contain wider geographical adventures and include the sites of the churches, houses, inns, brothels and fields known to 'Shakespearean' Londoners, we can explore where they were born, lived, died, worshipped, fought, drank and whored.

TUDOR LONDON

Administrative, social and economic life

'London' was a politically independent city within the county of Middlesex, which it dominated and eventually swallowed. It was not only the largest city in England but one of the largest in Europe and, by the end of the 17th century, in the world. In our period it comprised a large diverse area. The original London was the walled city, that area on the north bank of the River Thames, enclosed since Roman times and entered by the six city gates. Upstream from the city was Westminster, the main seat of royal government. The only bridge across the Thames from the city, London bridge, linked it to Southwark, an equally ancient settlement within the county of Surrey that was nevertheless incorporated into the city in 1550. The Dissolution of the monasteries in the 1530s resulted in opening up the sometimes extensive monastic precincts inside and around the city, and London as a whole was growing enormously. Development westwards along the riverside Strand virtually joined it to Westminster and other smaller villages. There was also ribbon development along the main routes running north and east of the city, even encroaching on natural boundaries such as rivers and marshlands.

Cheapside was the principal east–west street through the city and its commercial heart. The nodal point at its eastern end, the Royal Exchange completed in 1568, was probably its centre – much as it is today. This route continued eastwards along Cornhill and then Leadenhall out to Aldgate and beyond. The main north–south route, intersecting between Cornhill and Leadenhall, was the Gracechurch Street/Bishopsgate route that stretched way beyond London in both directions.

Since medieval times, the City of London had been divided into administrative wards, under the control of an elected alderman. There were 25 wards until the incorporation of Southwark as the 26th. Some stretched beyond the city walls and, like parishes, were divided into wards within and without. The City not only contained the Livery Companies, who controlled trade and commerce, but also its own militia, the trained bands. The lord mayor, elected annually from the aldermen and at the head of the City, was also, therefore, a very important person nationally. The relationship between the City and Westminster, representing national government, was closer, largely because of financial and political interdependence, than anywhere else in the country. The presence of the royal court, let alone the law courts, attracted great numbers to London generally.

The (Anglican) church played a more important role in everyday life in Shakespeare's time than it does today, at least in administrative if not spiritual terms, for attendance on Sunday was compulsory. At one time there were over 100 churches within the city alone and there was a dense network of small parishes. They were the focus of congregation, as well as community, and local records of births, marriages, deaths and local taxation were maintained by them.

London was more than just the administrative and financial centre of the country. It was also, due to the presence of the courts and the Inns of Court, its legal centre and, because of the great teaching hospitals, a medical centre which also resulted in a fringe of quackery. Nevertheless, commerce and trade expanded throughout this period. Clothing, and associated accessories, was one of the largest contributions to the economy of London – and vital to the theatre as well. The importance of the capital as a centre of ideas, enterprise and fashion cannot be underestimated.

The chronicler John Stow, to whom we owe so much for contemporary accounts of London life, noted warily the changes in his lifetime – the overcrowding and congestion. London's prosperity and renown led to a massive increase in population during this period. It grew from c 100,000 in the mid 16th century to over 200,000 a hundred years later – the same period when the population of England as a whole leapt from 2.7 million to 5.3 million. Immigration was mostly from rural parts of England (and Britain), but there were also foreign communities here, from the Netherlands, Italy and elsewhere. Their presence reflected the international importance of London as a major port.

There were, of course, consequences to this expansion, foremost being the availability of land and the growing demand for foodstuffs. Supply from the hinterland was cursed by natural disasters: years of poor harvest, such as 1586, 1590 and particularly 1594–5, created not just a famine but price rises and riots. Hoarders and rioters alike were treated harshly by the government. Shakespeare himself was accused of holding 80 bushels of grain in 1598 (though in Stratford rather than London). The maintenance of the court created a great need for provisions which might have enhanced a market in London, but was expensive for rural communities on the route of the annual royal 'progresses'. Imports of exotica, particularly fruits from more southerly parts of Europe, greatly expanded in this period and, for some, healthier diets emerged.

There was certainly a high rate of infant mortality, but overcrowding brought other problems, particularly in sanitation: the history of the whole period was beset by outbreaks of the plague (see Key dates, below) which had repercussions for the burgeoning theatrical life, as the authorities periodically banned playing in order to reduce infection spread by congestion. In one of the worst outbreaks, from the summer of 1592 to the beginning of 1594, it is estimated that London lost about 13% of its population.

In a large area with only limited sanitation, the dung of the city was at least removed by the 'scavengers', who cleaned the streets every now and again, and carted out to the hinterland as manure by 'nightsoilmen'. Thus the increase of suburban market gardening was part of a growing cycle. Water supply was in its infancy at this period.

New buildings in the city were increasingly made of brick with tiled roofs, though there were still a lot of prefabricated timber constructions. Most buildings in the city were shops, all with individual signs like inns, and differing trades settled in different areas. Many of the larger, older buildings, however, were increasingly divided into tenements, a fate that encompassed some redundant theatres too. Timber constructions, with thatched roofs, were more common in the suburbs and the danger of fire was a constant hazard. We shall see the fate of two theatrical conflagrations later on, but for more widespread disasters the fire that devastated the area on the

A map of London, Westminster and Southwark, *by Braun and Hogenburg, 1572*

north end of London bridge in 1633 was an ominous foretaste of the Great Fire of London that destroyed some 75% of the city in 1666, 24 years after our period. Most roadways in London were unpaved at the time, though the largest had gravelled surfaces. Congestion and road conditions became worse, not just because of greater numbers using them but because of the increased use of wheeled transport, wagons for trade and new-fangled carriages by the wealthy. In the age before mechanised transport, the vast majority of the population was accustomed to walking on foot, though horses were used, owned (like Philip Henslowe) or hired (like Christopher Marlowe), by as many as could afford it. An 18th-century myth had Shakespeare's first London job being that of holding the bridles of horsemen attending the Theatre in Shoreditch. With London bridge the only crossing of the Thames, the Company of Watermen had a very lucrative business ferrying great numbers, including theatrical revellers, along and across the river.

The large social network throughout London contributed to the plethora of inns, taverns, alehouses and other institutions. A prosperous city is always an incentive for crime, ranging from

fraudulent deals and loans to burglary, such as befell the Burbage brothers' houses in Holywell Lane in 1618, to the pickpocketing by the 'cut purses'. This petty crime was often attracted to the crowds at the theatres, as was prostitution. Thomas Platter, a visitor to London in 1599, wrote that prostitutes 'haunt the town in the taverns and the playhouses'. Nevertheless, pickpocketing and prostitution were linked in damnation of the theatre generally. Anthony Munday's 1580 description is typical of many: 'Whossoever shal visit the chappel of Satan, I meane the Theatre [in Shoreditch], shal finde ther no want of yong ruffins, no lacke of harlots, utterlie past shame, who presse to the fore-front of the scaffoldes'.

There had been 'legal' brothels in Bankside since medieval times and the girls – often Flemish, adding to Londoners' xenophobia – were described as 'Winchester's Geese' after the nearby London

London from Southwark, *Dutch school, 1626–55*

'house' of the Bishops of Winchester (Walk 4, location **3**). However, the brothels along Bankside were effectively suppressed in 1546 and the poor reputation of Bankside in our period was largely unwarranted, though the presence of bear baiting and the theatre did nothing to lift it and bad associations stuck. 1603, however, saw the opening on Bankside of 'Hollands leaguer', the most sumptuous and expensive brothel in London, way above the stews and common bawdy houses. It was rumoured to have been patronised by James I, but was closed down by soldiers on the orders of his son in 1631. Thomas Nashe pointed out in his 1592 description of the 'overspreading of vice, and suppression of virtue', that there were as many, if not more, brothels in the northern suburbs: 'our unclean sisters in Shorditch, the Spittle, Southwarke, Westminster and Turnbull streete' (properly Turnmill Street, whose northern end was known as Codpiece Row). Nashe was a playwright and poet, but was not above writing erotica too: his *The choice of valentines* described brothel activities in excess even of contemporary moral standards.

Shakespeare in London

As noted above, this book is concerned with the theatrical life of London in the whole 'Shakespearean' period, but a sketch of the limited evidence for where William Shakespeare himself lived, wrote and acted would seem opportune.

Shakespeare is known to have been in Stratford in 1585 and was in London by 1592. The intervening period, when his movements are unknown, is known as the 'lost years'. His appearance in the 1590s was attacked as 'this upstart crow, beautified with our feathers, who thinks himself the only Shake-scene in a country'. This description comes from the playwright Robert Greene, whose mocking of Shakespeare was provoked by jealousy and snobbery, but certainly confirms that Shakespeare's literary career had taken off.

It is uncertain where he was living in 1592, though the early 'theatrical area' of Shoreditch is a possibility. Shakespeare may have lived in Norton Folgate or Holywell Lane (Walk 3) and it is probable that his earliest plays were put on at the Theatre. He was certainly a member of the Lord Chamberlain's (acting) company in December 1594, when he and other fellow actors in the troupe were paid for performing before the Queen in Greenwich. From this time, wherever he was in London, he remained as actor and writer with the same company throughout.

The first real evidence for where Shakespeare lived in London comes from October 1597, when he defaulted on his taxes in the parish of St Helen's, Bishopsgate (Walk 1, location **6**). It is not known exactly where he lodged but he was still recorded as a defaulter in February 1598. This time, however, he was listed as one who had either died or vacated the parish, and in fact a similar list of October 1598 notes that he was now in 'Surrey'. A reference from October 1600 narrows this down to him being in the Liberty of the Clink, on the Bankside in Southwark, ostensibly, as we

KEY DATES Those which directly relate to theatre and other entertainment are in red type

	Year	(theatre, in red)
Elizabeth became queen	1558	
plague	1563	
	1564	birth of Shakespeare and Marlowe
	1567	construction of the Red Lion
	1575	construction of the Newington Butts playhouse
Martin Frobisher discovered Frobisher Bay in Canada	1576	construction of the Theatre
Raphael Holinshed published his *Chronicles of England, Scotland and Ireland*	1577	construction of the Curtain
Francis Drake sailed around the world in the Golden Hinde	1580	
earthquake		
Drake knighted by Queen Elizabeth on the Golden Hinde at Deptford	1581	
English parliament passed laws against Catholicism		
plague	1582	William Shakespeare married Anne Hathaway
Francis Throckmorton arrested for plotting the overthrow of Queen Elizabeth I	1583	collapse of bear garden no. 3, succeeded by 3A
Raleigh founded first American colony, named Virginia after England's virgin queen	1584	
English colonists founded first settlement in America at Roanoke Island, N Carolina	1585	
Anthony Babington arrested for plotting the overthrow of Queen Elizabeth I		
Elizabeth supported Netherlands against Spain to avenge murder of William of Orange		
	1586	death of John Brayne
execution of Mary, Queen of Scots	1587	construction of the Rose playhouse
Sir Frances Drake sank the Spanish fleet at Cadiz		
Spanish Armada	1588	death of comic actor Richard Tarlton
Hakluyt's *Principle navigations, voyages and discoveries of the English nation* published	1589	
Sir John Harrington invented the water closet; one made for the Queen in 1596		
death of 'spy master' Sir Francis Walsingham	1590	
	1592	Rose playhouse remodelled
	1593	Christopher Marlowe murdered in Deptford
	1593–4	most playhouses closed because of plague
	1595	construction of the Swan
	1597	'Isle of Dogs' play banned
		death of James Burbage
	1598	conversion of the Boar's Head inn to a playhouse
		Theatre pulled down
	1599	construction of the Globe playhouse
	1600	construction of the Fortune playhouse
	1600	William Kempe dances his jig to Norwich in 'Nine Daies'
Robert, Earl of Essex, attempts to overthrow the Queen	1601	
death of Queen Elizabeth at Richmond; James I became King	1603	
plague		
Gunpowder Plot	1605	
	1606	Rose playhouse pulled down
first recorded appearance of Halley's Comet	1607	Red Bull inn converted into a playhouse
	1608	Blackfriars theatre acquired by the King's Men
	1608–10	most playhouses closed because of plague
	1609	Shakespeare's sonnets published
King James Bible published	1611	
	1613	Globe playhouse burned down
	1614	construction of the Hope playhouse/bear-baiting ring
		Globe playhouse rebuilt
	1616	death of William Shakespeare
		death of Philip Henslowe
	1617	Pocahontas attended court masque; later buried in Gravesend
Sir Walter Ralegh executed	1618	'misogynist' first used in play *Swetnam the woman-hater*
Mayflower Pilgrims set sail from London for Massachusetts	1620	
	1621	Fortune playhouse burnt down
	1623	Shakespeare's widow Anne, died
		1st folio edition of Shakespeare's plays published
death of King James I; Charles I became king	1625	
plague		
	1626	second Fortune playhouse opened
plague	1630	
plague	1636	
English Civil War broke out	1642	Parliament closed all the playhouses and theatres

noted above, in Surrey. Second-hand evidence from the 18th century suggested that Shakespeare lived near the bear garden there, right within the 'new' theatrical area of London that had largely superseded Shoreditch by this time.

Many actors still lived in Shoreditch and 'commuted' to work in Bankside. Shakespeare appears to have commuted in the opposite direction, for he is recorded as acting in Ben Jonson's play *Every man in his humour*, which was performed at the Curtain in late 1598. Shakespeare was probably still in the Bankside area when the Globe, in which he had a financial as well as professional interest, was built there in 1599. He is recorded acting in another Jonson play, *Sejanus*, put on at the Globe in 1603 and was amongst those confirmed as a member of the company, now renamed the King's Men, in May of the same year.

Shakespeare crossed back into the city by 1604, for in that year at least, he was lodging with the Mountjoy family in Silver Street in the parish of St Olave (Walk 1, location **9**). In the same year Shakespeare is listed amongst the King's Men attending the entry of James I into London. He was also named in the will of his fellow player Augustine Phillips, who died in May 1605, being left 30 shillings in gold. It is not certain how long Shakespeare stayed in Silver Street, but throughout his life in London it appears he always lived in rented lodgings, perhaps because his increasing wealth allowed him to buy properties back in his home town. It was only at the end of his time in London that he bought a property here: the Blackfriars gatehouse, in March 1613 (Walk 1, location **24**). However, this seems to have been an investment, for in that year it is thought that he finally left London and retired back to Stratford where he died on 23 April 1616.

Shakespeare and his friends at the Mermaid Tavern *(Walk 1, location **12**)*, by John Faed 1851: *Shakespeare seated in the centre, to his left Sir Walter Raleigh, leaning on the shoulder of the Earl of Southampton; seated in the right foreground with his back to the spectator is Sir Robert Cotton, with Thomas Dekker on his right; figures seated behind Shakespeare are Ben Jonson, John Donne, and Samuel Daniel; seated at the back of the table is Francis Bacon, and with him are John Fletcher, Lord Dorset and William Camden; standing in the background are Francis Beaumont, with hand extended, and John Selden with Joshua Sylvester on the spectator's extreme left*

History and development

The history of dramatic performance in Britain is outside the scope of this book, though religious spectacles, street theatre and fairground booths form part of the ancestry of the Elizabethan stage. There is plenty of evidence for playing in London from medieval times, either in the open air, in places like Smithfield or Clerkenwell, or in the great mercantile halls of the city. Commercial playing started in the late 1530s and was certainly established in London by the 1540s, when actors themselves were hiring large halls.

The growth of London, with its court, commerce and growing population that we saw above, provided the incentives for the establishment and development of theatre there. London had the largest audiences, ready-made with a thirst for leisure and entertainment, large enough to sustain the acting companies and the theatres themselves. These criteria, together with the flowering of early modern drama, created by Shakespeare and his contemporaries, made London the first home of the professional theatre.

The playwright Thomas Heywood was immensely proud of his adoptive city and very conscious of its theatrical pre-eminence. He compared it with ancient Rome, but stressed this international importance, borne out by contemporary accounts.

> Playing is an ornament to the Citty, which strangers of all Nations, repairing hither, report of in their Countries, beholding them here with some admiration: for what variety of entertainment can there be in any Citty of Christendome, more than in London?

The written history of this theatrical period itself began in the 17th century, within living memory of the people and some of the buildings. Richard Flecknoe published his *Discourse of the English stage* in 1664 and James Wright his *Historia histrionica, an historical account of the English stage* in 1699. Neither book is completely accurate and both are patchy, but they represent the beginnings of an enquiry that took off seriously in the late 18th century, with Edmund Malone's massive *Works of Shakespeare* of 1790, which reproduced and discussed many documents, such as those in Dulwich College. There followed numerous 19th-century accounts that led to the distinctive branch of literary scholarship concerned with the history of the English theatre. New discoveries of further documents squirreled away in various archives continue to be made today. The archaeological excavations of theatrical venues, which began on the south bank over 20 years ago, have continued throughout London and further discoveries are still possible.

The history of control of the theatres is preserved in governmental and municipal accounts: largely the papers of the Privy Council, the City Remembrances and the Session Records of Middlesex and Surrey.

One of the most useful sources comes from the interminable lawsuits which Elizabethans indulged in – amongst the various financial and managerial disputes are often descriptions of the

Performance at the modern Globe

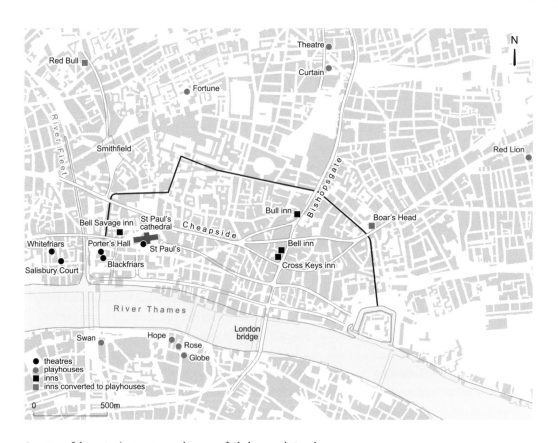

Location of the major 'entertainment' venues of Shakespeare's London

buildings or parts of them. The greatest treasures are from those concerning the Theatre and the Boar's Head, but many other venues had minor disputes that have provided snippets. The theatre owners must all have had accounts of their dealings but, uniquely, only those belonging to Philip Henslowe, owner of the Rose, Fortune and Hope but with interests in others, survive in Dulwich College, where they were deposited by its founder Edward Alleyn, Henslowe's stepson-in-law. His Rose accounts must have started in 1587, but these are lost and only those beginning in 1592 survive today, in a volume known as *Henslowe's diary*.

The Henslowe accounts also contain the only two surviving building contracts – for the Fortune and the Hope. Others must have existed, though these two provide a lineage: the Fortune contract says that the building is to be based on the Globe, and the Hope on the Swan. Most contemporary private accounts refer to events rather than the buildings, or only do so in passing. Many of the accounts by visiting foreigners, such as Johann De Witt, Thomas Platter, Orazio Busoni, Paul Hentzner and others, describe the playhouses in particular as buildings of a type unseen elsewhere. Little detail is seen on contemporary maps and panoramas, but a drawing of the Swan dated to *c* 1595/6 is the only view of a playhouse interior (p 84). Analysis of surviving stage directions has also provided clues about stages and scenery.

The rich language of the Shakespearean era is a delight and much quoted here, but some phrases demand explanation. In building terms, for example, a stand or standing usually refers to the galleries, though a scaffold can mean either the galleries or the stage. Degrees, meaning tiered seating, is another common term for galleries. The backdrop to the stage is sometimes called the *scenae frons*, after classical Roman descriptions. There is often mention of a 'discovery space' where the drawing-back of a curtain over a doorway in the *scena* would reveal further action. Behind the stage proper was the 'tiring house', where actors would get 'attired' or dressed.

It was only with the arrival of archaeology on the Shakespearean stage that concrete evidence for the shape, size and development of the playhouses emerged. Nevertheless, these buildings had been lost for 400 years and it is only the foundations and floors that have been exposed by archaeological excavation; details of the superstructure have not advanced much more than those left by the documentary accounts. The area of the largest excavation was that at the Rose in 1989, thus making it, with Henslowe's accounts, doubly unique. A small area in the north-east part of the Globe was found in the same year, but an excavation on the site of the Boar's Head in 1999 (Walk 2, location **3**) failed to identify any of the remains of that playhouse. The third Bankside bear-baiting ring was found in 1996, and its eventual successor, the Hope, in 1999. An excavation immediately south of the Theatre, in 2002, found associated buildings but structural elements of that playhouse were only found in 2008, followed by further work in 2010 and 2011. In October 2011 small areas of the Curtain were found, suggesting that further remains are preserved at the site. As a postscript we have included the fifth, or Davies's, bear-baiting ring of 1662, remains of which were found in 2004. Apart from the analysis that spatial and structural archaeological remains have provided, a wealth of objects were also discovered, which largely represent the detritus of everyday theatre life.

The phenomenon that was the 'Shakespearean' theatre in London can be divided into three categories of building, each discussed in more detail later. Firstly there were the inns within the city that hosted occasional playing. The permanent venues were the open-air playhouses, mostly purpose-built, and the indoor theatres, mostly adaptations of existing buildings. Two inns outside the city were 'converted' into permanent 'playhouses', but this was a fairly late phenomenon and indeed followed the major development of playhouses. Many of these venues were successful, some were short-lived, some burnt down and some aborted before they were finished. At the same time, as had been the custom for many years before, the professional companies were invited, albeit for rewards, to play at whichever palace the monarch was holding court. They were also engaged to play at private functions, such as the dining revels at the Inns of Court.

The explosion of theatres and playhouses in 16th-century London was a very localised phenomenon, particularly architecturally. There were other venues around Britain but usually in temporarily adapted buildings – the halls of great houses or the universities.

Few Elizabethan Englishmen would have been acquainted at first hand with the great theatres of ancient Greece and Rome, or even those of Renaissance Italy, though many were aware of them and of contemporary vernacular parallels. The *corral* playhouses in Spain started appearing in the 1570s. They were square or rectangular and some even survive today. The Ottoneum in Kassel in Germany was a permanent stone structure built in 1604–7, but the square timber theatre in Gdansk of *c* 1613 was based on the London Fortune. Both these playhouses were known to, and occasionally used by, touring English players.

According to numerous contemporary accounts, including the Fortune and Hope building contracts, the playhouse buildings had three tiers of galleries surrounding an open yard into which projected the stage. Behind the stage was the tiring house, which also served as a storage space and management offices.

Most timber-framed buildings of the time were largely prefabricated off-site and assembled when the foundations were completed. Economy of construction, however, is most clearly illustrated by evidence for reused materials. Until inflation caused a reversal in the 19th century, material was a far more expensive component in a building project than labour. Perhaps the clearest example of this is the second-hand timber (albeit from a former playhouse) used to build the Globe. The 'penthowsse shed' added to the Rose in 1592 was made out of 'owld tymber' and archaeological work found other reused ship's timbers there.

Permanent theatre may be said to have begun with the 'Act for the punishment of vagabonds' of 1572, which required all actors to be in permanent repertory companies under the patronage of great nobles. In 1604, under James I, it was reissued as the 'Act for punishment of rogues, vagabonds and sturdy beggars', which now emphasised royal patronage. The 1572 act provided some security for those players who were under influential patronage. A company of Lord Leicester's Men were established in 1574, with James Burbage at their head, and those under the names of Lords Sussex, Warwick, Essex and Oxford followed thereafter. All spent time, as players always had, touring the country, but also relishing the opportunity of playing at court in or near London. Conscious of what they had unleashed, the Queen's Privy Council, whose grasp on national power overrode the courts' and parliament's opposition, kept a careful eye on the companies. Their eye was the Master of the Revels, first appointed in 1545 as a royal courtier in control of the Office of Revels. In 1574 there was a 'calling together of sundry players and supervising, fitting and reforming their matters'. This was the beginning of a scrutiny, or censorship, of play texts to be performed, firstly at court, but then in all public places where rehearsals were also monitored. A fee for licensing plays by the Office of Revels is often recorded throughout Henslowe's papers. The Office was also responsible for selecting plays, and companies, for presentation at court. For most of our period the Master was Sir John Tylney, appointed in 1579. His long Mastership ended with his death in 1610 and he was succeeded by his nephew, Sir George Buck, who had been his deputy for the last few years. At one point the dramatist John Lyly had hoped for the post and a few years later Ben Jonson was said to have been interested too. Buck was succeeded in 1622 by Sir John Astley, who sold the office to Sir Henry Herbert, brother of the poet George Herbert.

The Office of Revels itself provided carpenters and painters to create and decorate performance spaces and tailors would make the costumes. The increase in royal pageants in the Tudor period needed storerooms for material and after a brief spell in the buildings of the former Black Friars they moved to St John's Gate (Walk 3, location 9) in 1560. The Office moved from St John's in 1608 to occupy the cloister in the former Whitefriars, immediately east of the hall where the theatre was established two years earlier. A few years later it moved again to St Peter's Hill, which led down to the river from St Paul's Churchyard.

Other 'government departments' associated with performances at court included the Office of Works. This had the responsibility for the construction and maintenance of royal properties, including palace theatre spaces. Its relationship with the Revels can be illustrated by the career of Sir Thomas Blagrave, who was Acting Master of the Revels in 1573–9 and Surveyor of the Queen's Works 1578–90 under Queen Elizabeth. The other associated department was the King's Wardrobe, which kept the royal jewels, clothes and arms, and was increasingly associated with the Office of Revels in providing for performances and masques. Edward III had established the Wardrobe in 1361, with offices and storerooms just west of Blackfriars, where it remained until destroyed in the Great Fire of 1666 (Walk 1, location 19).

The City authorities, as much as most municipalities in the country, were sceptical of playing and sought to restrict any such congregational activities. Apart from playing, these could include bowling alleys, puppetry and animal baiting, all of which might have corrupting influences conducive to gambling or worse.

The greatest opposition was expressed by the Church, since these activities brought competition to divine attendance – though it should be noted that many players and playwrights were themselves devout. The more puritan wing of the Church went much further by decrying the profanity of the stage, though it was the preconceived association with the other evils described

Queen Elizabeth I, c 1575
(unknown artist)

above that created the greatest fury. Nevertheless, the playwright Thomas Dekker admitted the collusion of the theatre and prostitution in his 1608 description of the underworld, stating that 'pay thy tuppence to a player' and 'in his gallery mayest thou sit by a harlot'.

There are hundreds of examples of this fury, one being Anthony Munday's 1580 description of the Theatre in Shoreditch as a 'consultorie house of Satan', and theatres clearly contained 'light and lewd disposed persons, [such] as harlots, cutpurses, cozeners [swindlers] pilferers &c who under colour of hearing plays, devised divers and ungodly conspiracies'. Stephen Gosson remarked, with apparent historical precedent, that 'Our theatres and playhouses in London are as ful of adulterie as they were in Rome'. Many poor women ended up in Bridewell, ostensibly a refuge for destitute women but in reality a prison for prostitutes (Walk 5, location **1**). The governor's accounts, however, furnish us with many details of prostitution at the theatres.

Actually, the authorities were not all necessarily puritans themselves, though they shared some of their concerns. They were worried about dangers to public health, where crowded infectious conditions, particularly in hot summers, invited outbreaks of the plague, which intermittently killed thousands of Londoners in bad years. Occasional closures of the theatres meant nothing worse than that Londoners were denied a few months' entertainment and that the players had to go on tour.

Their main concern, as Robert Ashton points out, was with public order and the fear of disorder and riot arising from anti-social behaviour, which might be whipped up by suggestive, theatrical activity. Even the Privy Council periodically banned plays that were perceived to be politically dangerous, such as the *Isle of Dogs* at the Swan, *Richard II* and the *The game of chess* at the Globe.

Although the 1572 Act changed the nature of playing, there was still a lack of permanent and secure venues in which actors could perform. It is often remarked that the playhouses, in particular, were situated outside the city because of Puritan opposition; but, though there may have been some civic concern, their location was much more to do with the cost, availability and development potential in the less crowded suburbs. Conversely, the indoor theatres within and adjacent to the city, supposedly given more toleration because of an undoubtedly higher social composition, were all located within existing buildings. Neither was the distinction between urban and suburban strictly valid, since the playhouses were all situated in, admittedly slightly less crowded, built-up areas.

The first playhouse, the Red Lion, may have been some distance out of town, but the quibbles that John Brayne had with his builders do suggest that he knew what he was doing in terms of location and construction. His next venture, with his brother-in-law player, James Burbage, at the Theatre in 1576, would seem to address the issue of a permanent home, particularly in the light of the 1572 Act. Players, or their companies, usually had limited resources and the construction of new purpose-built theatres was a hazardous commercial venture, more often undertaken by speculators, which is where Brayne may have come in. The player James Savage, building (or converting) a new playhouse in Newington Butts at the same time, was perhaps the first 'player developer'. We do not know enough about the Curtain, but Burbage may have started Leicester's Men off at the Theatre. In 1583 Tilney was asked to choose 'a companie of players for her Majestie', which clearly took the pick of the available bunch resulting in the formation of the Queen's Men, who certainly played at the Theatre in the 1580s with greater security from the puritan diatribes. Romantic narratives had been the staple diet in these early playhouses and the Queen's star player was the clown Richard Tarlton, whose extempore, and often smutty, outbursts and jigs delighted the simple audiences. By the time Tarlton died in 1588, there were new dynamic dramas in blank verse, such as Kyd's *Spanish tragedy* and Marlowe's *Tamburlaine*, which represented a change in tastes. This might explain the impetus, after a gap of 11 years, for a new playhouse, the Rose, on the south bank.

The comic actor, Richard Tarlton

There were different types of theatre management. We are not sure how the earliest ones operated, though Jerome Savage was the lead player in Warwick's Men and probably ran the Newington Butts playhouse as a company venture. At the Theatre, James Burbage was in the same situation with Leicester's Men. At the Rose, Henslowe, not an actor but an entrepreneur, rented his playing space to acting companies. He probably had contracts with them and was ever ready to lend them money for props and costumes, though he was not above legal action when players deserted – as some did to the Swan in 1595. Langley, therefore, was probably the same type of landlord. A change came in, certainly by the time that the Globe was built, when the Burbage brothers formed a partnership of sharers (shareholders in the modern sense) with the senior players of the Lord Chamberlain's Men. This system slowly developed in other venues, when selling shares produced ready assets for the initial development. Alleyn sold shares in the Fortune, and Beeston, almost reluctantly, did the same at the Phoenix. Nevertheless, Richard Heton, who took over management of Salisbury Court theatre in 1637, issued a manifesto that distinctly adhered to the original style of management, allowing him to 'hire and fire' his actors.

The competition and rivalry that developed between the different theatres and playhouses was as much to do with the playwrights and their productions. The Rose might have appeared as a breath of fresh air, compared to the old stale drama at the earlier playhouses. The boys' companies, in the smaller indoor theatres, below, could not compete with the larger playhouses in the new heroic genre of Kyd and Marlowe. In November 1588, however, the country was rocked by a writer under the pseudonym Martin Marprelate, who issued pamphlets violently denouncing the Anglican Church. The Church itself counter-attacked with 'anti-Martin' plays commissioned from well-known writers such as John Lyly, Thomas Nashe and Robert Greene. The affair fizzled out after a couple of years, but the authorities were so shaken by national discord that an even firmer eye was kept on all theatrical activity. From the summer of 1594, the newly-established Chamberlain's Men, resident at the Theatre, and the Admiral's Men, resident at the Rose, were the two main playing companies. It is probable that they were the only two licensed companies and for the next six years they were the only ones invited to play at court. There were other venues in London at the time, but they lacked any permanent acting companies.

Even after this time the heroic genre was still paramount, but by the end of the century different tastes were emerging. Jigs, hitherto danced at the end of a play, were largely abandoned and henceforth only appeared at the remaining playhouses in north London. Writing styles changed, certainly with Shakespeare's success with the Chamberlain's Men causing William Kempe, Tarlton's successor as clown, to leave the company and move to the Rose in its last years. There was also a market now for 'local' London plays of which Thomas Dekker's *Shoemaker's holiday* of 1599 was one of the earliest. Dekker was also one of the major figures in the 'war of the theatres', which was largely a rivalry between Dekker, John Marston and Thomas Middleton on one side, who were satirising what they perceived as Ben Jonson's pride. Marston's *Histriomastix* was answered by Jonson's *Every man out of his humour* and so on, until Dekker completed the sequence

Portrait of a 21-year-old Corpus Christi student dated 1585 and thought to be of Christopher Marlowe

William Shakespeare, portrait attributed to John Taylor

with *Satiromastix* in 1601. Nevertheless, little permanent harm was done as Marston and Jonson, together with George Chapman, collaborated in writing *Eastward ho* in 1605, but its apparent anti-Scottish satire landed Jonson and Chapman in jail – though Marston escaped.

The divergence of tastes became obvious with the emergence of the indoor theatres, whose entry prices alone created social differences in audience composition. The Whitefriars and Blackfriars were in almost the richest part of London, 'scituated in the bosome of the Cittie', with a ready audience amongst the gentlemen scholars at the nearby Inns of Court. The Curtain, Fortune and Red Bull were situated in the poorest parts, and produced popular or 'citizen' drama. However, they were still successful and the jibes about the Red Bull's lack of sophistication were probably exaggerated. The most successful company was the Chamberlain's Men, now the King's Men, who from 1608 had two venues, the Globe used during the summer and the Blackfriars during the winter. Although there was a social difference in the two locations, there is plenty of evidence that the same play could be performed at both venues.

Playwrights were often actors too and usually wrote, often in collaboration, for companies rather than specific venues; different stages could be adapted as needs be. Their 'playbooks' were seldom published and were jealously guarded by the various companies, under the control of the 'book-keeper', for whom they represented quite an investment. However, play texts were usually included in the annual Stationers' Register which 'registered' the right of the printer to publish it. This was maintained by the Stationers' Company of London and an important source for the play texts of the period. They were sometimes not recorded until a year or so after performance, but occasionally provide the performance venue and usually the author. Most printers and booksellers were located in St Paul's Churchyard, the roadway just south of the cathedral.

Playwrights at the time were usually not so well known as the players. Richard Tarlton was one of the theatre's earliest 'stars', and his jibes, jokes and improvisation brought him almost national popularity. Then there were the giants of the stage, like Edward Alleyn, who excelled in the bombastic roles that Christopher Marlowe created for him. His fame and acumen made him very rich, and he is as much remembered for his founding of Dulwich College. His main rival was Richard Burbage, the son of James, for whom Shakespeare wrote some of his greatest tragedies. He was particularly noted for the realism he engendered on the stage. A eulogy written after his death in 1619 noted:

> He's gone and with him what a world are dead.
> Which he review'd, to be revived so,
> No more young Hamlet, old Hieronimo
> Kind Lear, the Grieved Moor, and more beside,
> That lived in him have now for ever died.

Audience behaviour had changed since the days when the groundlings in the yard had slanging matches with the likes of Tarlton on the stage. Nevertheless, even by 1602 Shakespeare, himself an actor too, was famous enough for the following story of his relation to Burbage to have circulated.

Portrait of Edward Alleyn (1566–1626), dated 1626

Richard Burbage (?1573–1619), early 17th century; possibly a self-portrait

> Upon a time when Burbidge played Richard III there was a citizen grew so far in liking
> with him, that before she went from the play she appointed him to come that night unto
> her by the name of Richard III. Shakespeare, overhearing their conclusion, went before,
> was entertained and at his game ere Burbage came. Then message being brought that
> Richard III was at the door, Shakespeare caused return to be made that William the
> Conqueror was before Richard III.

Playwrights and actors had their rivalries shown in, for example, the war of words between
Robert Greene and Shakespeare, and the (fatal) duel between Ben Jonson and Gabriel Spencer in
Hoxton Fields (Walk 3, location 4). Few were as financially successful as Alleyn; Thomas Dekker,
for example, was continually being imprisoned for debt.

Due to the popular demand that the playhouses and theatres created, there had to be a constant
supply of new plays. Plays were performed six days a week – revivals and reworked older favourites
were not enough. Rehearsals could be minimal and actors usually learnt only their own lines,
relying on cues from the prompter. Printed 'playbills', announcing the impending production of
a (new) play, would be pasted up or distributed around town. They would name the date, venue,
playing company and the title of the play, but seldom the playwright. Despite what we know of
them from contemporary references, none survive for the playhouses or theatres, but an undated
example, advertising a bear baiting is preserved in the Henslowe papers. When the day arrived the
'last call' would be blown on a trumpet atop the building, as seen at the Swan. This was clearly
an early practice as, already in 1578, a sermon thundered at the 'competition' of the playhouse
drawing away 'audiences' from their devotions: 'Will not a fylthye play, wyth the blast of a
trumpette, sooner call thyther a thousande, than an houres tolling of a bell, bring to the sermon
a hundred'. The other form of announcement, also seen at the Swan and in other well-known
illustrations, was the flying of a flag, as a 1612 text records: 'Each play-house advanceth his flagge
in the aire, whither quickly at the waving thereof are summoned whole troops of men, women,
and children'.

In 1599 Thomas Platter recorded that playhouse performances commenced at about 2pm and
a poem by Sir John Davies, a few years earlier, suggests that they were open until 6pm. Although
drama was clearly the main entertainment, there were also songs and dances set to music, usually at
the end of a play. Many of the playhouses and theatres boasted a 'music room, usually backstage',
and the Henslowe papers record instruments owned by the Admiral's Company.

In 1596 William Lambarde noted that entrance to the playhouses (and bear-baiting rings) required
the visitor to 'first pay one pennie at the gate, another at the entrie of the Scaffolde, and a thirde
for a quiet standing'. Three years later Thomas Platter, in describing the playhouses, recorded that:

> There are, however, separate galleries and there one stands more comfortably and moreover
> one can sit, but one pays more for it. Thus anyone who remains on the level standing pays
> only one English penny: but if he wants to sit, he is let in at a further door, and there he
> gives another penny. If he desires to sit on a cushion in the most comfortable place of all,

where he not only sees everything well, but can also be seen, then he gives yet another English penny at another door.

This system is confirmed by the Swan drawing (p 84), which shows an *ingressus*, or internal doorway, up into the galleries, and by excavation evidence from the Theatre and the Rose. The 'third penny' for a more exclusive place seems to be related to those lords' or gentlemen's rooms whose locations are uncertain. Money was collected by the 'gatherers', stationed at the main and internal doorways, and placed in 'money boxes'. At the end of the day, these were broken open and emptied into what at the Theatre was described as 'The Commone boxe', which had a lock and key. This was obviously kept backstage, in a room now known as the 'box office'. A similar system operated at the more expensive indoor theatres, like the Blackfriars, which had a 'Doorkeeper at the Play-house door, with his Boxe like a church-warden'.

Henry Peacham, in a warning of the dangers of London, recounted a story (possibly apocryphal) of a lady at a theatre in the 1630s.

> A tradesman's wife of the Exchange, one day when her husband was following some business in the city, desired him he would give her leave to go see a play; which she had not done in seven years. He bade her take his apprentice along with her, and go; but especially to have a care of her purse; which she warranted him she would. Sitting in a box, among some gallants and gallant wenches, and returning when the play was done, returned to her husband and told him she had lost her purse. 'Wife, quoth he, did I not give you warning of it? How much money was there in it?' Quoth she, 'Truly, four pieces, six shillings and a silver tooth-picker'. Quoth her husband 'where did you put it?' 'Under my petticoat, between that and my smock.' 'What,' quoth he, 'did you feel no body's hand there?' 'Yes,' quoth she, 'I felt one's hand there, but I did not think he had come for that'.

Apart from the presence of cut-purses and prostitutes relieving one of money and goods, there could be institutional swindling, such as at the Swan in 1602 or the Hope in 1614, when the audience paid to get in but there was no performance.

You could even be minding your own business at a play and be rudely interrupted by the press gang. Soldiers were wanted for campaigns in Flanders in 1602 and the London authorities were desperately trying to fulfill their national quota. The writer Philip Gawdy recorded how desperate they were.

> Ther hath bene great pressing of late, and straunge, as ever was knowen in England, only in London, and my L. Mayor and the rest of the Londiners have done so contrary to their Instructions from the Lordes of the councell ... All the playe howses wer beset in one daye and very many pressed from thence, so that in all ther ar pressed ffowre thowsand besydes fyve hundred voluntaryes, and all for flaunders.

Affrays, as well as accidents, at the playhouses and theatres could be a danger too. Apart from brawls, there were occasionally life-threatening dangers. At the Fortune in June 1613, one Nicholas

Bestney, son of a magistrate, was stabbed in a fight. There could be accidents too, though the first account, at an unknown playhouse, may be apocryphal. An earlier, 1587 letter from Gawdy almost gleefully describes this event, to illustrate the (moral and physical) danger emanating from the playhouses.

> My Lord Admyrall his men and players having a devyse in ther playe to tye one of their fellows to a poste and so to shote him to deathe, having borrowed their callyvers one of the players handes swerved his peece being charged with bullet missed the fellowe he aymed at and killed a child, and a woman great with child forthwith, and hurt another man in the head very soore.

At the Red Bull in March 1623, a felt maker's apprentice, John Gill, was on the stage (albeit as a member of the audience), when he was accidentally hurt by an actor's sword.

As if that was not bad enough, there were natural disasters to contend with too. The third bear garden on Bankside collapsed in January 1583 with great loss of life (p 154) and in August 1599 a house in St John Street, Clerkenwell, where a 'puppet play' was being performed, fell down killing six people outright and wounding 30 or 40 more. There were also the fires that burned down the Globe in 1613 and the Fortune in 1621. Although the fire at the Globe only took two hours to burn the building to the ground, there were no casualties. 'Only one man had his breeches set on fire, that would perhaps have broiled him, if he had not by the benefit of a provident wit put it out with bottle ale.' Another disaster that befell the playhouses (and much of south-east England) was the earthquake of 6 April 1580, reported by a number of writers, including Richard Tarlton, who mention damage in various areas of London including, according to Thomas Churchyard, at the Theatre and the Curtain.

> A number being at the theatre and the curtayne in Hollywell, beholding the playes, were so shaken, especially those that stoode in the hyghest roomes and standings, that they were not a little dismayed, considering, that they coulde no waye shift for themselves, unlesse they woulde, by leaping, hazarde their lives or limmes, as some did in deede, leaping from the lowest standings.

The playing companies

The many playing companies, established under royal or aristocratic patronage, which graced the London stages actually spent as much time playing in the country outside. Many players were actually kept within noble households from the early 16th century, though we try to define a London period for them here. Confusingly, they switched names, venues and personnel so much within our period, that it is difficult to keep track of them. Royalty and nobles changed their own titles, some companies seemingly disappeared only to re-emerge at a later date; many amalgamated –

sometimes only temporarily. The players, and playwrights, often switched allegiance. As Andrew Gurr has said, they were virtually playing a game of 'musical playhouses'.

The accompanying table illustrates the main companies of our period with, as far as can be established, their foundations, change of names and the inns, playhouses and theatres where they performed. Many of these companies also played at court and other private venues.

NAME	DATE FOUNDED	VENUE(S)	DATE DISSOLVED OR TRANSFERRED
Children of the Chapel; later known as the Revels Children	medieval	1600–08 2nd Blackfriars (1610–11 Whitefriars}	dissolved 1609
Warwick's Men	c 1575	Newington	dissolved 1580
Sussex's Men	1570s	mostly provincial but great success at the Rose 1590s then back to the provinces	dissolved 1609
Leicester's Men	1572	?Theatre	dissolved 1588
Pembroke's Men	1575	Theatre	dissolved 1593
Pembroke's men revived	1595	Swan	dissolved 1597
Children of Paul's	1575 1599	St Paul's playhouse	1590 1606
Howard's Men	1576	not known	became Admiral's Men 1590
Admiral's Men	1590	Theatre, Rose, Fortune	became Prince Henry's 1603
Prince Henry's Men	1603	not known	became Palsgrave's men 1613
Palsgrave's Men	1613	Fortune	became Prince Charles's [II] men 1631
Prince Charles's [II] Men	1631	Salisbury Court, Red Bull, Fortune	
Oxford's Men	1579	absorbed Warwick's; mostly played in the country but also performed at court; ? Newington, Theatre	joined Worcester's to form Queen Anne's 1603
Worcester's Men	158?	Rose	joined Oxford's to form Queen Anne's 1603
Queen Anne's Men	1603	not known	
Queen's Men	1583	Bull, Bell, Theatre	dissolved ?1594
Strange's Men	1583	Cross Keys, Rose, Newington	dissolved 1594
Chamberlain's Men	1594	Newington, Theatre, Curtain, Globe (as Hunsdon's 1596, at Swan)	became King's Men 1603
King's Men	1603	Globe, Blackfriars	
Queen Anne's Men	1603	Boar's Head, Curtain, Red Bull, Phoenix	became Revels Company 1619
Revels Company	1619	Red Bull	dissolved 1623
Duke of York's Men	1608	not known	became Prince Charles's [I] Men 1612
Prince Charles's [I] Men	1612	Hope, Red Bull, Phoenix, Curtain	dissolved 1625
Lady Elizabeth's Men	1611	Swan, Phoenix	became Queen Henrietta Maria's Men 1625
Queen Henrietta Maria's Men	1625	Phoenix, Salisbury Court	

THE CITY INNS

Introduction

Today we drink in a public house, or pub, but there were a number of different drinking establishments in Shakespeare's time. An inn was originally the town house of a lord, a bishop or a rich merchant, but it had come to mean anywhere that provided accommodation, where your carriage would deposit you or where you would stable your horse, as well as food and drink. Their form varied but commonly they comprised a number of buildings, linked by alleyways and courtyards, all ultimately deriving from the medieval courtyard house. There were also the smaller establishments such as the taverns that sold wine and the cheaper alehouses that sold only beer. The most ephemeral were the tippling houses, many of which were unlicensed and consequently often shut down. Most of the larger establishments would once have had their own 'brewhouse', but by the 16th century a division between wholesale brewers and retail victuallers was developing.

Inns, being valuable properties often owned by rich and influential citizens, were less stringently regulated than the taverns and alehouses, because the Company of Innholders had long provided some self-regulation. Nevertheless, the association of playing meant that they were frowned on by the increasingly anti-theatre authorities. A Court Order of February 1569 allowed innkeepers to present plays if licensed and only if they produced bonds for £40 – a lot of money. Interestingly, this was the first attempt to target owners rather than the actual players. Thereafter numerous regulations were concerned with overcrowding, for fear of the plague, and with performances that competed with church attendance. Increasingly, therefore, such playing was only allowed between November and March, and only for a couple of hours in the afternoon.

As we saw above, there had been commercial dramatic performances in London for many years. These took place within a variety of venues but mostly, it appears, within indoor halls such as those of the livery companies. Inns were occasionally used and there are references to plays being put on at two of them outside the city: the Saracen's Head in Islington (Walk 3) and the Boar's Head outside Aldgate (Walk 2, location **3**), both in 1557. Interestingly, there is no evidence for playing in specific London inns after 1557 until the mid 1570s, which is when the purpose-built playhouses began to appear. This means that the four inns described here were competitors, rather than antecedents, of the playhouses. Like these earlier venues, the four inns listed below only had occasional performances and did not cease being inns; they were inns before, during and after their period of hosting plays, though the opportunity to provide victualling to playgoers cannot be denied. In contrast, the later Boar's Head and Red Bull were permanently converted into playhouses and specifically ceased being inns. Indeed, they were converted long after the open 'amphitheatre' form of playhouse had taken architectural root.

The preamble of an Act of London's Common Council from December 1574 contains the usual concerns about playing, 'the inordinate haunting of great multitudes of people ... to

The George in Borough High Street

playes, enterludes and shows, namely occasions of affrays and quarrels, evil practices and incontinence', but here related to 'the great inns' which are physically described as 'having chambers and secret places adjoining their open stages and galleries'.

For many years it was assumed that these inn performances took place within an open yard. Part of the audience will have been in the remaining yard space, as well as in the three tiers of galleries, similar to those at the surviving George in Borough High Street, Southwark (Walk 4, location **17**) – much like the open-air playhouses. However, if there was only one yard, any playing would seriously hamper the normal traffic of the inn's day-to-day business. John Taylor' *Carrier's cosmography*, published in 1637, is a sort of 'timetable' that shows just how heavy the traffic in and out of London was in the early 17th century, almost certainly similar to the 1570s. Moreover the stabling of the horses would usually be off a yard. The evidence from most provincial inns is predominantly of indoor playing and rarely for yard playing. Where there were multiple yards in a larger establishment, such a yard could be used. There is evidence that two of the four inns discussed here, the Bell Savage and the Bull, hosted performances in yards, whilst those at the Bell and Cross Keys must have been indoors. Nevertheless, any stages in the yards must have been temporary affairs, perhaps on trestles. Many inns also hosted fencing displays, as part of the qualifications for the London Company of the Masters of Defence; these were unlikely to have taken place indoors and indeed such displays are recorded at the Bell Savage and Bull (below), but not at the other two. They are also recorded as taking place at the Theatre and Curtain playhouses, particularly in 1582–3, when the plague was rampant in the city, forcing the fencers to find similarly spaced venues outside.

The Bell Savage

The Bell, or Bel, Savage inn was situated on the northern side of Ludgate Hill, just outside the city walls – but within its jurisdiction – abutting the Fleet prison (Walk 1, location **17**). It dated back to at least 1420 and was originally called the Bell; Savage was thought to have been an early innkeeper.

Fencing displays at the Bell Savage were known as early as 1562 when one of the fencers was accidentally killed. The first indication of plays being performed there is from George Gascoigne's *The glasse of government* of 1575 and a Bridewell account recounts a couple having a drink before 'they went to a playe at the Bell savedge' in 1576. William Lambarde's *Perambulation of Kent*, also dating from 1576, has an important description of London's entertainment at the time.

> No more than suche as goe to Parisgarden, the Bell Savage, or some suche common place, to behold Beare Bayting, Enterludes or Fence playe, can account of any pleasant spectacle unlesse they first pay one penny at the gate, another at the entrie of the scaffolde, and a third for a quiet standing.

Paris Garden was a famous centre of bear-baiting rings and the passage certainly suggests that the Bell Savage was well enough known for 'enterludes' or plays by then. Moreover, it is important for the description of a three-tiered entrance procedure, paying progressively more for better accommodation. It was the same system as that used in the playhouses until the beginning of the next century; Lambarde's second edition of 1596 adds the Theatre.

There is no evidence of any specific acting company performing at the Bell Savage, though a 1633 account stating that Christopher Marlowe's *Dr Faustus* was performed here in 'Queen Elizabeth's days' may be fictional. Richard Tarlton, the famous clown, had visited fencing displays here and gave his last 'jest' – impromptu recitals prompted by requests from the audience – in 1588. The only properly attested, and illustrated, show here was by the performing horse Marroccus in 1595.

The original layout of the Bell Savage is not known; there was no plan of it that predates its destruction in the Great Fire of 1666. Two yards are shown on Ogilby and Morgan's map of 1676. The larger triangular stabling yard was to the north, surrounded by the inn proper, and abutted onto the walls of the Fleet prison to the north-west. The narrower but longer yard was to the south, running north–south with the entrance to the stabling yard at its north end. This is shown as *c* 32ft (*c* 10m) wide (east–west) and 100ft (*c* 30m) long (north–south) on the 1676 map, surrounded partly by the inn and partly by other houses and shops. The southern-most yard might have been used for playing here, as this would not have disrupted access to the main buildings and other yard, allowing the inn to maintain its primary function. However, it has also been noted that there was originally a third yard on the western side, not rebuilt after the fire, that would have been better suited for playing.

Interestingly, there is evidence for a stage at the Bell Savage in 1590, albeit used for a fencing bout 'to be played at the Bell Savage upon the scaffold, where he that went in his flight faster

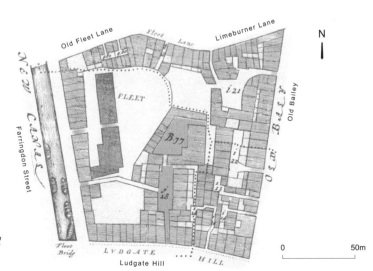

Detail from Ogilby and Morgan map, 1676, showing the rebuilt Bell Savage

William Bankes and his performing horse Maroccus Extaticus *at the Bell Savage in 1595*

back than he ought … should be in danger to break his neck off the scaffold'. The scaffold here means the stage and that it was unusually high off the ground. Otherwise the only indication of the yard is the illustration to *Marroccus Extaticus* which does not, obviously, include a stage, but clearly shows people standing in a gallery.

The Bull

The Bull inn in Bishopsgate was the largest of the four inns discussed here (Walk 1, location **5**). Fencing bouts were recorded there from 1573 and it appears to have been one of the most popular venues for this up to the 1590s. The earliest record of the Bull as an occasional playhouse is from 1578 when John Florio wrote:

> Where shall we goe?
> To see a playe at the Bull, or els to some other place.

In 1583 the new Queen's Company of players was licensed to play 'at the sygnes of the Bull in Bushoppesgate streete and the sygne of the Bell in Gratiousstreete, and nowhere els within this Cittye ... upon Wednesdays and Saturdays only', presumably alternately. Tarlton was a member of the Queen's and they are said to have 'oftentimes' played at 'the bull in Bishops-gate-street' and Tarlton once had a pippin (apple) thrown at him on the stage there. The writer Robert Greene mentions a 'playe at the Bull within Bishopsgate during the Christmas holydaies' in a pamphlet of the 1590s. In 1594 it was said that 'plays and interludes were continually acted' there.

This inn survived the Great Fire so its appearance on the Ogilby and Morgan map is as it was in the 1570s. This shows that it was quite a large complex stretching from Bishopsgate to Broad Street.

Detail from Ogilby and Morgan map of 1676, showing the Bull inn

Here there were three yards, the easternmost was entered through a long passageway from Bishopsgate and another eventually led to Broad Street. A third, however, the northernmost, had only one entranceway and was not, therefore, a throughway. According to the map, it was an irregular rectangle measuring *c* 45 x 35ft (*c* 14 x 11m), which would have been the obvious place for a playing yard.

The Bell

The Bell, which also dated back to the 14th century, was a little to the south of the Bull and just north of the Cross Keys (Walk 1, location **3**). Bell Alley, its original access, still exists, though confusingly a plaque in its entranceway commemorates the Cross Keys whose entrance was some 25m further south. Also, just on the northern side of Bull Alley is a newly established Cross Keys inn.

There are no records of fencing displays at the Bell and the first note of playing there was in a Bridewell prison account about an adulterous couple who 'went to a play at the bell in Gratious street' in May 1576. According to an account of the Revels Office, an otherwise unidentified play called *Cutwell* was performed there in February 1577. Interesting new evidence also reveals that at 'the Bell … in Graycious street … a certain interlude called '*A playe to be played*' was to be performed by the appointment of the said John Brayne and James Burbage' in January 1578. Brayne and Burbage were proprietors of the newly opened Theatre, but it seems that they hired the Bell for this particular production, which was to include the two sons of John Hinds whose acting and musical prowess was well known. In the event the boys were absent and it is not known if the production happened. As we have seen at the Bull, the Queen's Company was also licensed to play at the Bell from 1583. Tarlton had been playing there before he strolled down to the Cross Keys.

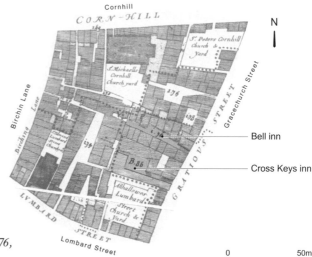

Bell inn

Cross Keys inn

Detail from Ogilby and Morgan map of 1676, showing the Cross Keys and the Bell inns

The Bell only had a single long yard in the middle of a passageway/alley that ran westwards from Bishopsgate towards St Michael's churchyard. This was limited space for traffic and the yard, only 20ft (6m) wide according to the Ogilby and Morgan map, would hardly have been available for any form of performance. Playing must have been elsewhere; here we have evidence from a lawsuit of 1597 (by which time playing at the inns had stopped) that there was at least one indoor hall, on the first floor, almost certainly at the south side of the Bishopsgate entrance. The Bell was consumed in the Great Fire of 1666, but the representation of its layout on the Ogilby and Morgan map of 1676 is thought to reflect an accurate rebuilding of it.

The Cross Keys

This was situated on the west side of Gracechurch Street just north of its junction with Lombard Street (Walk 1, location **4**). It had only one alleyway that eventually led out to the south-west. The yard was small and obviously full of traffic that would have left no room for playing.

The Cross Keys was certainly in use in the summer of 1579 as James Burbage was arrested 'as he came down Grace Street towards the Crosse Keys there to [see] a playe'. We should also note that the performing horse Marroccus also appeared at the Cross Keys, where Tarlton (who died in 1588), having just come from the Bull, saw him. The first evidence for any company there was from November 1589 when the Lord Mayor tried to ban 'all plays within the City' and ordered two companies, the Lord Admiral's Company and the Lord Strange's Players to desist, but the latter 'in very contemptuous manner departing from me, went to the cross keys and played that afternoon, to the greate offense of the better sorte'. In 1594 the Lord Chamberlain noted that 'my nowe companie of Players have bin accustomed for the better exercise of their qualities ... to plaie this winter time within the Citye at the Crosse keys in Gracious street' and it should be noted that the new Chamberlain's Company was largely founded from former members of Lord Strange's now defunct company.

This interesting but poorly documented period of playing within the city inns came to an end in the 1590s. In November 1596 people living in the smart Blackfriars area complained about James Burbage's plans to build a playhouse there as 'all players being banished by the lord mayor from playing within the Cittie by reason of the great inconveniences and ill rule that followeth them, they now think to plant themselves in the liberties'. Certainly no playing in the city inns is heard of after this date, but no definitive ban has been found. However, a Privy Council Order of June 1600 was quite explicit: 'it is forbidden that anie stage plaies shalbe plaied, as sometimes they have bin, in any common inn for publique assemblie in or near about the Cittie'.

THE PLAYHOUSES

Introduction

'Playhowsse' was the most commonly used word for theatres generally in this period. It usually referred to the open-air type of building like the Globe, described, by Johann De Witt in 1595/6, as 'amphitheatres' on account of ancient parallels. There was also a difference in terms of 'public' and 'private' playhouses/theatres and this distinction between outdoor 'playhouses' and indoor 'theatres' (as opposed to theatre generally) is used for convenience in this book to differentiate between the two types of building. It was also a bit of a misnomer, as both venues were open to anybody, though the difference in entrance prices certainly reflected differing classes of audience. The playhouses were larger and more crowded than the theatres; the largest, latest playhouse could hold up to 3000 spectators. At their most basic, these buildings were polygonal wooden structures with three tiers of galleries and an open yard into which projected a raised stage. There were the 'groundlings' standing in the yard and a seated audience in the galleries, as well as higher priced 'boxes' – often referred to as lords' or gentlemen's rooms. The central yard was open to the skies without any protection from rain and even the early stages had no, or very little, cover over them.

Cuthbert Burbage stated in 1635 that his father 'was the first builder of playehowses, and was himselfe in his younger yeeres a player'. He was referring to the building of the Theatre in 1576, but the statement is not quite true: documents discovered in the 1980s reveal that the first, the Red Lion, was built by John Brayne out in Stepney in 1567. Moreover, the second such playhouse, the unnamed one in Newington Butts, was in fact started a little before the Theatre, which now takes third place. Actually Cuthbert would have known about the Red Lion at least, as Brayne was his uncle, but loyalty to his father must have been a factor in his statement. We can see another reason for the statement today, because these two earlier playhouses were, in the first case, probably temporary and, in the second, almost certainly a converted house. If the playhouse type was defined by cost, size, permanence and influence, then the Theatre can be counted as the 'first'. It was certainly the first to be built in the now familiar polygonal form followed by others into the 17th century. Another asset was that the Theatre was situated much closer to the city, for wider availability and accessibility to audiences. Its success might be measured by the appearance the next year of the Curtain, only 200 yards (183m) down the road, and the Rose on the south bank ten years later. Despite the timespan the three appear to have been of similar dimensions and design.

Improvements in design and staging had certainly been made to the Rose, but it appears that with the Bankside Swan of 1595 there was a distinct development in size and grandeur. A Dutch visitor Johann De Witt recorded that of the four playhouses he saw in London in 1595/6 – the Theatre, Curtain, Rose and the Swan (the Newington Butts playhouse was probably no longer in operation by this time) – the two northern ones were distinctly tattier. He then noted and famously sketched the Swan because it was by far the largest and most magnificent, probably because it was also the newest. The two others of this group, the Globe of 1599 and the Hope of 1600, appear to have been the same size and the Globe was certainly said to have been magnificent.

Chronologically, the Fortune of 1600 comes between the Globe and the Hope, but as it was 80 foot square (24.4m), it does not fit easily into the development of the polygonal playhouses. Moreover, the two inns fully converted into playhouses, the Boars Head and the Red Bull, were also certainly rectangular.

Mention will also be made of two abortive attempts at playhouse construction, the George inn which was to be converted into a playhouse and the unnamed project in Nightingale Lane which was probably a new construction. There is no one year when all these playhouses existed together and their evolution was slightly haphazard.

The Red Lion, Whitechapel, 1567

In 1567 the 26-year-old John Brayne, Citizen and Freeman of the Grocers' Company, embarked on what is now recognised as the first public playhouse of the 'Shakespearean' era. All we know about it, however, comes from two court cases brought by the luckless Brayne – later described by Edward Alleyn's brother John as 'a plain and simple man' – whose legally complicated theatrical career we will come across again. Brayne was the brother-in-law of the older James Burbage; they both lived in the same city parish of St Stephen, Coleman Street. It has been speculated that Burbage's acting career, with the Earl of Leicester's Company, had already taken off by this date and that it was he that encouraged Brayne to build a playhouse. From what we know of Burbage, it is hard to dismiss any interest he might have had in this project.

Amongst the bizarre aspects of this scheme was the decision to build it about a mile outside the city walls at the far end of Stepney 'in the parish of St Mary Matfellon, otherwise called Whitechapel without Aldgate' (Walk 2, location 7). However, there may have been influencing factors. The plague, always a recurrent theme in the history of London, had been particularly bad in 1563 and Bishop Grindall of London thought that it might perhaps have been caused, and certainly exacerbated, by the profusion of plays and players in the city. In 1565, therefore, the Court of Aldermen prohibited professional playing in any 'taverns innes, victualling houses or in enny other place or places' where money might be 'demanded colleted or gatherede'. There was some softening of the ban the next year when the Lord Mayor allowed playing, but only through a licence costing the great sum of £40.

There might have been some sense, therefore, in establishing 'any other place' outside the city, in a small but prestigious area already well known for its fairs and the annual mustering of the London militia. It was a popular location for city revellers and there is indeed evidence that a play was performed there in 1501 – though probably at a private royal audience.

Performance at the modern Globe

The playhouse was to be situated within the 'court or yard lying on the south side of the garden belonging to the messuage or farmhouse called and known by the name of the sign of the Red Lion'. This farmhouse may also have already had a history of providing refreshments and entertainments in the area, and the creation of a playhouse there might have been an attractive idea. It was to be ready for a play called *The story of Samson* to be performed there on 8 July 1567. Brayne employed two carpenters to build the venue: William Sylvester to construct the audience 'scaffolds', or galleries, and John Reynolds the stage. From here on, the project spiralled downwards.

By 15 July, Brayne went to the Carpenters' Company to complain about deficiencies in Sylvester's scaffolds. Although there is no description of the actual scaffolds, a deputation from the Carpenters' Company went to inspect them and secured promises that they would be completed satisfactorily by the coming Saturday. Over a year later Brayne then sued Reynolds for costs over the construction of the stage. Here there are at least fragmentary details, which were copied into the legal dispute. The galleries were already under way by the time Reynolds was contracted to 'frame, make, or build and set up' a 'stage for interludes of plays', which was to be 'in height from the ground five feet of assize and shall be in lengthe north and south forty foot of assize and shall be in breadth east and west thirty foot of assize'. There would also be a 'certain space or void part of the same stage left unboarded in such convenient place' to be determined by John Brayne. Reynolds was also to 'make, frame and set up' a 30ft (9m) wooden turret set on the ground but rising up through the stage. It was to have a little room at the top, 7ft (2.1m) high. This part of the building was to be ready on 8 July, though Reynolds later said that it had, in fact, been finished early.

There is no further evidence for performances or use of the Red Lion as a playhouse. It may have lasted just for the summer of 1567 or been used for a couple of years. It seems to have been an expensive mistake – one that Brayne would not unfortunately learn from. Nevertheless, these few details provide some idea about the form of our first playhouse. As it was situated in the yard or court, we surmise that it was rectangular, though there was no mention of a building as a whole and perhaps it was only meant to be temporary, or at least, seasonal. We know little of the galleries but the stage dimensions (12.2 x 9.1m) reveal it to be larger than many of its successors and it is the only stage whose height (1.5m) was recorded. Moreover, it appears to have had a trapdoor which is an early indication of staging potential. The 9m turret or tower, with its 2m top room, may be reminiscent of medieval features or it might be the precursor of the later tiring houses with their little huts on top.

Newington Butts, 1576

The unnamed playhouse was situated in a field called Lurklane at Newington Butts – today the Elephant and Castle area (Walk 4, location **21**). The owners of the land, as they had been owners of the whole area for hundreds of years, were the Dean and Chapter of Canterbury Cathedral. Richard Hicks, a 'yeoman of her majesty's guard', took a lease on a large plot of land in 1566; he promptly enclosed part of the Lurklane field and built a messuage or tenement on it. This was clearly an investment, as Hicks almost certainly lived in the city. He had other property interests, however, as he also leased land near the Curtain and must have known his fellow guardsman, Henry Laneman.

The description is mostly consistent in its account of there being one building, though by 1596, Canterbury described the site as containing 'one messuage or tenement heretofore by one Richard Hicks, deceased, erected and built upon parcel of the said lands, now called the playhouse, with all houses gardens or orchards thereto adjoining'.

Jerome Savage, a leading player with the Earl of Warwick's company, took a sub-lease on the Lurklane property at an unknown date before 1576, for on 25 March of that year he extended it to 30 years with Hicks. Savage had probably been there for a while and is recorded there in the Sewer Commission records in 1576, 1577 and 1578.

Warwick's Men had only really come into being in early 1575 and for the next five years they appeared to be quite successful and performed at court in the winters of 1575–6 and 1578–9. Other well-known actors in the company were the Dutton brothers, John and Lawrence. It is possible then that Savage, with an acting company behind him, had converted Hick's 'messuage or tenement' into a playhouse in 1575 or early 1576 – before Burbage's leasehold of the Theatre site, which was a new rather than refreshed lease, was signed on 13 April 1576.

In 1577 Savage brought an action against Hicks and his son-in-law Peter Hunningborne, who were trying to oust him from the property. They pretended that by an earlier agreement – which, of course, they could not produce – Hicks had promised the site to Hunningborne. As part of their defence they claimed that Savage was a 'very lewd fellow and liveth by no other trade than the playing of stage plays and interludes' and that this 'lewd and loose life' had been noted by the parish priest and other honest neighbours. This invective was clearly designed to appeal to the anti-theatre faction – indeed the vicar of Newington at the time, Stephen Bateman, was a well-known Puritan. However, it also indicates that this lewd behaviour – for which we might read 'acting' – had been going on some time, which further suggests an early construction of the playhouse. Hicks can hardly, therefore, have created the playhouse himself, as he would have been subject to the same opprobrium. However, since Hunningborne was clearly running it a few years later, it has been suggested that they saw a successful business opportunity and became covetous.

Although no court decision is recorded, Savage was still there in 1578 so the attempt to oust him had failed. However, Warwick's Men dissolved in 1580, partly because the Duttons left it to join the newly formed Earl of Oxford's company, and Savage, newly married, also moved away from the area. It is possible that the new company moved into the playhouse then, perhaps under a new arrangement with Hunningborne. Curiously, it is only from this year that we have the first mention of its operation. In May 1580 the Privy Council complained that 'certain players do play sundry days every week at Newington Butts' in contravention to an earlier order that all playhouses close until Michaelmas (29 September) 'for avoiding of infection'. In 1586 they wrote to the Surrey justices to restrain playing in Newington, again because of the plague.

There is evidence that at some time in early 1593 Lord Strange's Men were playing at Newington three days a week, while their normal venue, the Rose, was temporarily closed. This comes in an undated response of the Privy Council allowing the company to return to the Rose. The reasons given, possible exaggerations to favour the Rose, were that Newington was some way away and that there had not been much playing there for a while. Our last notice of playing at Newington was also related to a temporary closure of the Rose. The Lord Admiral's and the Lord Chamberlain's companies were to play there alternately in June 1594.

These references are interesting for a number of reasons. Firstly they suggest that Philip Henslowe had some arrangement with the Newington playhouse, whether as a tenant or even manager. Secondly, his list of what plays were put on there in 1594 shows that the repertoire included works by Christopher Marlowe and William Shakespeare. Lastly, therefore, it is probable that Shakespeare acted there, possibly in 1593 and almost certainly in 1594.

There can be little known about the building itself, but if it was a converted 'tenement or house' it was probably rectangular, with an open yard area. In April 1577, however, Hunningborne went to the site to 'view the reparacions' which, since playing had been going on for at least a year, may have meant alterations or improvements which, as we will see below, was common to most playhouses. Hunningborne was denied entry at the time, scuffling with Savage, but later said that his interest was in living there. This was almost certainly a ploy, though since the building had been converted he might have meant a reconversion.

It seems probable that the 1594 performances were the last in Newington and that Hunningborne had wearied of the place, for soon after the Canterbury owners leased the property out to one Paul Buck. This new lease included the clause that 'he shall convert the playhouse to some other use uppon the saide grownde and not suffer anie playes there after Michaelmas next'. Buck seems to have been swift in complying, as the description in another Canterbury document of April 1595 refers to the site as comprising a 'mansion house and tenement latelie builded by the foresaide Richard Hicks'. Another Sewer Commission inspection of October 1599 recorded that the site comprised 'the houses where the old playhouse did stand', which suggests a reconversion.

The exact location of the playhouse plot can be calculated by recourse to later documents. After wartime damage, the whole Elephant and Castle area was completely remodelled in the 1960s and the site of the playhouse now lies below the traffic roundabout (Walk 4, location **21**). Any archaeological work in the area is highly unlikely, whatever state any buried remains may be in. The site remains important, however, as a development from the Red Lion, in that identifiable personalities, players and plays are associated with the building. Indeed it is also the first playhouse to be built, albeit converted, by a player.

The Theatre, Shoreditch, 1576

The Theatre has always been prominent in the list of 'Shakespeare's playhouses', partly because it was thought to be the first such built and because of Shakespeare's known association with the building. Shoreditch is often, therefore, regarded as the earliest home of the playhouse development. John Stow wrote in 1603 that there were there 'two houses for the shewe of activities, Comeddies, tragedies and histories for recreation. The one of them is named the Curtayn in Holy well, the other the Theatre. They are on the bak-syde of Hollywell towards the filde.' Another contributory factor to the fame of the Theatre is the wealth of information gleaned from legal documents first published a hundred years ago. The location of the site has been known for almost as long, though it is only within the last decade that archaeological excavations have revealed part of it.

As we saw above, the licensing of players under the protection of a great lord was made in 1572. In 1574 the Earl of Leicester confirmed his patronage of a company of actors with the actor James Burbage at its head. Such protection was certainly necessary in London, where the greatest profits were to be had, so that the establishment of a permanent purpose-built venue was the next step.

How Burbage came across the property in Shoreditch is uncertain, though it has been suggested that Hugh Richards, one of the tenants at the site, actually lived in the same Coleman Street parish in the city as the Burbages and probably knew them. In any case, Burbage took out a 21-year lease on 13 April 1576 on a site that lay within the precinct of the former Holywell Priory, dissolved in 1539 (Walk 3, location **1**). To the west lay the open Finsbury, or Holywell, fields, but to the east and south was the prosperous settlement of Shoreditch. The leasehold comprised an area situated between the modern Curtain Road on the west and New Inn Broadway on the east, and from New Inn Yard on the south to the northern end of New Inn Broadway. From the outset, Burbage was clear about his intended use of the site: he would 'erect or set up in the gardens or void ground a theatre or playing place'. The garden or empty space was behind the street frontage; excavations have shown that there were considerable remains associated with the former priory in this area, though it was clearly demolished before the lease was signed. There were other buildings within the leasehold that Burbage agreed to repair and maintain at a cost of £200 within the next 10 years.

James Burbage had nothing like enough money for the project and persuaded his younger brother-in-law, John Brayne, to supply most of the necessary funds. Burbage promised that they would be partners and would share the profits. Nothing was ever written down but the two of them were often regarded as partners by others. Nevertheless, 'Brayne did think himself aggrieved … of the said James Burbage'. This led to prolonged legal action and fisticuffs. John Grigges, the carpenter who later built the Rose (below), testified that it was mostly John Brayne's money that paid for the construction of the Theatre and that he 'hyred workmen, provided Tymber and all

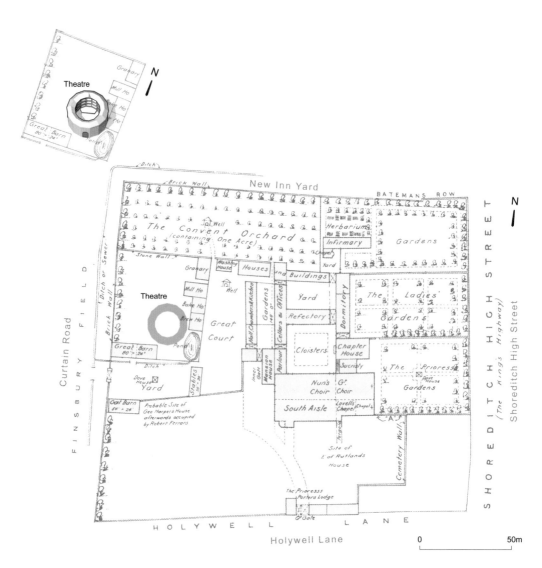

Medieval Holywell Priory in a conjectural plan of 1922, with the Theatre superimposed; inset detail of the Theatre reconstruction

other nedefull thinges for ther building of the said Theatre'. In the end, the Theatre cost about £700 to build, but Griggs also noted that so desperate was their financial situation, that they were putting on plays there even before the building was fully finished in order to produce income. Financial problems continued for many years and the property was mortgaged on more than one occasion.

The earliest evidence that it was in use was on 1 August 1577, though what might have been played or performed is not certain. The earliest fencing match attested at the Theatre was on the 25 of the same month, followed by many others up to the 1590s. The Theatre must have been attracting audiences from an early date and if 'disturbances' are any indication, it was also a popular venue for most of its life. Already in October 1577, there was said to be a 'brabble' there. 'Illicit assemblies of people to hear and see certain ... plays and interludes put into effect' at 'a certain place called the Theatre in Hollywell' were reported on 21 February 1580, causing 'great affrays, reviling, tumult and near insurrections, and divers other malefactions'. Another 'great disorder was committed at the theatre' in April of the same year, though a 'brawl at the Theatre door' in June 1584 was caused by a discontented individual named Browne.

Any disturbances caused by crowds of playgoers were certainly matched by the violent behaviour of the Burbage family itself. James Burbage was described as a 'stubborn fellow' and we have seen him resorting to violence. He was particularly unscrupulous and he spent a lot of time trying to belittle Brayne, his wife and their sometime partner/creditor Robert Miles (no angel himself). When challenged for his unconscionable behaviour, Burbage retorted that 'he cared not a turd for Conscience', and when Margaret Brayne and Miles later tried to claim half the Theatre profits, they were chased away by Richard Burbage and his mother wielding broomsticks.

Within this rich and troubled history, the Theatre's legal and financial situation must have led to some uncertainty. A witness in one of the law cases remembered that in 1592 'the said James Burbage lost much money by that controversy and trouble, for it drove many of the players thence because of the disturbance of the possession'.

There were probably quite a number of acting companies that played at the Theatre, but direct evidence is scarce. It is probable, however, that the first intended tenants of the Theatre were Burbage's own company, Leicester's. When they played at court in March 1576 they were described as 'Burbage and his company'. If they were at the Theatre, it was only intermittently, since they are recorded on tour throughout the country and abroad most of the time, and it was the Earl of Oxford's Men who were playing there at the time of the riot in April 1580. Many of Leicester's Men defected to the newly-founded Queen's company in 1583, and it may have been from this year or shortly after that the Queen's appeared at the Theatre. They were there in 1584 and, at some time before his death in 1588, their comic star Richard Tarlton made lewd remarks at the Theatre to great applause. The Admiral's Men were there by 1590, when they might have performed Marlowe's *Dr Faustus*. After a row with Burbage the next year, they left for the Rose on Bankside. By 1594, however, the Lord Chamberlain's company were there, probably headed by Burbage's son Richard and many others, including Shakespeare, whose *Hamlet* was probably performed there in 1596.

There are numerous references, in passing, to structural components and elements in the lengthy legal accounts. These help to define the building as the usual timber-framed structure of the time, though it appears to have been so constructed that it could have been partitioned into tenements if necessary. Timber, wainscotting and 'suche like thinges' appear to have been reused from nearby buildings. £40 worth of ironwork was used, but there was timber, lead, brick, tile, lime and sand left over. Randolph May, a painter, worked in the building, which may suggest a decorated interior. There were frequent mentions of galleries entered by stairs through a door and with 'upper rooms'. There was a 'Theatre yard' in the centre and an 'attryring housse or place where the players make them readye', presumably backstage.

Like most buildings, there appears to have been 'further building and repairing of the Theatre or playhouse', in the winter of 1591–2. There are no details of this work, but it cost between £30 and £40. Although 'repairs' proper may well have been needed after 16 years, it is likely that improvements were made in order to maintain and enhance the Theatre's prominence; it is interesting to note that the five-year-old Rose on the Bankside was undergoing greatly more expensive refurbishment at precisely the same time.

The Theatre itself was only found in 2008 and, though further excavations continued in 2010 and 2011, only a small north-east segment has been revealed. Its location slightly further east than expected was, logically, nearer the roadway now known as New Inn Broadway. Within the limited area of excavation no trace of the outer wall itself was revealed, though two pads, one of brick to the north and one of ragstone to the north-east, mark its position and would have supported the main upright timbers of the frame. The better-defined line of the inner wall, represented by brick foundations, lay 12ft 6in (3.8m) from the line of the outer wall. There was also a square foundation pad, of randomly coursed bricks, ragstone and chalk blocks, on the line of the inner wall, which would have supported another one of the upright timbers there, thus marking the division between two bays. About 3m further west there was a distinct angle into the yard that might define the north-eastern edge of the stage. To the east of the inner wall pad was a short section of brick and tile floor projecting into the yard that may have been part of an *ingressus* or entrance into the galleries, appropriately in the centre of a bay. Abutting the inner wall was a slightly south-sloping gravel yard surface. It had a shallow eroded area parallel to the gallery wall that suggests rainwater erosion from the eaves of the overhanging roof.

Although the remains are limited, the angles of the wall foundations suggest that the building was a polygon of 14 sides with an external diameter of *c* 72ft (22m) (see pp 165 and 171 for reconstruction). These dimensions are very similar to those found at the Rose, which was a much larger and, therefore, better defined excavation. However, this logically means, of course, that the Rose must have been based on the earlier Theatre.

Elsewhere, the excavations revealed buildings to the north-east, which were probably those

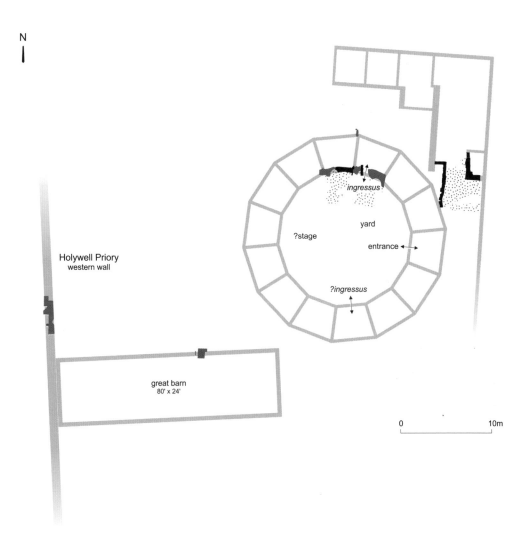

Plan of the excavated remains (in black) of the Theatre

The inner wall (dotted outline) and yard of the excavated remains of the Theatre, view looking south-east

old priory buildings noted in the 1576 lease, still occupied contemporaneously with the Theatre. Just south of these buildings and adjacent to what must be the north-east quadrant of the Theatre was a very fine cobbled yard surface, which may have served as a forecourt perhaps opening into New Inn Broadway. The entrance to the theatre itself would have been just to the south of the area of archaeological excavation.

Archaeological investigations in 2001–02 found traces of the western perimeter, or curtain, wall of the priory and a fragment of the 'Great Barne' – exactly where Braines had predicted it in 1917. This was known to measure 80 x 24ft (24.3 x 7.3m) and thought to abut onto the west wall of the priory complex. By the time that the Theatre was built, the barn had become rather dilapidated and, as Burbage was required to maintain these older buildings, it was propped up by the Theatre itself. The discovery of the Theatre slightly further east than conjectured meant that only the north-east corner of the barn could be near enough to be propped up by the Theatre. In one of the law cases, witnesses were asked whether the barn was indeed propped up by the Theatre and one testimony stated that 'one end of the Barne did fale to suche ruyne as that they weare Constrayned to underproppe yt wth Shores'. This would suggest that the location of the 'Great Barne' and its relation to the Theatre is correct.

The lease on the Theatre site was due to end in April 1597 and the Burbages started negotiating with the landlord, Giles Allen, for a new lease the year before. James Burbage died in February 1597, leaving his sons Cuthbert and Richard in debt. Allen, perhaps wary of the Burbages, demanded numerous conditions to be met, claiming that maintenance on the leasehold properties and even back rent had not been fully met. This deadlock continued until late 1598 when the Burbage sons realised that nothing further could be gained and decided to recoup some of their losses by dismantling the Theatre for its building material.

Meanwhile, the Lord Chamberlain's Men had moved to the Curtain down the road. Everard Guilpin's epic poem *Skialethia* captured the last moments of the troubled building:

> But see yonder,
> One like the unfrequented Theater
> Walkes in darke silence and vast solitude.

Giles Allen sued the Burbage brothers and their contractors for trespassing on the site, 'demolishing' the Theatre and taking away the timbers, as he believed that the building was now his. In fact, the original 1576 lease had allowed Burbage to 'take downe and carie away part of the saide new building' or carry away 'tymber and stuffe'. On or about 28 December 1598, 'Peeter Streete the Chefe carpenter' and 12 others 'did enter upon the premises and take down the saide buildinge' – ie the Theatre. The Street family had been neighbours of the Burbages in Coleman Street many years before (Walk 1, location **15**). After dismantling it they did 'take and carrye awaye from thence all the wood and timber ther of unto the Banckside in the parishe of St Marye Overyes and there erected a newe playe howse wth the said Timber and wood'. In fact the raw materials salvaged from the dismantled Theatre were then 'sett yt upp upon the premiss [ie the

Globe site] in an other forme and that they had covenanted with the Carpenter to that effect'.

It was not just Giles Allen who got it wrong in 1599. In the 20th century a myth grew up that the Globe was the old Theatre 're-erected', that the dimensions and layout of the Globe were exactly the same as the Theatre. Assumptions of the size of the Globe were transposed backwards to make the Theatre much larger than it really was. In the most extreme scenario, the Theatre was secretly dismantled overnight and its timbers slid across the frozen Thames to build the Globe before Giles Allen was aware of what was going on. Coming back to reality, the contemporary descriptions cited above are enough to dispel the Theatre into Globe myth – it would take quite a long while to remove the wooden pins from every single joint of such a building. Giles Allen did not wake up to find the Theatre gone; he was away in the country and only learnt about its demolition weeks later. The truth lies in the history of building projects, which shows that the most expensive component, up to the 19th century, was material rather than labour. Historical accounts are full of references to reused materials and nearly every archaeological excavation of structural remains from Roman to post-medieval reveals reused material from older buildings. Finally, we now know the relative sizes of the Theatre and the Globe, which shows that the former was considerably smaller than the latter.

The Curtain, Shoreditch, 1577

The history and location of the Curtain have presented problems to scholars for many years. The scant available evidence is ambiguous, but limited archaeological excavations in 2011, east of Curtain Road, revealed late 16th-century foundations that are probably the Curtain. As noted above John Stow wrote in 1603 that the 'Curtayn in Holy well' was near the Theatre, 'on the bak-syde of Hollywell towards the filde'. This would suggest that it was nearer Finsbury, or Holywell, Fields, east of Shoreditch High Street, and the name must derive from Curtain Road, itself from the curtain wall of Holywell Priory. However, other evidence suggests that it was south of Holywell Lane, thus south of the priory itself.

The site has generally been associated with the Curtain estate, or Close, recorded in 1567 and 1572, and with greater clarity in 1581 as a 'house, tenemente or lodge commonlie called the Curtayne' with a parcel of land. The site of this 'house' has been identified as the Curtain Court shown on 18th-century maps, which led Hackney Council to place a commemorative plaque to the playhouse on no. 18 Hewett Street (itself an 18th-century road) as an approximate location (Walk 3, location 2). Whether this was the same building as the playhouse still remains uncertain.

The Curtain is thought to have been built just after the Theatre, because it was not mentioned in an order of August 1577, which only mentions 'the Theatre and such like' (though this is not conclusive). The Curtain was certainly open for business by December of that year, when it is mentioned with its neighbour as a 'school for wickedness'; from this time on the two Shoreditch playhouses are frequently damned together. The Curtain was certainly hosting fencing matches from 1579.

Even if the Curtain was built in 1577, it has never been certain who built it. However, attention has focused on Henry Lanman or Laneman, a Yeoman of Her Majesties Guard and a minor courtier. By his own testimony he had 'the profittes of the playes done at the house called the Curten', which suggests a proprietorial role. Lanman was a tenant in Curtain Close in 1581, which means he leased one of the properties there. Another tenant there at the same time was Richard Hicks, another Yeoman Guard, who was probably the same Richard Hicks who was the (absentee) owner of the Newington Butts plot. Lanman certainly owned the Curtain in 1585, when he made a curious deal with Brayne and Burbage at the Theatre. The two playhouses were to share profits for a period of seven years, up to 1592, and Lanman described the Curtain as an 'easer' to the Theatre. It has been suggested that this might actually have been a protracted way for Burbage to buy the Curtain. At some point, possibly from 1592, shares in the building were sold off, as the wills of a number of actors, as late as the 1620s, record Curtain shares amongst their bequests. The Swiss visitor Thomas Platter, whose accounts have provided so much theatrical information for London at the time, went to see a play near Bishopsgate in late 1599 that can only have been at the Curtain.

The Privy Council tried to close down the Curtain in 1600 but it was still open in 1601. There was certainly some change by 1611 when the freehold changed hands and the 'Curtain ... wherein they used to keep stage plays, now or late in the tenure and occupation of Thomas Greene, his assignee or assigns'. As we have seen the assumption that the building was no longer a working playhouse is wrong. More interesting is that Greene, a leading member of the Queen's Men, appears to have had some management role in the Curtain in the year before he died. As theatrical performances tailed off there is much evidence for fencing displays at the Curtain, though a curious 'prognistication' for 1623 promised that:

> About this time, new playes will be in more request, then old; and if company come currant to the Bull and Curtaine, there will be more money gathered in one afternoon than will be given to Kingsland Spittle in a whole month. Also, if at this time about the houres of foure and five it waxe cloudy and then raine down-right, they shall sit dryer in the Galleries than those who are the understanding men in the yard.

Evidence for the dramatic history of the Curtain, and which acting companies occupied it, is equally sparse. Apart from the fact that it was open for business from 1577, the earliest record of a playing company there was in a March 1584 petition by the City to close down the Shoreditch playhouses. This mentions the Queen's Men (known to be at the Theatre) and Lord Arundell's Men, who must have been at the Curtain. The Lord Chamberlain's Men took up residence at the Curtain by September in 1598, when they left the Theatre and before they moved to the new Globe in mid 1599. Shakespeare was one of this company and thus will have known the Curtain, certainly; he is listed as an actor in Ben Jonson's *Every man in his humour* put on there in 1598. Moreover, it is almost certain that his plays *Romeo and Juliet* and *Henry V* were premiered at the Curtain. John Marston's satirical *Scourge of villainy* of 1598 hints at *Romeo and Juliet* receiving 'curtain plaudities'. If *Henry V* was indeed premiered here, then the prologue reference to 'this wooden O' would refer to the Curtain rather than the Globe.

The Queen's Men appear to have been at the Curtain in 1603–4. Another physical reference comes in the line of an audience 'that fill up this round circumference', from the epilogue of *The travels of the three English brothers* by William Rowley, John Day, and George Wilkins, performed by Queen Anne's Men at the Curtain in 1607. Rowley was also recorded as having 'played a woman's part at the Curtaine Play-house', though at an unknown date. A minor work by Wentworth Smith, *Hector of Germany,* was published in 1615 with the information 'As it hathe beene publickly acted at the Red Bull and at the Curtayne by a companie of young-men of this Cittie', who were probably an amateur company.

Intermittently from *c* 1620 until 1625 the Curtain was occupied by Prince Charles's [I] company and they might have performed the play or ballad '*The man in the moon drinks claret* as it was lately sung at the Curtain, Holy-well'.

It was only in the 1611 description (above) that there is a definition of the playhouse; 'that large messuage or tenemente, built of timber and thatched, now in decay, called the Curtaine'. Its polygonal shape, now the standard playhouse form, is hinted at in the dramatic descriptions of the 'wooden O' and the round circumference (above) but we now have graphic evidence too. An undated engraving, *The view of the cittye of London from the north towards the sowth*, was once thought to include a view of the Theatre but it has now been conclusively identified as the Curtain. This small representation is almost certainly stylised, but it appears to show a playhouse with three storeys and a single door at the base. Above, one can see a little tower, from which flies a flag, over the ridged hut that would be over the stage. The other interesting aspect of the view is that there appear to be two 'stair turrets' built onto either side of the building. This was an innovation in playhouse design that was to do with audience entry, discussed in more detail below. Nevertheless, they represent additions to the structure that suggest a renovation at some point, perhaps just after its reported decay. The orientation suggests that it did indeed front Curtain Road, with its stage opposite on its eastern side. There is also one possible piece of evidence about the building from *Hector of Germany*, played at the Curtain, which contains a stage direction to 'sit on the rails'. These are hardly likely to have been the low rails seen at the front edge of indoor stages in the 1630s and 40s, but might be the balustrades fronting the lords' rooms or 'boxes' adjacent to the stage. Sometime between 1611 and 1615, the Venetian Antonio Foscarini described the visit of his servant to the Curtain and mentioned audiences in the yard, in a 'box' and in the galleries.

A preliminary archaeological evaluation was undertaken in a small area south of Hewett Street and east of Curtain Road (at NGR 533284 182188). The modern ground surface lies at *c* 15.20m OD and the average height of what is probably the playhouse yard is at 12.10m OD, though there

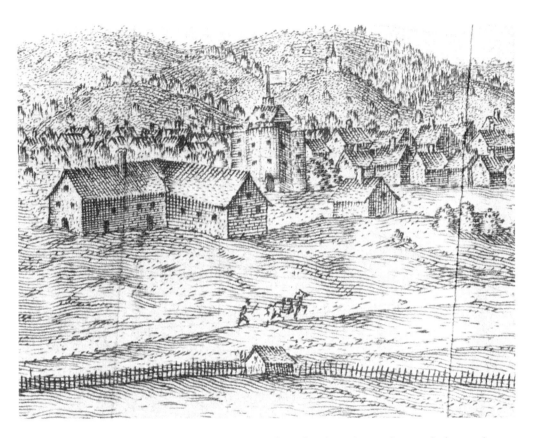

Detail from the Burden copy of The view of the cittye of London from the north towards the sowth, *c 1611, showing the Curtain – the tall polygonal building in the centre with a flag*

appears to be a slight slope down to the north – or centre – of the yard. Two long thin trenches were excavated along an alleyway running south off Hewett Street. This has, therefore, produced a section across the centre of the Curtain, north–south, revealing traces of the outer and inner walls either side of the yard.

At the southern end of the site was a short stretch of a narrow east–west brick wall and 3.8m north of this was a thicker wall that incorporated a relieving arch, suggesting that it either held a great weight or, possibly, an *ingressus*. The walls were of 16th-century brick, with between them patches of later brick flooring. The distance between these walls is similar to those gallery depths recorded at the Theatre, the Rose and the Globe, and thus they might be defined as the outer and inner walls of surrounding galleries. North of these two walls and laid up against the thicker inner wall was a gravel surface which probably represented the yard in the centre of the building.

Because of modern intrusions no excavation was possible immediately north of the gravel surface and another trench had to be excavated 8m further north. This revealed two possible foundation pads built of (probably reused) limestone blocks and bricks that might represent the line of the outer wall at the northern side of a playhouse building – similar to the outer wall pads found at the Rose playhouse. These pads marked the northern edge of another brick floor identical to that to the south. If the two pads at the northern end represent the line of the outer

The inner wall of the Curtain, possibly next to an ingressus, *with the gravelled yard surface abutting it; view looking south*

wall here, the full external diameter of the building would be *c* 72ft (22m), which is the same as the Theatre and the later Rose. The diameter of the yard would be in the region of 54ft (16.5m). It is possible that the difference in construction of what appears to be the outer wall was because of varying ground conditions. The flooring in between the gallery walls at the northern and southern ends is of mid to late 17th-century date, suggesting reuse of the building. The yard and the brick floors were sealed by a demolition dump dating to the early 18th century.

It is presumed that entrance to the building was from Curtain Road on the west and, in fact, the entrance to Curtain Close shown on the Chassereau map is at the centre point of our building. The stage would, therefore, have been to the east. All the remnant inner and outer walls are parallel without any angles, possibly because they were all located within a single bay due to the narrowness of the excavation trenches. An absolute identification of these remains with the Curtain playhouse – as opposed to another large 16th-century building – must be deferred until any further excavation. Nevertheless the location, size and typology of the remains make them a firm candidate for the Curtain.

The George, Whitechapel, 1580

This is the first of two aborted playhouses. It was also the third theatrical venture of John Brayne, undertaken just as his difficulties with his brother-in-law were beginning. Curiously, it appears to represent a return to Whitechapel, not that far from the scene of his first disastrous enterprise.

In January 1580 Brayne took a 25-year lease on the George inn (Walk 2, location **4**), for the surprisingly high rent of £30 a year. This was surprising because Brayne was certainly aware that the previous lessee, Reynold Rogers, had declined to renew his lease precisely because of the high cost of repairs and maintenance to the building. Brayne, however, thought he saw more in the property and was 'hoping that he might do some good upon it, intending to build a playhouse therein'. This would seem to indicate that he intended to convert the inn fully, rather than use it intermittently as a theatrical venue, like the earlier city inns. Work seems to have started early on, for Anthony Noble was hired for 'Carpentry work at the Inn without Aldgate called the George'. A 'painter' William Heron was another one of the later creditors who may have been involved in decoration there, which might suggest that the 'conversion' had progressed some way.

1580 was an unfortunate time to propose a new playhouse venture, even outside the city walls. Already, as we have seen, Brayne and Burbage had been held responsible for the riots at the Theatre in February of that year. In April the earthquake that shook the Theatre left the City authorities with no doubt as to its cause, namely that 'the players of plays, which are used at the Theatre and other such places … is a great hindrance of the service of God, who hath with his mighty hand so lately admonished us of our ernest repentance'. Even the Privy Council agreed that 'great resort of people to plays is thought to be very dangerous'.

A witness to another case regarding the George, 25 years later, recorded the end of the project by stating that Brayne was 'prohibited to proceed with his playhouse', though no further details were noted. Brayne then took on Robert Miles as a partner in running the George as an inn again. Brayne has been described as being 'afflicted with poor judgement' and by 1584 he had spent £240 on the rents, improvements and redemption of loans and mortgages on the property. Worse still, at the same time, he was arrested for non-payment of the work that the carpenter Noble had done four years previously.

He avoided a prison sentence by finding a surety on the debt paid by none other than James Burbage. This was a curious move by Burbage – because he later claimed that Brayne and Miles were trying to cheat him by creating a nest egg out of the George – one that backfired. Despite later problems with Miles, the Braynes appeared to have continued to live at the George and both died there, John in 1586 and his wife Margaret in 1592.

The Rose, Bankside, 1587

The Rose is one of the most intrinsically important playhouses of the 'Shakespearean' period, because historical and archaeological evidence means that we know more about it than any of the others. The Rose was owned by Philip Henslowe who was a successful businessman and, like anyone in his position, kept accounts – largely for the Rose but also for other assets in his vast property portfolio, which included the later Fortune and Hope playhouses as well. It is, of course, likely that all the other playhouse and theatre owners kept accounts, possibly varying in detail, but Henslowe's are unique because they (mostly) survive. This archive has been known about and published since the late 18th century and has continued to provide theatre historians with data on many aspects of Tudor entertainment. The amount of information is fantastic: it includes deeds and contracts, building expenses, and a miscellany of other documents. Perhaps most important is the list of more than 200 plays performed at the Rose between 1592 and 1603 by the Earl of Sussex's Men, the Queen's Men, the Lord Admiral's Men, Lord Strange's Men and the Earl of Worcester's Men. Two personalities in particular made the Rose famous. Most of Christopher Marlowes plays were performed there; he was probably the most important playwright before Shakespeare got into his stride. The leading actor, or star, at the Rose was Edward Alleyn and it is probable that Marlowe wrote many roles for him. Alleyn was also quite an entrepreneur and later founded Dulwich College.

In 1989 an archaeological excavation uncovered nearly three quarters of the Rose, and a great amount about the physical layout and development of the building was learnt. When this rich archaeological data was compared with the unique documentary sources, many of the obscure

Overhead view of the Rose excavations, looking north; both building phases are visible, along with intrusive 1950s concrete piles

passages there were revealed, explained and illuminated. Its archaeological importance to our subject is that the excavations covered a much greater area than any of the subsequent excavations on the other playhouses, theatres and baiting rings discussed here. Though they are all to an extent different, they can be usefully compared and contrasted with the Rose results.

A plot of land known as the Little Rose estate lay in the Bankside area on the south side of the Thames opposite the city (Walk 4, location **14**). It was quite a large site stretching from the river southwards to Maid or Maiden Lane (now Park Street). There were houses at the northern end and at least one other (which becomes important to the story) at the southern end. What lay in between is uncertain. though there may have been commercial fishponds there. It was owned by the parish of St Mildred's in Bread Street in the city (Walk 1, location **11**) and in March 1585 Philip Henslowe bought a 20-year lease on it. Only 18 months later he started building the playhouse.

Much of what we know about the Rose starts with the so called 'partnership document', drawn up between Henslowe and John Cholmley on 10 January 1587, in which they were to 'beniffyte somes of moneye proffitte and advauntage of a playe howse now in framinge and shortly to be erecked and sett uppe'. Although the document is not a building contract (such as survives for the later Fortune and Hope playhouses) it contains a number of important details. It mentions that the plot on which the playhouse was being built was 94ft square (28.7m square), which means that Henslowe had hived off the southern part of the leasehold specifically for this venture. Construction had clearly begun and was under the supervision of 'John Grygge carpenter'. The Rose appears to have been a popular venue by October 1587, when complaints were being made about playing on the sabbath on Bankside and the Rose was the only playhouse there at the time. In April 1588 the Sewer Commissioners described it as 'ye new plaie house', suggesting that it was still regarded as a novelty on Bankside. Similarly, the building marked as 'The play howse' on John Norden's map of London published in 1593 (though probably drawn earlier) must be the Rose as built in 1587.

The archaeological excavations uncovered two distinct building phases. Phase 1, which we presume is that originally constructed in 1587, is a simple affair. The building was a 14-sided polygon whose frame comprised two parallel rings of walls that formed the galleries, surrounding an open yard. There was an entrance at the southern end and a stage projecting into the yard at the northern end. As noted above, this design was almost certainly based on the Theatre in Shoreditch. John Grigg, the builder of the Rose knew the constructional history of the Theatre as shown by his testimony in the Burbage v Allen law case.

The shape of the playhouse was defined by the foundations of the outer wall, which consist of a series of pads, or piers, which were necessary to support the large upright timbers that would have framed the building. The outer sides of the 14 bays were an average of 5.0m apart, virtually the Tudor measurement of a rod – 16ft 6in. Each of these lengths had three piers, one in the centre and one at either end, two lengths thus sharing five piers, making 28 piers around the entire

Detail from John Norden's map of London showing 'The Playe howse' (the Rose), 1593

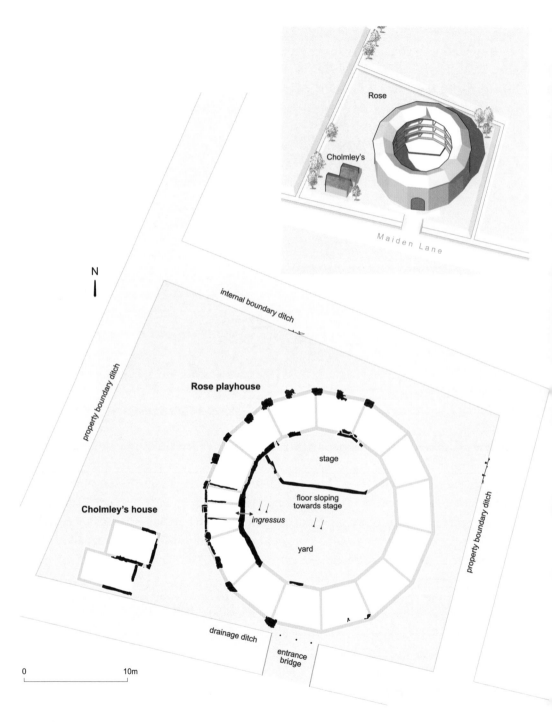

Rose

Cholmley's

Maiden Lane

N

internal boundary ditch

property boundary ditch

Rose playhouse

stage

floor sloping
towards stage

Cholmley's house

ingressus

yard

property boundary ditch

drainage ditch

entrance
bridge

0   10m

Plan of the excavated remains (in black) of the Rose, phase 1, 1587–92; reconstruction inset above

building. The piers were of varying regularity in size and were mostly built of mortared chalk blocks, though some had stone and brick pieces too. Between the piers, chalk blocks were laid along the wall lines. A low brick wall would be built over these chalk and stone foundations in order to protect them from the elements and the overlying wooden cill beams would be protected from the invariably damp ground conditions.

In contrast to the outer wall, the superstructure of the inner wall would have been an open framework, allowing a full view of the yard and stage. The inward thrust of a (roughly) circular building meant that these foundations had to be heavier and deeper. The foundations were thick and solid without any piers, though the angles showed that the bay frontages were some 11 ft (3.35m) wide. Only a few bricks of the superstructure survived.

Between the two walls at the northern end behind the stage, there appeared to have been a parallel foundation that might have been extra strengthening connected to the tiring house superstructure, with its hut above. In the western part of the galleries were two parallel east–west walls that we believe were part of an *ingressus* – an internal entrance from the yard into the galleries, as seen on the drawing of the Swan (p 84). There was also some surface wear on the yard just in front of these walls that suggests heavy traffic there. There were presumably steps up into the lower gallery and they may have had bars across, creating a sort of barrier or gateway similar to that shown in a drawing in the Henslowe papers (p 168). What might be similar features are recorded in the Fortune contract of 1600 (p 99) as the 'stronge yron pykes' that the lower galleries were to be 'laide over and fenced with'.

The stage was an irregular shape, a trapezoid covering an area of *c* 490 square ft (47.7m^2). It was tacked onto the inner wall of the frame; its rear, therefore, was clearly the same inner wall whose angles mirrored the external wall of the frame, thus providing, it seems, five planes. Its front wall was built of brick and timber with three sections: a long straight frontage of 8.08m and shorter wings (of *c* 3.0m) at either end. Within this stage area, behind the front wall, was a mortar surface below the level of the actual stage boards – creating an understage area that could have been used for storage or for a multitude of other purposes. We do not know how high the actual boards were and there was no evidence for the greater supports needed for a roof or cover over this stage; it seems to have been open to the elements. There might have been some form of cantilevered canopy extending from the rear wall, and the absence of any superstructure to the stage explains why the foundations of the front wall appear to be shallower than those of the frame. The tiring house, where the actors would get 'attired', was clearly that area of the frame of the building behind the stage and so useless for an audience. The five planes of the back wall, or *scenae frons*, of the stage suggests that there would have been at least two doors here, perhaps a larger third one in the centre.

The yard was the open area defined by the ring of the galleries, into which the stage projected. This was the part of the auditorium where the 'groundlings' stood, paying the cheapest entry prices. The area must often have been quite crowded, especially if people had to go through this area to gain access into the galleries via the *ingressus*. The floor of the yard was of mortar and had a distinct slope down towards the stage. Although this slope will have allowed the people at the back to see over the heads of those in front, it also seemed to have caused drainage problems, as the area right in front of the stage was much eroded with evidence of relaid surfaces there. However, the crowds pressing up to the front of the stage will have exacerbated this wear and it is a rare example of archaeology providing evidence for human behaviour – here interpreted as Tudor 'moshing'. There was evidence that sometime later on, but before the changes of phase 2, a new floor was laid across the whole yard.

Very little survived of the northern outer wall, largely due to later 17th- and 18th-century disturbance. However, there was a large timber drain that appears to have been built into the inner wall behind the stage. It is not clear where this drained from, but it was presumably connected to a pipe coming down from the stage building, though it sloped down to a ditch at the back of the building.

Little is known of the life and workings of the Rose in its first five years as any records that Henslowe kept for this period are lost. We know that the Admiral's Men arrived there, from the Theatre, in the summer of 1591, and it is likely that many of Christopher Marlowe's plays were performed at the Rose in this period, as they were also to be later on.

One of the earliest entries in Henslowe's new account book is 'A note of suche charges as I haue layd owt a bowte my playe howsse in the yeare of o^r lord 1592', which is an itemised list of building materials and costs totalling over £105. It had been thought that this entry referred to repairs, but it was only through the archaeological excavations that the nature of this work was finally revealed as a complete rebuilding of the northern, stage half of the playhouse that we defined as phase 2. It is interesting to note that the Theatre in Shoreditch was also undergoing alterations at the same time (above) and it looks as though this period was one of competition between the London playhouses, all striving to attract audiences, acting companies and playwrights through new building designs.

This rebuilding of the Rose was completed by 19 February 1592, when Henslowe's diary records that Lord Strange's Men began playing there. The first (known) performance, by the company, of Marlowe's *Jew of Malta* at the Rose was on 26 February 1592, but its author was certainly not present, for on that very day he was arrested and deported from Flushing on a coining charge. On 3 March another premiere saw Shakespeare's *Henry VI* at the Rose. The rebuilt playhouse appears with more detail on John Norden's map of 1600, though incorrectly labelled as 'The Stare', which is likely to have resulted from a misinterpretation of the rose motif on its sign or flag.

The excavations revealed that this phase was entirely concerned with a remodelling of the stage. This rebuilding did not affect the southern half of the building, but a brick cross wall, between the outer and inner wall just north of the *ingressus*, was probably inserted as a strengthening element during the construction of phase 2. This new stage was moved further back, 6ft 6in (2m) northwards. It was not much larger in area than the first but it was much more rectangular in shape and created a greater 'thrust' into the yard. More importantly, two column bases were now

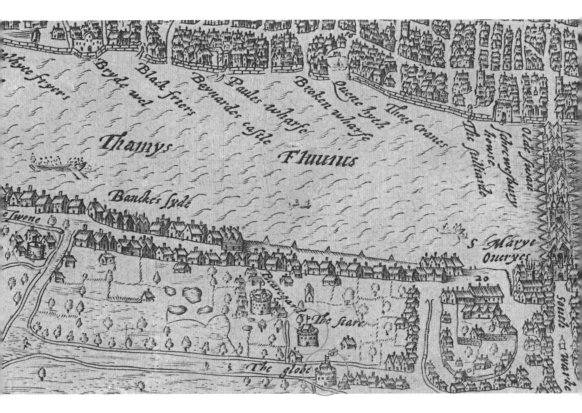

Detail from John Norden's map of London showing the Rose, mislabelled the 'Stare', as well as bear garden no. 3A, the Globe and Swan, 1600

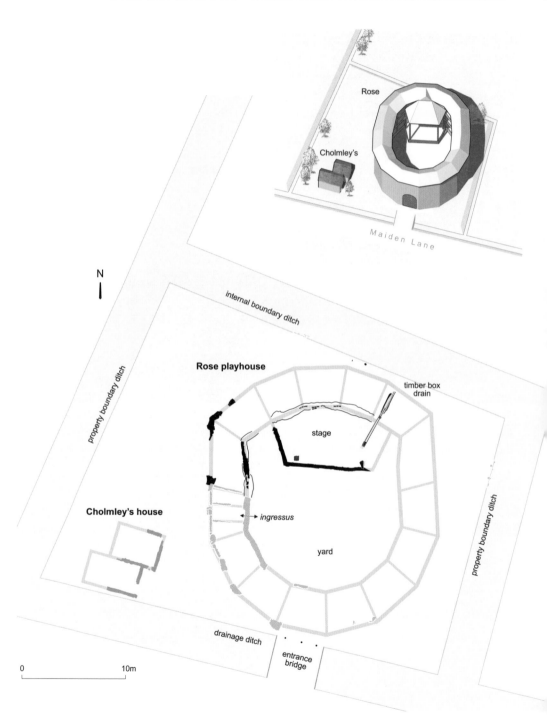

Plan of the excavated remains (in black) of the Rose, phase 2, 1592–1606; reconstruction inset above

built at the front of the stage that give us direct evidence for a permanent roof or cover over it. The new back wall behind the stage had much heavier foundations than the first, again stressing greater strength needed in this area, and it had three planes which suggests that there might have been three corresponding openings onto the stage.

Because the stage now had a roof, the galleries on either side had to be moved outwards in order to allow unimpeded sight of the stage itself from the upper galleries. Such a view would have been impossible in phase 1, had there been a roof or cover over that stage. Nothing remained of the new back wall, but its location must be the same depth as the area of new galleries found to the side. Henslowe also recorded payment for a 'penthowse shed' built against the building 'at the tyeringe howsse doore', though nothing identifiable as such was found in the excavations.

The yard was relaid with a homogenous conglomerate of silt, ash and clinker, with a high proportion of hazelnut shells, to form a much more durable, and distinctly more level, floor than the old sloping one. It turns out that hazel nut husks were the waste product of the soap-making industry and there was one such establishment nearby. It is a good illustration of the pragmatic nature of Tudor builders, utilising the waste of one industry as construction material for another. It was laid at a slightly higher level than the earlier one, as it covered the old stage frontage and the gallery fronts next to it.

Hazelnut shells from the second yard floor surface

The little house in the south-west corner of the playhouse site referred to in the 'partnership agreement' as the 'dwellinge howsse scittuate and standinge at the sowthe ende … adioyninge unto a lane there comonly called mayden Lane' and seen on both Norden map editions, was that occupied by John Cholmley who was 'to keepe victualinge in' to sell to theatregoers. The 'agreement' was actually a contract whereby Cholmley was to pay Henslowe £816 in instalments over the next eight years and it is clear that he was buying what we would now call a 'catering franchise'. He was ideally placed to go into business, with his new landlord, Philip Henslowe, becoming a partner in the playhouse concern. This building was also partially excavated to reveal a modest dwelling that was clearly older than the playhouse, but it had been modified at some time. We suggested that this related to the construction of the Rose next to it and its role as a bar or kiosk for the playhouse.

In February 1593, the Rose was closed because of fears about the spread of plague; the watermen of the Thames petitioned for its speedy reopening, because of their loss of business ferrying audiences across the Thames. The playhouse was not reopened until the end of the year, but its repertoire was seriously depleted by the death of such well-known playwrights as Robert Greene, Thomas Kyd and Christopher Marlowe. Nevertheless, on 23 January 1594, Sussex's Men gave what is probably the first performance of Shakespeare's *Titus Andronicus*.

The Rose continued to be one of the most successful playhouses in London, although it must have felt some competition with the opening of the Swan playhouse 500m upstream. It was perhaps in response to this new rival that Henslowe recorded spending money on carpentry supplies and for 'payntinge my stage' and 'doing it about' in March/April 1595. In June of the same year he paid for making a throne in the heavens, the underside of the stage roof – which had been added in 1592. This almost certainly means that machinery for ascents and descents was built enabling greater special effects. Improvements seem to have been made in 1602 when he paid for 'poleyes & worckmanshipp' to hang Absalom in Robert Peele's *David and Bathsheba*.

In 1597 Edward Alleyn retired from the stage, temporarily as it turned out, and the entries in Henslowe's *Diary* recorded less detail than before. The construction of the Globe in 1599 only 100 yards away proved to be a greater competitor. It is possible that Henslowe was already thinking ahead to new theatrical ventures – culminating in the move to the Fortune in 1600.

There were few performances at the Rose after 1600, when the Admiral's Men moved to the Fortune. In June 1603, Henslowe started negotiations with St Mildred's parish for a renewal of his lease of the Little Rose estate, due to expire in September 1605. However, as he learnt that a new lease would be at a greatly increased ground rent and a requirement to spend 100 marks (a notional value which equals £66 5s 6d) on building, he said that he would rather pull down the playhouse than accept such terms. Henslowe does not seem to have carried out this threat, as over the next few years, the Sewer Commission continued to fine him for not repairing the sewer along Maid Lane next to the playhouse. By January 1606, Henslowe had clearly abandoned the building and the land on which it stood, as the Commission noted that the property was back in

A reconstruction of Bankside c 1602 showing the Globe in the foreground and the Rose and bear garden no. 3A behind
(Faith Vardy)

the hands of the parish. In April, however, they referred to 'the Late playhouse in maidelane called the Rose', which implies that the building had disappeared between January and April. The archaeological results indicate that it was more likely to have been carefully dismantled, rather than wantonly demolished, for probable reuse of its timbers elsewhere.

Detail from John Norden's panorama showing bear garden no. 3A, upper left, the Rose, lower right, and the Globe, bottom right

The Swan, Bankside, 1595

The Swan was the second playhouse to be built on the south bank, after the Rose, but it represented a new development in playhouse construction, in size and ostentation. It also has an important position in theatre history because a sketch made in *c* 1595/6 is the only interior view of an early playhouse and provides most of what we know of the layout of the Swan. Thanks to a map of 1627, we know exactly where it was: on the east side of modern Hopton Street (Walk 4, location **9**). Despite this, it will never, regrettably, be found archaeologically. The site is occupied by Sampson House, a large modernist office block built in 1976–9. Crucially, the complex has deep and extensive basements which will have removed any archaeological deposits.

The site of the Swan lay within the manor of Paris Garden, situated at the east end of Bankside. The manor was a Crown possession, but was eventually bought by Francis Langley in May 1589 for £850. Langley was the nephew of Sir John Langley, Lord Mayor in 1576. He was apprenticed as draper, but actually made a – sort of – living from property deals and money lending, much of which was at the least unscrupulous. We will see that, although the Swan was the only theatrical venture that he owned, he was involved in many others.

Langley was certainly keen on realising the development potential of this large manor and must also have seen the success of the nearby Rose and the other playhouses in Shoreditch. Construction of the Swan appears to have been under way by November 1594, when the Lord Mayor had heard that Langley 'intended to erect a new stage or theatre (as they call it) for the exercising of plays upon the Bankside'. He lost no time in writing to Lord Burghley, the Queen's chief advisor, urging him to 'suppress all such places built for that kind of exercise than to erect any more of the same sort'. Nevertheless, it may be assumed that the playhouse was finished and open for business by the summer of 1595.

Certainly, two foreign visitors in London in 1595/6 stated that there were four playhouses about London: these must have been the Theatre, Curtain, Rose and Swan. The first was the German Prince Ludwig von Anhalt-Cöthen, followed by the Dutch scholar Johann De Witt. The latter made a famous sketch and left an account which noted that the two Shoreditch playhouses were not as fine as the two on the Bankside, and furthermore stated that the Swan was the largest and most magnificent of the four, capable of hosting an audience of three thousand. His famous drawing only survives as a copy made by his friend Aernout van Buchell (p 84). Studies have shown that compared to other De Witt drawings, Van Buchell was a very poor draughtsman – the layout and perspective of the drawing leaves quite a bit to be desired. Nevertheless, De Witt envisaged this strange building as a Roman amphitheatre and labelled it accordingly, based on the terms used by the Roman architectural writer Vitruvius.

Essentially it is similar to the earlier playhouses with an open yard – though in this case distinctly labelled as a flat or level (*planities*) arena – into which projects a stage, all surrounded by three tiers of galleries. Although the size of the stage may be an exaggeration, the tiring house

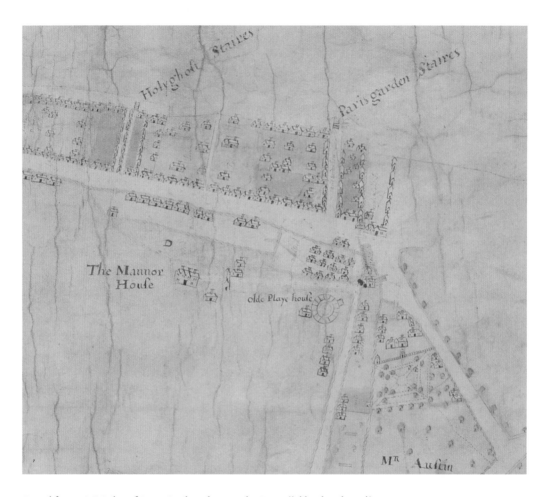

Detail from a 1627 plan of Paris Garden, showing the Swan ('olde Playe house')

(labelled here the *mimosum aedes* – 'actors house') projects forward from the circuit of the galleries. Again, it is not certain if this is an accurate representation, but if so, it would provide a little more room backstage. Perhaps it was a development on the earlier playhouses (certainly the Theatre and Rose). Nevertheless, it also has an *ingressus* or internal entrance 'doorway' into the galleries, which conforms to the early method of staggered entry, paying first to get into the yard, with further payment at the *ingressus* for better seats inside. The *orchestra* shown here next to the stage represents a 'box' or – lords' room. De Witt also wrote that the building was made of flint stones, which is unlikely for the superstructure and may have referred to the foundations. However, he recorded that the wooden pillars holding the stage were cleverly painted to resemble marble and it is just possible that the exterior was given a similar *trompe l'oeil* treatment.

The building contract for the Hope, built in 1613, stated that it was to be was to be based on the Swan. The Hope has been partially excavated and its external diameter may have been as much as 25m, which certainly would suggest that the Swan was larger than its predecessors; it is not far from the lower estimate for the diameter of the Globe and this may represent a new larger size for the new generation of playhouses. According to the scale of the 1627 map, however, the diameter of the Swan would be some 65ft (19.8m). This is implausibly small – De Witt stated that it was larger than the earlier three and we know the size of the Theatre, Curtain and Rose to be 72ft (22m), so that the Swan must have been bigger than that. The map was perhaps scaled only in terms of land measurements, with the buildings represented in a stylised fashion.

Some idea of the stage workings and rich furnishings of the Swan can be gauged by an event in 1602, when one Richard Vennar advertised a play called *England's joy* to be performed here. The story was to include the Queen 'taken up into heaven; when presently appears a throne of blessed souls; and beneath, under the stage, set forth with strange fire-works, diverse black and damned souls, wonderfully described in their several torments'. This would indicate hoisting mechanisms into the heavens, as well as a trapdoor in the stage. However, Vennar took the entrance money and then fled, and no such play appeared. Not unnaturally the cheated audience took their revenge on the building. 'In the meane time the common people, when they saw themselves deluded, revenged themselves upon the hangings, curtains, chairs, stooles, walles, and whatsoever came in theire way, very outragiously, and made great spoil.'

There is no direct evidence for any acting company there in 1595–6, but Philip Henslowe lent £9 to his actor nephew Francis to 'lay down for his half share with the company which he doth play withal' on 1 June 1595. Francis moved into one of Langley's newly-built tenements soon afterwards, where he stayed until 1598. A witness to the loan was another well-known player, George Atewell, and it is probable that the two of them, at least, were part of a company playing at the Swan since it opened. It has also been suggested that the Lord Hunsden's Men were at the Swan in 1596. This company was essentially the ex-Lord Chamberlain's company and would have counted Shakespeare amongst its personnel. Shakespeare was living on Bankside from this date and he certainly knew Langley, being a witness for him in a dispute with the Surrey

The interior of the Swan in 1595/6, as copied by Arendt van Buchell from a drawing by Johann De Witt

magistrates. This has caused some debate as to whether Shakespeare was mixed up in Langley's dubious affairs.

The Earl of Pembroke's company signed an agreement with Langley to play at the Swan for one year starting in February 1597. Francis Henslowe and Attewell may have been with this company; there were certainly some players who defected from the Rose to come to the Swan, including at least one young apprentice player who was made to return. In July they put on a now lost play by Thomas Nashe and Ben Jonson, called the *Isle of Dogs*, at the Swan. The Privy Council later described this as a 'lewd plaie that was plaied in one of the plaie howses on the Bancke side contanynge very seditious and slanderous matter'. Three of the offending actors Robert Shaa, Gabriel Spencer and Ben Jonson – who was also the co-author – were flung into the Marshalsea prison in Southwark (Walk 4, location **20**). All the playhouses were closed down, but it seems that this was based on an earlier Privy Council injunction of 28 July, which was merely one of the recurrent anti-theatre diatribes also concerned with the danger of 'multitudes' spreading plague. Nevertheless, they gave direction 'that not only no plays shall be used within London or about the city or in any public place during this time of summer, but that also those playhouses that are erected and built only for such purposes shall be plucked down'. In the event, the playhouses were not demolished; most reopened in October and the three actors were released. The Swan, however, remained closed, possibly because Langley had incurred the enmity of Lord Burghley through other dubious deals. Most of the players decamped to join the company at the Rose, whereupon Langley sued them for breach of contract. The players described Langley as 'of a greedy desire and dishonest disposition' and the case eventually fizzled out, with Henslowe paying the costs of 'his' actors. It is possible that the rump of Pembroke's Men stayed on at the Swan for a few months, but from the summer of 1598 it is uncertain who, if anyone, played at the Swan over the next decade.

Langley built further tenements in the area, perhaps to restore income, and created complicated deals in order to sell the whole manor of Paris Garden to the Browker family in early 1602. Nevertheless, because of his continued legal and financial adventures, he died a bankrupt in July 1602. The Swan was intended to be used for the *England's joy* scam in November of that year and by March 1606 it was leased by one Alexander Walshe, though it is uncertain what he did there.

The newly founded Lady Elizabeth's Men were playing at the Swan intermittently in 1611–14, when they moved to the Hope. They certainly made 'articles of agreement' with Philip Henslowe in August 1611, which suggested that Henslowe had some arrangement with the Swan. The company is recorded to have performed Middleton's *A chaste maid in Cheapside* there in 1613. If the building had been largely unused for a number of years, and perhaps devoid of much of its furnishings since 1602, there will have been a need for refurbishment and improvements. One of these may have been the addition of the stair turret seen on the 1627 plan and noted as one of the Swan features to be copied at the Hope in 1613.

There is evidence that players at the Swan paid towards the poor of Paris Garden in the year 1621, but we do not know who they were. After this, there are only a couple of records of fencing matches at the Swan. It was described as 'ye olde play house' on the 1627 plan and as 'fallen in decay' in 1632. The last recorded use of the building was in 1634, when it was used as a temporary venue for the Court of Requests (involved in a hearing about the Globe) and it has been noted that such men 'would not take official evidence in a hovel', indicating perhaps another (slight) refurbishment.

The Swan represented an important development in the history of the London playhouses. However, as William Ingram has pointed out, its success as a business venture never matched its opulence, almost certainly because of the disarming personality of its owner.

The Boar's Head, Aldgate, 1598

The Boar's Head inn had existed since at least the beginning of the 16th century. It was situated just outside the city beyond Aldgate, on the north side of Whitechapel High Street (Walk 2, location **3**), and by the 1590s it was part of a larger estate owned by the Poley family. On 28 November 1594, Oliver Woodliffe took out a 21-year lease on the inn and its outbuildings. As we saw above, the Privy Council banned a 'lewd play' from being performed there in 1557, though that may have been a one-off event. This time, Woodliffe intended to convert the premises into a permanent playhouse and the lease notes that, apart from other improvements, he would build a tiring house and stage within seven years.

Like other theatrical venues of the period, most of what we know about the Boar's Head comes from lengthy lawsuits between the various warring parties. The whole story was brilliantly recounted by the late Herbert Berry.

Woodliffe arranged for the building of a tiring house with galleries above at the western edge of the property, overlooking a stage which apparently occupied most of the yard. In April 1598 Woodliffe subleased most of the eastern part of the site to Richard Samwell, in order that he should add new galleries to the north and south; these were narrow spaces built on posts above the yard, so that there was standing room below. He was also to adapt an existing gallery on the east. Woodliffe was to remain a silent partner and then left London, travelling abroad. It is not certain which carpenter built the playhouse that opened in the summer of 1598, but it must have been fairly basic, and we have no information on what plays were performed by what company during this first, short, period of operations.

Woodliffe returned the next year and saw that there was a greater potential in rebuilding and enlarging the playhouse. This work was then undertaken in July and August 1599 by the carpenter, John Mago. Firstly a new gallery was to be added above the existing eastern one both now *c* 8ft

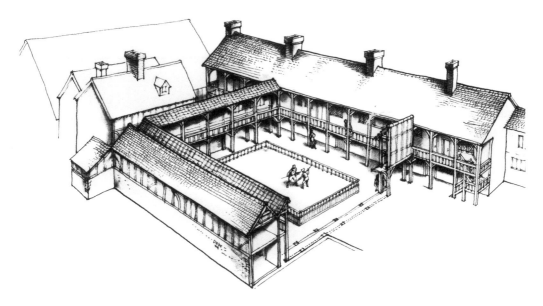

Reconstruction of the Boar's Head playhouse 1598 (C Walter Hodges)

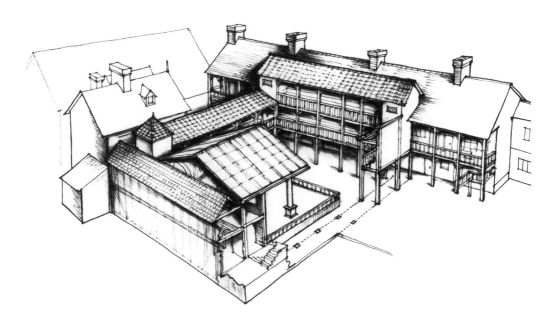

Reconstruction of the Boar's Head playhouse 1599 (C Walter Hodges)

(2.4m) deep. The north and south galleries were enlarged, now to a depth of *c* 6ft (1.8m), and leading into the eastern galleries; they only abutted, without access, to the western gallery which was now *c* 7ft (2.1m) deep. The stage was moved slightly westwards and it now measured *c* 39ft (11.9m) wide (north–south) by 25ft (8.8m). Woodliffe now had Mago build the 'stage tyringe houses & the galleryes over & about the stage with the coverings over them'.

The playhouse now appeared to be complete, albeit smaller than the purpose-built ones, and Lord Derby's Men became the resident players. Samwell was soon in debt and finally sold his share to Robert Browne, the leader of Derby's Men. Woodliffe followed suit in November and sold his part to Francis Langley. In fact Woodliffe and Langley were the same sort of unpleasant people and they hoped to get control of the rest of the property, now in Browne's hands, by arguing that the new galleries were built over the yard, which was in the Woodliffe/Langley domain. True to form, Langley embarked on a campaign of harrassment against Samwell and Browne, including lawsuits and the not-so-legal-use of his thugs to threaten Samwell's family.

In 1601 Browne, now *de facto* manager of the site, brought in Lord Worcester's Men to play at the Boar's Head. Their stay was clearly successful, for in the next spring the Privy Council wrote to the Lord Mayor that 'the house called the Boar's Head is the place they have especially used and

Portrait of Joan Alleyn (c 1573–1623), 1596;
stepdaughter of Philip Henslowe and Edward
Alleyn's first wife; a number of letters written
between Edward and Joan Alleyn survive

do like best, we do pray and require you that the said house, namely the Boar's Head, may be assigned unto them'. However, they had a row with Browne in August and moved to the Rose. Langley died in July 1602 and in 1603 there was a particularly bad outbreak of the plague which carried off both Woodliffe and Browne, after which the lawsuits fizzled out. Joan Alleyn wrote to her husband Edward, on tour in the provinces, that 'Browne of the Boar's Head is dead and died very poore'. Browne's widow Susan then married Thomas Greene the leading player with Worcester's Men, who now became the Queen's Men and, though they maintained an interest in the Boar's Head, they moved on to the next inn conversion, the Red Bull, in 1607. The Boar's Head was henceforth a peaceable though minor playhouse, mostly occupied by the Duke of Lennox's Men and then Prince Charles's [I] Men – which may have been the same company.

In 1616 the original leases expired and the Poley family started to sell off the whole estate. It was slowly developed over the next century, though the site is recognisable on early maps. In November 1999 a small excavation was undertaken at the site, but such was the extent of modern basements that only very small areas of medieval and Tudor occupation were noted, which could not conclusively be identified with the Boar's Head. The plot still lies vacant and undeveloped, and any future work elsewhere on the site might yet bear fruit.

The Globe, Bankside, 1599 and 1614

The Globe, known as 'The Glory of the Banke' (Bankside) is the most famous playhouse of the period. Its fame, of course, derives from it being known as Shakespeare's (own) playhouse and the venue where many of his plays were first performed. It appears in countless maps and views – not all contemporary – and there are many replica Globes all over the world. The most recent is that on the modern riverside (Walk 4, location **6**), 300 yards north-west of the original (Walk 4, location **15**).

Following the end of the lease on the Theatre and the failure of negotiations for a new one, the Burbage brothers, Richard and Cuthbert, took a 31-year lease on a piece of land owned by Nicholas Brend on the south side of Maid Lane – only 100 yards south-east of the Rose. The lease was dated 21 February 1599, but backdated to Christmas 1598. The lease was divided into two half-shares, one half to the Burbage brothers and the other half to five players: William Shakespeare, John Hemmings, Augustine Phillips, Thomas Pope and William Kemp. With Richard Burbage, these were the main players, or 'sharers' of the Lord Chamberlain's company, who moved into the Globe after their departure from the Theatre and a brief spell at the Curtain. The company, with a change of name to the King's Men in 1603, were to stay at the Globe for the rest of the period.

The Globe has become a victim of its own success and fame, as so many assumptions have

Detail from Hollar's pencil sketch of c 1644 for his Long view of London, *looking west, showing the second Globe*

been made about it. In fact there are far fewer details of the building than many of the others in this book. As we saw above, the dismantling of the Theatre and the reuse of its timbers at the Globe site created a mythology about the size of both buildings. The timbers of the Theatre were indeed used in the construction of the Globe but, because it was much bigger than the Theatre, more material was needed. In 1635 it was said that 'the Leassees thereupon spent about Seaven Hundred pounds in building a Playhowse Called the Globe'. This figure actually included repairs and maintenance, but was still a great amount of money and a lot of it must have represented buying more building material.

It is a fair assumption though, that the carpenter Peter Street – who masterminded the dismantling of the Theatre in late 1598, and in January 1600 was contracted to build the Fortune, with details to be based on 'the late erected Plaiehowse on the Banck in the saide parishe of Ste Saviours called the Globe' – actually built the Globe.

If construction of the Globe started in early 1599, when all materials were ready, it may well have been completed by 16 May, when an inquisition into the property of Nicholas Brend's father referred to a newly-built 'house' with a garden on the site. It was certainly completed before the end of 1599, when Thomas Platter saw *Julius Caesar* (probably Shakespeare's) at the Globe in September; Ben Jonson's *Every man out of his humour* was performed there at about the same time. A more serious event happened in February 1601, when supporters of the Earl of Essex paid the Chamberlain's Men 'forty shillings above the ordinary' to perform Shakespeare's *Richard II*. The story of Richard being deposed and murdered by the adherents of Henry IV was seen as incitement for Essex's plan to depose the queen. In the event, the players, who had thought the play too old, were absolved of any complicity, though Essex was executed before the month was out. The first Globe can clearly be seen on John Norden's map of 1600 (p 75).

After a successful 14 years the Globe burned down on 29 June 1613, when the thatched roof caught fire during a performance of Shakespeare's *Henry VIII* or *All is true*. There were a number of contemporary accounts of this famous fire. Sir John Chamberlain wrote that it 'burn'd ... down to the ground in less than two hours, with a dwellinge house-adjoining, and it was a great marvaile and fair grace of God, that the people had so little harm, having but two narrow doors to get out'. The speed of destruction was corroborated by other writers and the dwelling house was elsewhere defined as the tap house. We assume that the two doors were the main front door and a back, stage, door. Apart from the safety of the audience and actors, it was inferred that no valuables such as play texts were lost, for another description, by Sir Henry Wotton, confirms that 'nothing did perish but wood and straw'. Ben Jonson's poem *An execration upon Vulcan* includes the lines

> See the world's ruins! nothing but the piles
>
> Left, and wit since to cover it with tiles.

The original lease of the Globe site was due to expire at Christmas 1629, but the players negotiated a 6-year extension at the same rent in October 1613, when they were planning the rebuilding of the burned playhouse. After a new rent was agreed they would 'reedifie & new build the said Playhouse', which they probably started at the beginning of the new year. The first Globe was built with limited means, albeit with rising costs, but the second was much more magnificent and cost twice as much as the first. Sir John Chamberlain wrote that 'I hear much speech of this new playhouse which is said to be the fairest that ever was in England'. Nevertheless, documentary accounts suggest that the new building was built on the foundations of the old one and thus was at least of the same size and plan as the first Globe. The players themselves, in a lawsuit of 1632, said that the second Globe was 'erected, built, and set up ... in the same place where the former house stood'. In 1635 the local parish also confirmed that the Globe was 'built by the company of players with timber about twenty years past upon an old foundation'. As we will see, the limited excavation evidence suggests that the second playhouse was indeed built on the foundations of the first. The only reliable view of the second Globe and the rebuilt tap house is the engraving by Hollar, which has had its labels reversed.

The archaeological excavations of 1989 unearthed only a very small and disturbed part of the north-east segment of the Globe playhouse, next to the 1830s Anchor Terrace building. However, it is necessary to describe the remains of both the first and second Globes to gauge the layout and development of the building. A short stretch of the outer wall foundations, of chalk and ragstone set around timber stakes, survived to the north and was overlain by burnt debris suggesting fire damage. The brickwork of the outer wall was partly over the burnt debris, indicating that it was from the second structure even though it was indeed over the line of the earlier foundations. Some 12ft 6in (3.8m) parallel to the west was another short stretch of the inner wall, but this was very similar to the outer brickwork and any possibly earlier foundations were not revealed. This suggests that the destruction of the first Globe was almost complete, though damaged elements would have been removed before reconstruction.

The other structural elements found appear to be of the second Globe, though whether they replicated earlier features cannot be known. In between the inner and outer walls were three fragmentary stretches of what might have been strengthening cross walls. These were surrounded by a 'surface' of hazel nuts, like the yard floor at the Rose. Just west of the inner wall, therefore within the yard, were two parallel walls clearly contemporary with the inner wall. These walls might be interpreted as providing supports for an internal entrance into the galleries. However, they are clearly different from the *ingressus* illustrated at the Swan (p 84) or the same feature at the Rose, and possibly at the Theatre. Nevertheless, as these walls were built in 1614, they may represent a development on the earlier form of internal entry. There were certainly plenty of tile fragments found that confirmed Jonson's observation on the new roof.

The excavations did, however, uncover fairly clear evidence for a new form of external entrance, known as the stair tower, illustrated on both the Hope and, precisely in this location, on the second Globe in Hollar's engraving. The archaeological evidence shows the feature extending c 6ft 6in (2m) from the main wall of the playhouse and c 15ft 9in (4.8m) in length. There is a

Detail from Hollar's Long view *of 1647 showing the Globe incorrectly labelled 'Beere bayting house' (the Hope) and vice versa*

View of the second Globe excavations looking south-east; fragments of the outer wall and attached stair tower can be seen in the centre

central break in its outer wall that may be associated with an entrance. Its build, however, exactly matches the construction associated with the second Globe, whose brickwork it tightly abuts. Internally, the space for any stairs must have been quite cramped. Apart from the stair towers, the second Globe also had a tiring house door. This was noted in a later income dispute between the lessees and other actors, indicating that there was still a private entrance of sorts via this door.

Using the archaeological remains of both first and second Globes, it is possible to produce some dimensions. Firstly the bays of the galleries appear to be similar to those at the earlier playhouses. The outer length of each bay was based on a rod of 16ft 6in (5.02m) and the inner length was 10ft 6in (3.2m), with the depth at 12ft 6in (3.8m). The limited remains, however, could not give precise dimensions for the whole building, though it was clearly bigger than the earliest playhouses. Analysis suggests that the Globe was either a 16-sided polygon with a diameter of 84ft 6in (25.75m) or an 18-sided polygon at *c* 95ft (29m), with a feeling that the lower estimate is more realistic.

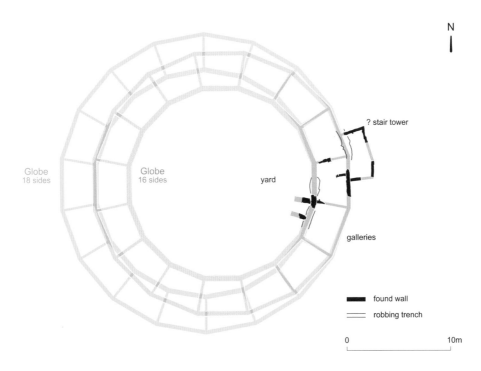

Reconstructed plan of the Globe with 16 and 18 sides

From at least 1616 the King's Men regarded the Globe as their second home, preferring the more exclusive Blackfriars theatre. Nevertheless, there were new plays by the likes of Beaumont, Fletcher, Massinger, Webster, Heywood, Davenant and Shirley. But it was Thomas Middleton's *A game of chess*, put on at the Globe in August 1624, that became not just a roaring success but a diplomatic scandal. The play was a comment on the failed marriage negotiations between Prince Charles and the Spanish infanta, distinctly anti-Spanish in tone, and was particularly mocking of the former Spanish ambassador to London. The current ambassador then complained to the English government and wrote an account to the Spanish one. The theatrical interest in this letter lies in its statement that the Globe had an audience of 3000 watching this satirical play. The Privy Council, worried about diplomatic rifts, immediately banned the play and effectively finished Middleton's career as a playwright.

Between 1632 and 1637 the players fought a protracted case against the landowner Sir Matthew Brend, to force him to honour a promise of a further nine-year extension that he had made whilst still a minor. Brend wanted to recover the land in order to build tenements, which he reckoned were more profitable than the playhouse. Meanwhile, in 1635 a dispute arose about shares in the building, because very few now belonged to players. Share ownership was rearranged but they were still now predominantly held by non-actors.

The Globe will have closed in 1642 in accordance with the parliamentary orders prohibiting all playing. The players' lease of the land ran out at Christmas 1644, but they may have abandoned the playhouse before this. Brend probably pulled down the Globe soon after he recovered the land, but no definitive date for its disappearance has been found in any documentary sources. Demolition deposits over the remains of the Globe, uncovered in the excavations, could only be broadly dated to the mid 17th century. There were persistent reports of fragments of the Globe being still visible in the mid 18th century. However, these were usually not on the site now identified as the Globe or were wishful inventions associated with an emerging Shakespeare mania.

The Fortune, Cripplegate, 1600 and 1623

After 13 years of fairly successful theatrical activity on Bankside, Philip Henslowe had seen competition emerge first with the Swan, but more recently with the nearer Globe. It has been speculated that a move to fresh pastures had been envisaged as early as 1597 and an indication of early planning can perhaps be seen by the swiftness with which the Fortune project was realised. Henslowe's stepdaughter's husband, Edward Alleyn, was the prime mover in the new venture and on 22 December 1599 he bought the lease of a plot of land in the parish of St Giles without Cripplegate – being about a quarter of a mile outside the city walls (Walk 3, location **5**). A building contract was signed with the carpenter, Peter Street, on 8 January 1600 'ffor the erectinge,

Frontispiece of Middleton's play A game of chess, *performed at the second Globe in 1624*

building & settinge upp of a new house and Stadge for a Plaiehouse in and uppon a certeine plott or parcell of grounde appoynted out for that purpose', but it appears that the locals became concerned about a playhouse in their midst very quickly. Alleyn then got the Earl of Notttingham, his patron as the Lord Admiral, to write to the Middlesex Justices on 12 January, wherein he noted that 'my servant, Edward Alleyn ... hath taken a plot of ground ... very fit and convenient, for the building of a new house there and hath provided timber and other necessaries for the effecting thereof'. Nottingham laid it on well, stating that his servant and playing company were esteemed by the Queen, and begging them to support the project. The Privy Council, though, was still uncertain and wrote to the Middlesex authorities to reject the idea. Pressure seems to have been brought to bear because in early April the parishioners wrote to the Council saying that they would be now content enough to tolerate a playhouse, because, firstly, it was very remote from any population centre that 'none could be annoyed thereby' and, secondly, because the builders would contribute generously to the parish poor, at a time when their own funds were hard stretched. The Privy Council bought this too, responding swiftly that, as the Queen was fond of this servant and company, they would require the Middlesex justices to 'permit and suffer the said Edward Alleyn to proceed in the effecting and finishing of the same new house'.

Careful analysis of construction payments reveal that preparation and building were going on at the same time. However, costs spiralled and the work continued for some time after the completion date of 25 July specified in the contract. Alleyn later said that he was still spending money on the building over the next eight years.

The plot was situated between Golding Lane on the west and Whitecross Street on the east. From west–east, the plot measured, according to a 1656 survey, 415ft (126.5m), though its north–south dimensions are uncertain. As with many other theatre properties, most of the land could generate other income, whilst the playhouse would occupy only a defined area within. In this case it is probable that the Fortune playhouse was sited just behind the properties fronting Golden Lane and, again according to the 1656 survey, the 'late playhouse and Tapphouse belonging to ye same standeth upon a piece of ground' measuring only 127ft (38.7m) east–west by 129ft (39.3m) north–south.

The famous building contract does not actually provide as much detail as one supposes, because many will have been 'prefigured in a plott therof drawen', and there must have been an understanding between client and carpenter over many other aspects of the building. Nevertheless, many of the details were to be as in 'the late erected Plaiehowse on the Banck in the saide parishe of Ste Saviours called the Globe'. The implication, as noted above, was that Peter Streete had just built the Globe. The main difference, however, was that the Fortune was to be square, 80 x 80ft (24.4m²). Other important measurements tell us that the yard would be 55ft square (16.8m²) which means that the gallery depth was 12ft 6in (3.8m), which was the same as the Theatre, Curtain, Rose, Globe and Hope. The stage was to 'conteine in lengthe Fortie and Three foote of lawfull assize and in breadth extende to the middle of the yarde of the saide howse'. As we have the yard

Building contract for the Fortune, 1600

Tsubouchi Memorial Theatre Museum at Waseda University, Tokyo, Japan; built in 1928, this building was designed as a replica of the Fortune

dimensions, the stage, probably rectangular, would be 43ft (13.1m) by 27ft 6in (8.4m).

The phrase 'with suchelike steares, conveyances & divisions withoute & within, as are made & contryved in and to the late erected Plaiehowse ... called the Globe' has been assumed by many to mean that there were external stair towers at the Fortune. However, there is much ambiguity in this phrase and, moreover, the stair tower(s) at the Globe were only part of the second Globe of 1614.

There were to be three tiers of galleries and their heights were to be 12ft (3.66m) high for the lowest, 11ft (3.35m) for the middle and 9ft (2.75m) for the uppermost. There was a touch of Renaissance influence in the building as 'all the princypall and maine postes of the saide fframe and Stadge forwarde shalbe square and wrought palasterwise, with carved proporcions called Satiers to be placed & sett on the topp of every of the same postes'. Indeed it was noted that these embellishments were not amongst those details to be copied from the Globe. Interestingly, the main window that Street made six years later at the bear garden gatehouse was framed by 'twoe carved Satyres'.

The Admiral's Men were performing at the Fortune by the autumn of 1600 in full competition with the Globe. The company, which became the Prince Henry's Company in 1603, had a good stock of plays and players, but the reputation of the Fortune declined over the years. In 1612 we find that 'certayne lewde Jigges songes and daunces used and accustomed at the play-house called the Fortune in Gouldinglane, divers cutt-purses and other lewde and ill disposed persons in great multitudes doe resorte thither at th'end of euerye playe many tymes causinge tumultes and outrages wherebye His Majesties peace is often broke and much mischiefe like to ensue thereby'.

There were some successes: the prologue to *The roaring girl* by Thomas Dekker and Thomas Middleton announced that it 'shall fill with laughter our vast theatre' at its first performance there in 1610. It dramatised the life of Mary Frith, a well-known cross-dressing underworld figure, who actually appeared to see the play wearing a sword and smoking a cigar. This, and other racy dramas, did nothing to improve the reputation of the Fortune. But in July 1621 the Spanish ambassador Count Gondomar went to 'a common play' there, after which the players entertained him to a banquet in the adjoining garden. This was the same ambassador who was so savagely satirised in *The game of chess* at the rival Globe just three years later (above).

On the business side, Alleyn leased half of the property to Henslowe in 1601, so that it would be a joint venture, but managed to buy the freehold of the property in 1610. After Henslowe's death in 1616, he retrieved the half lease. Alleyn also began selling shares in the Fortune to players and in 1618 he leased the entire building to the resident company – who had been renamed the Palgrave's Men in 1612.

On the night of Sunday 9 December 1621, the Fortune burned down in two hours. This time it was a greater disaster than the loss of the Globe eight years earlier, as all the players' 'apparel and playbooks [were] lost, whereby the poor companions are quite undone'. As in 1613 it was 'intended to be erected and sett vpp a new playhouse', though this time it would take a number

Frontispiece of Middleton and Dekker's
The roaring girl, *performed at the Fortune*

of years to come to fruition and it was not finished until the summer of 1623.

There is no surviving contract for the new building, but some details are found in various sharers' papers. The carpenter Anthony Jarman and the bricklayer Thomas Wigpitt were engaged 'for the new building and erecting of a playhouse in Golding lane aforesaid according to a plottforme by them allready drawne'. Alleyn had shown this plot or plan, also lost, to the Earl of Arundel in June 1622.

James Wright's *Historia histrionica* referred to the second Fortune as 'a large, round [probably polygonal] Brick Building'. Although doubt has been cast on this late, 1699 source, the Dankerts map indeed shows a 'round' building probably on the site of the first. Moreover, a survey of the building done in 1656 (by Edward Jarman, architect son of Anthony) describes much of the, now decayed, material:

> the Tyling not secured and ye foundation of ye sd play house not kept in good repair
> great pt of ye sayd play house: is ffallen to ye ground, the tymber thereof much decayed

and Rotten: and the Brick walls soe Rent: and torne ... ye whole structure is in noe condition capable of Repaire but in greate danger of ffalling, to ye Hazzard of Passengers ... [a] greate pt of ye tymber is Rotten, ye Tyles much broaken and decayed and ye brick walls much shaken'.

They concluded that the cost of demolition would be much cheaper that any restoration or rebuilding. There was a mention of 'two gates', when the place was raided for playing illegally in 1643, which as in the earlier playhouses must have been the front and back doors.

There was a great plague in 1625 and a hitherto unknown company, The King and Queen of Bohemia's Players, took up residency once it abated. The last years of the Fortune were noted for riots and bawdy shows, but respectable, though overtly political, plays written by the likes of Massinger and Davenant, were still put on there.

The Fortune will have closed in September 1642, along with all the other theatres, but, as noted above, there was still some illicit playing. It was still, just, standing in 1656 but clearly pulled down shortly afterwards.

The 1656 survey suggested that it would be more profitable to the owners, Dulwich College, if they 'Cutt a streete of twenty fower foote wyde from whitecrosstreete to Goulding laine' which would be lined with tenements. It is most likely that there was a gap in the Golden Lane street frontage allowing access into the Fortune built in 1600. With the final disappearance of the second Fortune, this opening would have been extended as the 'Playhouse Yard' shown on the Ogilby and Morgan map of 1676 (Walk 3, location **5**). It was renamed Fortune Street in 1936 and thereby defines the location of the playhouse.

Detail from Cornelius Dankerts' map of c 1645 (attributed to Augustine Ryther) showing the second Fortune

Wapping, 1600

On 1 April 1600, the Middlesex authorities demanded a £40 'recognizance' or bond, from 'John Wolf, of Eastsmithfield, Co Midd, stationer', because he 'hath begun to erect and build a playhouse in Nightingale Lane near East Smithfield aforesaid, contrary to Her Majesty's proclamation and orders set down in Her Highness's Court of Starchamber. If therefore the said John Wolf do not proceed any further in building or erecting of the same playhouse, unless he shall procure sufficient warrant' from the Privy Council, he would be let off. Although no further decisions were noted, the inference is that he did indeed, abandon the project.

East Smithfield is actually a roadway just to the east of the Tower of London in Wapping; it also became an alternative name for the (southern part of the) parish of St Botolph without Aldgate. Nightingale Lane, now Thomas More Street, runs south from East Smithfield. Though exactly where the projected playhouse was started is difficult to say: perhaps half way down below the 'glittering glass Swedish bank' (Walk 2, location **6**).

John Wolf, or Wolfe, was a well-known printer and publisher with a large and diverse portfolio that included Marlowe's poems and the first edition of John Stow's *Survey of London*. He was about 52 when this playhouse episode began, and he died the next year, but it was not the first time that he had brushed against the law. Regrettably, we know nothing else about how he acquired land in Nightingale Lane or any other details of his intended playhouse. Nevertheless, it was certainly not the first theatrical venture in the area: the Boar's Head, just to the north, had been renovated and improved just a year before, and the earlier aborted playhouse, the George inn, was nearby, with the 1567 Red Lion further east. Its brief appearance also showed the continued attraction of theatrical investment, despite official opposition.

It would seem that Wolfe must at least have started laying the foundations of this playhouse. These might have revealed a shape and size indicating where such a project lay in the development and evolution of playhouses at this date. However, because of continued building development in Thomas More Street, there is little chance that such remains survive.

The Red Bull, Clerkenwell, 1606

Much further west of the Fortune, this new venture was situated in the fashionable district of Clerkenwell, over 500 yards (457m) north of the city (Walk 3, location **6**), but it was to gain a poor reputation in dramatic terms. In December 1604, Aaron Holland bought a 30-year lease on an inn 'commonly called or known by the name or sign of the Red Bull at the upper end of St John Street'. He was described as a 'servant' of the Earl of Devonshire (the former Baron Mountjoy), who was certainly a patron of various poets and may thus have had theatrical connections.

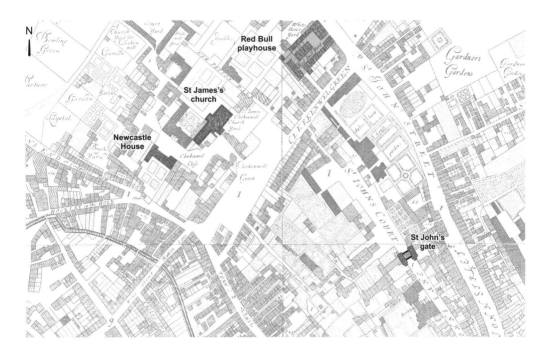

Detail from Ogilby and Morgan's map of 1676 showing the Clerkenwell area

Holland's motives though, were not new and he intended from the start to convert the building into a playhouse, much as the Boar's Head in Aldgate had been. With some acumen Holland procured the patronage of the Queen's brother, the Duke of Holstein, 'to selecte and gather a Company of Comedians to attend his Grace here or elsewhere'. He also found a player, Martin Slater, who promised to lead a ducal playing company to perform in the venture. However, neither choice turned out to be satisfactory, as Holstein left England under a cloud in May 1605; Slater's own company, the Queen's Men, disowned him. Nevertheless Slater stayed and certainly helped to win over the parish with the usual promises of contributions to the parish poor and improvements to 'pavements and highways', thus, it appears, winning permission from the Privy Council to proceed with the project. The next step was to finance it and Holland divided the cost into 18 shares to be sold. In the event, we only know of one such sale, to another Queen's player, Thomas Swinnerton. Swinnerton eventually sold his share to Philip Stone in 1609, who in turn sold it on to Thomas Woodford in 1612; this brought troubles as we shall see below.

The property that Holland had leased included 'courts, gardens, cellars, ways and liberties thereunto belonging'. Presumably funds were ready by the beginning of 1607 when Holland 'to his great charge and expenses, did erect and set up in and upon part of the said premises divers buildings and galleries for a playhouse to present and play comedies, tragedies and other matters of that quality'. As in other playhouses, gatherers would take payment from 'every person that should come and take place, sit or stand in any the said rooms or galleries, or upon the stage, in the said playhouse'. Apart from dramatic performances, the Red Bull also hosted fencing displays, like many of the other venues.

By the autumn of that year, the Queen's Men had left the Boar's Head and came to the Red Bull, where they were to spend the next ten years. The company put on the popular *The travels of three English brothers* by Day, Rowley and Shirley in 1607. They also gave the first performance of John Webster's *The white devil* there in 1612; this was initially a flop though subsequently recognised as a great play.

The leader of the Queen's Men, Thomas Greene, now took over half the 18 shares from Holland, though he later sold two of them to Christopher Beeston. After Greene died in 1612, Beeston took over the management of the company, but he was clearly not up to the job and the company brought an action against him. More seriously, Woodford, now a major investor in the playhouse, sued Holland for what he saw was a poor return. This case went on for many years and its accounts tell us much about the Red Bull, but by 1623 Holland was ruined and left the entire venture.

We know very little about the actual building, though Slater later described how Holland had 'altered some stables and other rooms, being before a square court[yard] in an inn, to turn them into galleries'. Holland's own descriptions above refer to galleries and rooms, which suggests that the place conformed to the basic playhouse design of the period.

The main entrance to the playhouse was almost certainly that of the original inn, from St John's Street on the east. In fact it was in a room over 'the Great Gate' that Holland and Woodford discussed their finances, suggesting a 'management' office. However, this is unlikely to have been a 'backstage' area, as the stage would usually have been opposite the main entrance. A recently rediscovered sketch seems to confirm this by showing a turret-type structure, almost certainly over a tiring house, on the east side. What changes had been made by the 1680s, however, when the premises had long since stopped being theatrical, are unknown.

William Prynne, in his *Histriomastix* published in 1630, wrote of 'two old playhouses being also lately re-edified', which are assumed to refer to the Fortune and the Red Bull. As we have seen, most playhouses were altered, modified or even rebuilt throughout their lives. There are no other indications of what 're-edification' might have taken place at the Red Bull, but it might have involved a roof or cover – either a larger one over the stage or possibly over the whole yard – transforming the playhouse into an indoor venue. A 'Plott or Survey' of the site of 1679 suggests that the building was of brick, though whether this was from the original or a later building is uncertain. James Wright, in 1699, stated that 'The Globe, Fortune and Bull were large Houses, and lay partly open to the Weather, and there they alwaies Acted by Daylight'. This has been taken to refer to the Red Bull, but the inference for it being roofed is also suggested by a late engraving of its stage, which shows two chandeliers hanging from somewhere over the stage (p 108). These might possibly be used for performances in the late afternoon, but the 12 candles, footlights, at the front of the stage are much more indicative of an indoor theatre. The engraving clearly shows a rectangular stage with an audience on three sides. Also of interest is that there appears to be only one entrance onto the stage from a 'tiring house', which also has a balcony reminiscent of the Swan (p 84). Holland's own testimony of 1623, noted above, refers to audience (presumably sitting) 'upon the stage', again much more common in indoor venues. When Samuel Pepys attended a performance there after the Restoration, he was led 'up to the tireing-room' and 'at last into the

Title page of John Cooke's Greene's tu quoque *or* The city gallant *(1614), performed at the Red Bull and probably portraying Thomas Greene in the title role*

Frontispiece of Kirkman's The wits, *showing the stage of the Red Bull*

Pitt, where I think there was not above ten more than myself, and not one hundred in the whole house'. If the building had not been changed since reopening, Pepys's description does not square well with an open-air playhouse. He also noted that there was a 'musique-room' somewhere, presumably backstage. George Reynolds, who undertook an important analysis of the plays performed at the Red Bull, found so many instances of mechanical staging devices and, particularly, fireworks 'than one would expect in a theatre lighted by daylight and made of wood'.

There was quite a succession of acting companies at the Red Bull after the Queen's Men left in 1617 – though they returned in 1619 as the Revels Company. These included the Prince Charles's [I] Men as well as the Palgrave's who came over from the Fortune. There was some stability in 1634 when a new company, Prince Charles's [II] (possibly under the patronage of the Prince's tutor, the Earl of Newcastle, who lived nearby), occupied the playhouse until its closure in 1642.

There were highly regarded actors at the Red Bull, including Thomas Greene, Richard Perkins and the comic Andrew Cane. The place was also revolutionary in having women performing on its stage in November 1629. They were with a French acting company specifically licensed to play for one day, though their presence attracted the usual puritan opprobrium. In 1639 a 'scandalous and libellous play', *The whore new vamped*, which apparently mocked City officials, was performed at the Red Bull, but there do not appear to have been any lasting repercussions.

The Red Bull had its fair share of rioting, such as by felt makers' apprentices in 1610 and others in 1638, and a pickpocket was arrested there in 1613. Nevertheless, the reputation that the Red Bull (and the Fortune) had for unsophisticated plays and audiences is probably exaggerated.

Although it was officially closed in 1642, there were a number of instances of illegal playing at the Red Bull after this and during the interregnum. Indeed, Andrew Cane was arrested there in 1650 for performing. At the Restoration, the playhouse opened again and, as noted above, Pepys went there on 23 March 1661, but it had lost much of its glamour and he was not impressed.

The Hope, Bankside, 1613

The new Globe playhouse of 1599 had swiftly outshone the Rose, and Philip Henslowe did not renew the lease on the Little Rose Estate in 1604. When the Globe burned down on 30 June 1613, Henslowe might well have seen it as divine retribution. His last major building project, which marked a 'theatrical' return to Bankside, was the Hope playhouse (just to the north-west of where the Rose stood), which is often thought to have been prompted by the Globe fire. Actually, the building contract for the Hope – which still survives at Dulwich College – was signed on 29 August 1613, only two months after the destruction of the Globe. He may have been thinking about a new venture for some time, though perhaps the disappearance of the Globe accelerated his plans.

Amongst Henslowe's various properties on Bankside was bear garden no. 3A, which he bought in 1594. The Hope contract was between Henslowe and Jacob Meade on one side, and the carpenter Gilbert Katherens on the other; the first item was the demolition of the old bear garden and its stable for bulls and horses, although the new building was situated just to the south of the bear garden. However, the Hope was to serve a dual purpose, spelled out in functional as well as constructional terms: 'to erect, builde, and sett upp one other Game place or Plaiehouse fitt & convenient in all thinges, bothe for players to playe in, and for the game of Beares and Bulls to be bayted in the same, and also a fitt and convenient Tyre house and a stage to be taken and carried awaie, and to stand upon tressells good, substanciall, and sufficient for the carryinge and bearinge of suche a stage … And shall also builde the Heavens all over the saide stage, to be borne or carryd without any postes or supporters to be fixed or sett upon the saide stage'. The Hollar engraving of the Hope clearly shows what must be a cantilevered roof over the removable stage on the southern side of the building (p 93). The main entrance must have been on the northern side, but a later document also mentions 'the doore goinge into the Bearegarden out of Maidelane' which must have been 'a stage entrance'. Although the stables and animal pens were to the west, it is not certain how they entered the Hope itself.

There may a have been practical reasons why it was to be a dual-purpose building – apart from profit. The conservative authorities might not have sanctioned yet another playhouse development on Bankside, but one aligned with animal baiting – one of King James I's favourite pastimes – may have been more politically acceptable.

The contract specified that the new building was to be built 'the same of suche large compasse, fforme, widenes, and height as the Plaie house called the Swan'. Although the Swan was almost 20 years old, it is possible that it had been refurbished in 1611 and by 1613 it was the only surviving playhouse in the area. The Hope, like many buildings of the time, was to be largely constructed from reused materials, both from the old buildings as well as 'olde tymber' bought by Henslowe from a demolished property in Thames Street.

There were also to be 'two Boxes in the lowermost storie fitt and decent for gentlemen to sitt in' as well as 'particions betwn the Rommes' as at the Swan. Although the height of the main timber posts in the lowest galleries was given as 12ft (3.7m), there are no other measurements that may help us with a reconstruction of the building. Katherens was also to build a new bull house and stable, and all these buildings were to be roofed in new English tiles – clearly remembering the combustibility of the thatch at the Globe.

The Hope contract specified completion by 31 November, but there is no evidence that it was open until the next year, 1614, by which time there was renewed competition from a rebuilt Globe. The first recorded use of the Hope was in October 1614, when the poet John Taylor and William Fennor were to have a 'triall of Wit'; but Fennor never turned up, whereupon the disappointed audience gave vent to their feelings – just as the Swan audience had done in similar circumstances 12 years before:

One swears and stormes, another laughs and smiles,
Another madly would pluck off the tiles.
Som runne to'th doore to get againe their coyne,
And some doo shift, and some againe purloine.
One valiantly stept out upon the stage,
And would teare downe the hangings in his rage ...

After this, Taylor continued, 'came the players, and they play'd an act'. These players were most likely to be the Lady Elizabeth's company, who will have moved from the Swan to the Hope, probably on its completion. Their first recorded appearance, however, was in the premiere of Ben Jonson's *Bartholemew fair* on 31 October 1614. The stage directions for what was probably the Hope's most famous production included a series of stalls, booths and stocks on the stage, with the central booth probably being used as a 'discovery place'.

As noted above, the Hope was specifically built as a dual-purpose arena with animal baiting originally taking place on Sundays and Thursdays, though it appears that there was increasingly more baiting than playing. The actors became more and more dissatisfied with these arrangements

Ben Jonson, portrait by Abraham van Blyenberch c 1617

The Hope playhouse as found in the initial archaeological evaluation, looking east

and Jonson had quipped that the Hope was 'as durty as Smithfield and as stinking every whit'. The players finally drew up *Articles of grievance* against Henslowe in February 1615 and eventually left the Hope in 1617. There were hardly any plays presented at the Hope after this date and it soon reverted to its old name of the Bear Garden with baiting being the main activity there. In 1625 a boy was 'kilde in the Beargarden', though we know not from what cause. However, there are references to prize fighting, fencing displays and, most oddly, for exhibiting a camel there in 1632. It was closed by order of Parliament in 1653 and a late addition to Stow's *Survey* notes that it was 'pulled downe to make tenements by Thomas Walker, a petticoate maker in Cannon street, on Tuesday, the 25 day of March 1656'. The seven remaining bears were 'shot to death … by a Company of Souldiers'.

There was an archaeological excavation of the Hope site between 1999 and 2001 but very little was found, as most of the building lay outside the site limits. Two parallel stretches of brick walls uncovered apparently formed the north-eastern part of a polygonal structure, but represent just less than a quarter of the whole. Furthermore, these walls have been reused, with later brickwork in the form of a vaulted stairway giving access to a flue associated with a late 17th-century glass furnace.

The two walls are both 0.48m thick and built out of early 17th-century brick. The innermost has angles that suggest a yard with a diameter of some 52ft (16m), slightly larger than the yard of the Rose. However, the two walls of the Hope are only 5ft 10in (1.55m) apart, which cannot possibly be a full gallery depth. The gallery depths at the Theatre, Curtain, Rose and Globe are all *c* 12ft 6in (3.8m). If, however, the 'outer' wall at the Hope was actually a middle wall of three, perhaps for extra strength, and a lost outer wall was equidistant at another 5ft (1.55m), then an external diameter to the building would be in the region of 83ft (25.4m). This is close to the lower estimate of the Globe diameter and might, therefore, provide a dimension for the same 'large compass or wideness as the playhouse called the Swan'. Abutting the inner wall of the Hope was a mortar surface, though it is uncertain if this was the original yard floor.

The excavations also revealed, to the west, large deposits of animal bone, principally comprising the disarticulated remains of several horses, dogs and bears, most butchered and defleshed. It was known that there were two ponds, one that was used to wash the bears and another old pond that was used for the disposal of dead dogs.

In the same area, the excavations found remains of a substantial wooden structure erected above the waterlogged 'pond', with a floor level at a similar height to the possible yard of the Hope. This may have been an internal partition wall to a stable or kennel associated with the Hope. Construction of new partitioned stables was mentioned in the building contract and its location was noted in a 1620 law case: 'where the bull house now stands was anciently a doggyard belonging to the [earlier] beargarden'.

THE
TRAGEDY
of
MESSALLINA
by
N. RICHARDS

London printed
for
Dan. Frere.
1 6 4 0

MESSALLINA

SILIVS

Introduction

There had been dramatic performances indoors for many years – in private houses, the city inns, the great institutional halls and at the royal palaces. These would all have been on temporary stages and the construction of purpose-built permanent indoor theatres was a later phenomenon.

It is convenient to use the term 'theatre' here in specifically referring to the indoor venues, though it might be noted that the neighbours of the Blackfriars referred to it as a 'common playhouse'. As we have noted, the terms public and private are misnomers, but for the 'private' indoor theatres this certainly reflected a higher entrance price and it may have been an allusion to the earlier performance within private houses. Nevertheless, the theatres were all situated in the more fashionable areas of London, at the western edge of the city and beyond; this certainly and deliberately indicated richer audiences. Entrance fees to the theatres were much more expensive than the playhouses, which immediately created social differences between the two.

They were all, with the probable exception of the Phoenix, built or adapted within existing buildings. This also produced improvements conducive to more sedate audiences, protection from the elements perhaps being the most obvious. It also meant that there had to be artificial lighting. This had an impact on performance with the introduction of the 'interval', made necessary by the need to trim candle wicks. The fact that most of them were on the first floor of these existing buildings means that there is no scope for archaeological analysis, though their locations can be generally determined.

The audience capacity within the theatres was much smaller, perhaps by a quarter, than the playhouses; this lessened the extent of crowding. Moreover, there was no standing in the central 'pit' (as opposed to 'yard'), but benches arranged around or in front of the stage which often had low rails at its edge. Seating in the pit was actually more expensive than in the galleries, there was usually only space enough for one tier. There were certainly 'boxes', lords' or gentlemen's rooms, here too, at the side of the stage; but a more ostentatious 'seat' was on a stool at the edge of the stage itself, where a young gallant may 'see and be seen'. There was no such room on the playhouse stages and they were banned at the Salisbury Court theatre in 1639, on account of its small size. On popular occasions there was clearly 'standing room only', which provoked a famous row at the Blackfriars in 1632, when Lord Thurles stood at the edge of the stage blocking the view from a box occupied by Lady Essex and her stepson, a captain in the army.

> This Captaine attending and accompanying my Lady of Essex in a boxe in the playhouse at the blackfryers, the said lord coming upon the stage, stood before them and hindred their sight. Captain Essex told his lordship, they had payd for their places as well as hee, and therfore intreated him not to deprive them of the benefit of it. Whereupon the lord stood up yet higher and hindred more their sight. Then Capt. Essex with his hand putt

The title page of Messalina, *1640, showing an indoor stage (bottom centre)*

him a little by. The lord then drewe his sword and ran full butt at him, though hee missed
him, and might have slaine the Countesse as well as him.

Despite the social and architectural superiority of the theatres, therefore, affrays were not limited to
the hoi poloi of the playhouses.

The restrictions of an existing space meant that attention was given to the stage, with elaborate
scenery and mechanical devices, though there will have been no posts on the stage supporting any
'covers'. However, since we know that the same plays were often performed at both playhouses
and the theatres, the differences cannot have been great. The King's Men used the Globe in the
summer and the second Blackfriars in the winter.

The earliest indoor 'theatres' were those occupied by 'boys'' or 'children's' companies. These
were the choir boys from the Chapel Royal (the itinerant choir for the various royal chapels), the
Children of Windsor (the choir of St George's chapel in Windsor castle) and the Children of St Paul's
Cathedral, who, since the beginning of the 16th century had been involved in royal pageants and,
increasingly, with secular drama. The boys would be given a traditional grammar school education,
with added singing and acting instruction. Their 'masters' were increasingly entrepreneurial and,
it is probable, quite exploitative. Well-trained boys were in great demand and one unfortunate,
from St Paul's, was kidnapped in 1575 and another, from Salisbury Court, in 1632. By this time
they established their own indoor premises – at the same time that the adult companies began to
erect the outdoor playhouses. Their own plays were now being written by many of the leading
playwrights of the period – John Lyly, John Marston, Thomas Dekker, Thomas Middleton, George
Chapman, John Webster, Ben Jonson, Francis Beaumont and John Fletcher, though not Shakespeare
himself – augmented by well-known musicians, such as John Dowland and Phillip Rosseter.

St Paul's, 1575

A playhouse was established in a small upper chamber against the south side of the nave of the
cathedral in 1575 by Sebastian Westcott (Walk 1, location **16**). Little is known of the room except
that it measured a maximum of 29ft (8.8m) east–west but, of necessity, 'the stage is so very little'.
A number of plays are known to have been performed by the boys here and at court, but they
were closed down in 1591 purportedly for their involvement with the Marprelate controversy.

They were allowed to recommence acting by the autumn of 1599, though the new master, Giles
Peers, took on Thomas Woodford to look after the dramatic side from 1603. However, the two of
them came to blows and Woodford moved on to other theatrical escapades. Peers's next partner
was Edward Kirkham, previously manager of the children at the second Blackfriars theatre, but no
further performances were recorded after 1606. Indeed it was said that when the King's Men occupied
the Blackfriars from 1608 they bribed the boys' master to keep their little playhouse closed.

View of old St Paul's; the theatre is thought to have been in a building in the angle of the south aisle and the south transept, in the chapter house precinct

The first Blackfriars, 1576

Two indoor theatres were established in succession in the former Dominican friary of Black Friars (Walk 1). The first was relatively short-lived and unsuccessful, lasting from 1576/77 until 1584.

The first proper theatre in Blackfriars began in the winter of 1576–7 after Richard Farrant took out a 21-year lease on part of the old friary buildings, principally the monastic dining hall and buttery (food and drink storage rooms), which was occupied in the 1550s by the Master of the Revels. Farrant was in effect master of two companies of child actors and singers, the Children of Windsor and the Children of the Chapel Royal. In 1576 he was looking for a permanent London home for the Chapel Royal choristers and he was probably familiar with the Blackfriars property, since he would have used the 'Revels equipment' (stored at Blackfriars) for private royal performances. Farrant's new Blackfriars property was primarily a boarding school for the choristers, rather than a public theatre, though he funded the school (and no doubt made a personal profit) by allowing the public to pay to view rehearsals for the exclusive royal performances that were held at court. None of Farrant's plays has survived (indeed it is not certain if he actually wrote them), but titles such as *King Xerxes* suggest a taste in classical history, and these performances were enhanced by music for a solo chorister accompanied by a viol consort. The boarding-school theatre turned out to be relatively short lived: the freeholder, Sir William More, claimed that Farrant had misled him over the purpose of the building and that the crowds of playgoers were 'to the offence of the precinct [of Blackfriars]'. After Farrant's death in 1580, the Earl of Oxford gave his patronage to the children managed now by Henry Evans, the playwright John Lyly and the musician William Hunnis. Four years later, More managed to evict the new company and transform the theatre into tenements.

Farrant seems to have built his rehearsal and performance hall by adapting the old friars' refectory or dining hall, situated above the buttery and with an internal space of about 46 x 25ft (14 x 7.5m) (Walk 1, location **22**). The theatre scholar, Irwin Smith, has skilfully reconstructed aspects of the theatre, using the evidence of the lease and contemporary stage directions in *Campaspe* and *Sapho and Phao*, two early plays by John Lyly that were performed here. There was a 'platform' or main stage with a trapdoor in the floor and a 'discovery space' at the rear. There is no evidence, positive or negative, for an 'above' or upper stage platform and there seem not to have been any galleries for spectators, since the room almost certainly lacked sufficient width to allow good sight lines.

The second Blackfriars, 1600 and 1609

The second theatre operated from 1600–42 and, from 1609, it was a particularly successful venue, celebrated in its day and famous thereafter, as the home of the King's Men, Shakespeare's company.

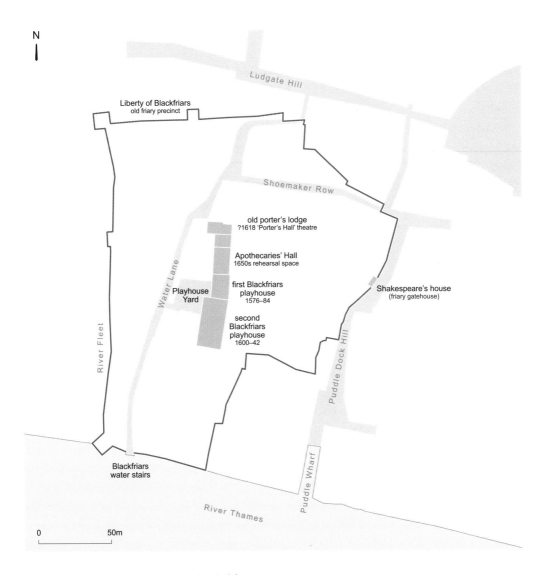

Location of the various theatres within the Blackfriars precincts

Its story begins in February 1596, when James Burbage purchased the freehold of the parliament hall building from Sir William More for £600 (although it would not be fully paid for until 1605). This was the large first-floor hall just south of the buttery, where the first Blackfriars was; previously this had been used for sittings of parliament and was where the papal enquiry into the marriage between Henry VIII and Katherine of Aragon had convened (Walk 1, location **23**). In 1596, however, the aristocratic residents of the area objected to the impending presence of a 'common playhouse' in their midst and managed to get the Privy Council to forbid 'the use of the said house for plays'.

By 1600, Henry Evans managed to obtain permission to open the theatre, not as the home of a company of adult players but with the return to Blackfriars of the Children of the Chapel Royal. This proved to be successful at first and Thomas Middleton even urged young gallants 'to call in at the Blackfriars, where he should see a nest of boys able to ravish a man'. Thereafter, a series of gaffes blighted the theatre, the Children and their managers. In 1605 offence was caused by the perceived anti-Scottish tone of *Eastward hoe*; under Robert Keysar's management in 1606 John Day's *Isle of Guls* offended parliament, and in 1608 George Chapman's play the *Duke of Byron* upset the French ambassador. A bad plague the same year sealed the fate of the Children's theatre and the lease was soon surrendered to the Burbages.

The Burbage family then launched a new consortium to run the theatre as the indoor venue of the King's Men, in parallel with their outdoor building, the Globe playhouse. The seven leaseholder-directors included the brothers Cuthbert and Richard Burbage, with Henry Evans, William Shakespeare, John Heminges, Henry Condell and William Slye, and the revived theatre ran successfully from 1609 until the end of playing in 1642.

Careful detective work has revealed how Burbage and his successors transformed the hall into a theatre. The first act was stripping away the various partitions and subdivisions of the parliament hall that had been inserted after the closure of the friary in 1538. Burbage thus obtained a huge space – some 101 x 46ft (31 x 14m) internally – for the stage and auditorium. The company built galleries along the sides of the auditorium to increase seating capacity, including several private boxes. The large platform stage had a smaller rear stage behind a curtain and, behind that, the 'tiring-house' for the actors to change and where scenery and props were stored during the performance. The promoters also made full use of the height of the medieval hall, constructing a complicated upper stage structure with galleries, a balcony, a musicians' room and an upper storey known as the 'top'.

Subsequent theatre scholars have debated the evidence for the internal layout. How big was the actual stage area? Were the galleries curved rather than rectangular, creating a U-shaped, more classical auditorium? How many levels of gallery were there in this huge hall? How many spectators sat above or even on the stage? In the absence of any definitive evidence for the layout of the theatre, that reconstructed in Staunton, Virginia, by the American Shakespeare Center is the most plausible. In fact we know very little of the internal arrangement of the parliament hall, or its

The 2009 performance of A comedy of errors *at the reconstructed second Blackfriars in Staunton, Virginia*

original date of construction (?14th century). A description of the subdivided hall in 1571 suggests that it had been partitioned *down the length* of the hall, perhaps making use of a central row of slender stone columns (the Franciscan friars' refectory hall in Paris is a surviving example of this arrangement).

This second Blackfriars theatre was, of course, the stage for which Shakespeare wrote his late plays, including *The winter's tale, Cymbeline* and *The tempest*. Can the smaller and more exclusive setting of the Blackfriars theatre (compared to the outdoor Globe playhouse) be detected in these more reflective, more musical romances? The Blackfriars was also the venue for collaborative works by Shakespeare and John Fletcher, including *Henry VIII,* the king whose first marriage had been investigated in the very same hall 85 years earlier. Other premieres at Blackfriars include John Webster's macabre *The Duchess of Malfi* (1612) and Ben Johnson's *The alchemist* (1610).

*The actor and playwright
John Fletcher (1579–1625)
by unknown artist c 1620*

Whitefriars, 1606

The Carmelite friary of 'White Friars' lay to the west of the River Fleet and had been suppressed in 1538. The former friary became a 'peculiar', neither a proper parish nor, until 1608, under the control of the City of London authorities. The short-lived theatre established here in the early 17th century (Walk 5, location **4**) is, like others, mostly known through complicated lawsuits.

On 1 December 1606, Thomas Woodford, the 'entrepreneur' we have already met at the Red Bull and Blackfriars, took an eight-year sub-lease on the site from Sir Anthony Ashley (long-suffering brother-in-law of Francis Langley). Ashley's lease probably ran out after the eight years too; later leases were obtained from the landlord Lord Buckhurst (son of the Earl of Dorset). In 1608 Woodford took on Michael Drayton, the poet and playwright, as a partner and created a wider partnership of a number of sharers. Among these were minor playwrights Lording Barry and John Mason, as well as the actor Martin Slater who had just been involved in setting up the Red Bull. In time-honoured fashion, most of the sharers fell out over debts, borrowing money from Woodford who was soon in control of the project.

The theatre was first used by a company known as the Children of the King's Revels and later by the Children of the Queen's Revels, these were child actors, not choristers like the St Paul's children. The playhouse was in business by September 1607 and the Children revived performances of Thomas Middleton's *The family of love*, as well as staging the first productions of less enduring plays, such as Lording Barry's *Ram Alley* (whose title referred to a notorious nearby passage). However, the Children were poorly – and probably dishonestly – managed by Woodford until spring 1608, when the enterprise collapsed in a mass of lawsuits. A bad plague the same year no doubt played a part in its demise.

The second company of children, moving from the neighbouring Blackfriars theatre under the management of Robert Keysar, took over the venue with rather more success in the period 1609–14. The Children of the Queen's Revels were a cut above their predecessors and they had considerable success with plays such as Ben Jonson's *Epicoene* (a Whitefriars premiere), and Beaumont and Fletcher's *Coxcomb* and *Cupid's revenge*. Local residents were not, however, happy about the new theatre on their doorstep: at a meeting in December 1609 men of the neighbouring parish complained that the new 'playhouse in the [Whitefriars] precinct [is] not fitting there to be, nor tolerable'. In 1613 the Children combined with an adult company, Lady Elizabeth's; the latter may have been after winter quarters at the Whitefriars, in the same way that the King's Men successfully used the second Blackfriars. Lady Elizabeth's were also playing at the Swan – which might have been intended as their 'summer home' – though with the end of the Whitefriars' lease in 1614 they moved to the Hope.

The original lease described the property as 'a messuage or mansion house parcel of the late dissolved monastery called the Whitefriars in Fleet Street'. There was also a description of 'the rooms of which house are thirteen in number, three below, and ten above; that is to say, the great hall, the kitchen by the yard, and a cellar, with all the rooms from the Master of the Revels's office as the same are now severed and divided'. Also included were 'divers playbooks, apparel and other furnitures and necessaries used and employed in and about the said messuage ... by the Children of the revels there being, in making and setting forth plays, shows, interludes and suchlike' which gives an indication of what a playing company, even a children's one, needed.

The two most likely candidates for this 'great hall' theatre are the friars' refectory or their library. Given that the former hall was demolished and redeveloped in the 1540s it is very likely that Thomas Woodford leased and adapted the old monastic library building, situated at the end of a lane leading south from Fleet Street. The medieval library had been repaired in 1507 and, soon after the friary was closed in 1538, a surveyor recorded that it had a lead-covered roof and that it was 32 yards long (29.3m, probably an external measurement along the north side). It must, therefore, have been a great stone hall, much of which may have been double height, that is, without a first floor.

A detailed survey of the Whitefriars precinct dating to *c* 1627 shows the long narrow 'The Hale' (hall) where the theatre was located. In this survey the internal measurements of the theatre are *c* 90 x 17ft (27.4 x 5.2m), not including the 8ft (2.4m) wide passage at the west end. There is also some useful archaeological evidence: two walls of the theatre building were still visible in the 1920s, preserved in the basement of a solicitor's office on Bouverie Street.

Perhaps providing the most important evidence of all are the actual plays that were written for this theatre. The theatre scholar Jean MacIntyre has studied those plays – particularly the works of Nathan Field (p 127), an actor-writer with the Queen's Revels – to give us an insight into the arrangement of the stage. Using this range of evidence, we can attempt a reconstruction of the theatre.

One of the two walls seen in the 1920s was an internal wall and we can guess that most of the superstructure of this dividing wall would have been demolished in the early 17th century, in order to enlarge the theatre space; the front of the stage platform may have rested on the demolished wall stub. This hypothesis would create an auditorium space of about 56 x 17ft (17 x 5m), with space for *c* 21 rows of seven seats. The space over the passage at the west end would be an obvious place to site a gallery (providing another three rows of seven seats), since it would be difficult to have longitudinal galleries without completely cutting off the sight lines for the majority of the audience. The auditorium would thus only seat about 170 people, although it is possible that a short gallery on one of the sides (or over part of the stage) could have brought this seating capacity to nearer 200 spectators.

The 'platform' or main stage is reconstructed with a depth of 15ft (4.7m) to form an almost square space (with the width being the 17ft (5m) width of the building). The 'discovery' or rear stage area probably occupied almost the full width of the building, allowing space for a corridor on each side connecting the platform to the 'tiring house' or backstage area. The actual doors into the platform are described as 'studies' in Jonson's *Epicoene* (1609), and these were presumably sturdy wooden structures, sort of kiosks, perhaps supporting the 'above' or upper platform over

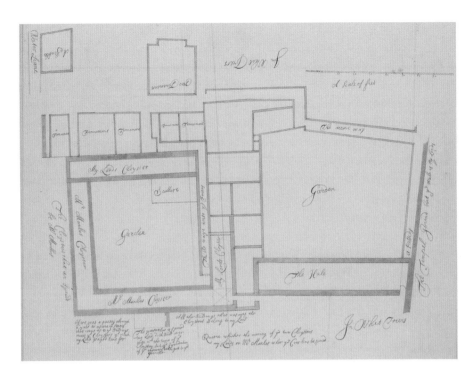

19th-century tracing of a survey of Whitefriars of c 1627; the building marked 'The Hale' (hall) is the Whitefriars theatre, the old library of the Carmelite White Friars (north to the bottom)

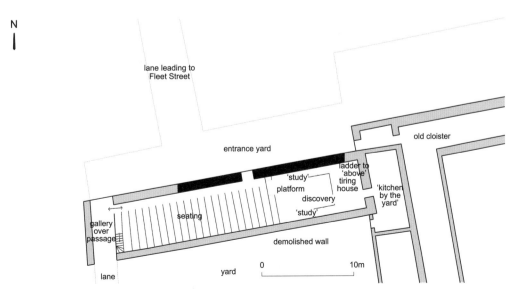

Reconstruction plan of the Whitefriars theatre of 1606–14; archaeologically recorded walls in black tone

the discovery. The discovery – curtained at the front to allow scene changes – would thus be about 11ft (3.5m) wide and perhaps 8ft (2.5m) deep, with a fairly wide rear door to allow props to be carried on and off. This leaves remarkably little space for the tiring house; perhaps part of the old cloister wing to the east ('the kitchen by the yard') was used as an additional facility. The 'above' or upper platform must have been quite small, because the scripts show that no more than three actors used it at a time and, furthermore, that it was quite hard to access (there was generally a minute's worth of dialogue to give time for an actor to exit the stage and get up to the above).

Porter's Hall, Blackfriars, 1615

Philip Rosseter, the court lutenist, had been appointed manager of the Children of the Queen's Revels back in 1609 at the Whitefriars. With the closure of that theatre, Rosseter endeavoured to find a new home for the Children and, initially, the Lady Elizabeth's Men, but this story is of another failed project – albeit with interesting twists.

Rosseter started off well by finding some partners, Phillip Kingman, Robert Jones and Ralph Reeve, and taking a lease on 'divers buildings, cellars, sollars [upper rooms], chambers and yards for the building of a playhouse thereupon for the better practising of the said Children of the Revels. All which premises are scituate and being within the precinct of the Blacke ffryers neere Puddlewharfe in the suburbs called by the name Lady Saunders house or otherwise Porter's Hall'. More importantly he secured from the King a royal patent of 3 June 1615, which gave 'licence and authoritie unto the said Phllip Rosseter, Phillip Kingman, Robert Jones and Ralph Reeve at their proper costs and charges to erect build and sett up in and upon the said premises before mentioned one convenient playhouse fore the said Children of the Revels ... and for the Prince's Players and for Lady Elizabeth's Players'. Shortly afterwards Kingman and Jones appear to have sold their shares to Philip Henslowe, who provided 'advice expences and aid' to pull down some of the older 'messuages or tenements' (including the Lady Saunders house) there and 'indeavoured to build a playhouse there'. Henslowe died in January 1616, but Edward Alleyn, his stepson-in-law, noted that Henslowe had spent £200 and that he, Alleyn, had later spent over £2000 on the project. The name of the theatre suggests that the building was the old porter's lodge of the Dominican Black Friars, that is to say the building immediately north-west of Apothecaries' Hall (Walk 1, location **21**).

The appearance of Henslowe and Alleyn would certainly have brought experience and influence to the project, but forces were already ranging against them. In August 1615, the inhabitants of Blackfriars wrote to the Lord Mayor complaining that a(nother) playhouse in the area would bring 'greate annoyance, danger and inconvenience' to the 'divers noblemen and gentlemen of quality' who lived there. They then listed the usual fears of drunkeness and noise introduced by the wrong sort of people, and disturbance to church services. They were supported by Sir Edward

Coke, the powerful anti-theatrical judge, who also wrote to the Lord Mayor, who now wrote to the Privy Council seeking an annulment of the King's licence. He noted that Rosseter and his partners were already 'erectinge a newe Playhouse' on the site 'with speede', which brought some urgency to the matter. The Privy Council acted fast and instructed the partners to stop the project. Their arguments included the dubious claim that the original royal licence was not for any playhouse development 'within the cittie', they were also, of course, conscious that the 'king's plaiers have a howse already' within the Blackfriars precinct.

Despite such restrictions, a year later the Lord Mayor learnt with horror that the playhouse was operating in one form or another and that Rosseter was about to approach the King if he could proceed again with the playhouse project. By January 1617 the Privy Council had informed the king that 'certain persons ... have latelie erected and made fitt a building, which is almost if not fully finished'. There must have been further injunctions, for no more is heard of performances there. Nothing is known of the construction or layout of the Porter's Hall playhouse and it was probably converted to other uses; certainly Edward Alleyn continued to own 'divers tenements' there for many years. The only inferences that there were performances there are in first editions of two plays: Beaumont and Fletcher's *The scornful lady* (1616) stated that the Children of the Queen's Revels acted it there and Nathan Field's *Amends for ladies* (1618) was acted there by both the 'Prince's Servants' and the company of which he was principal actor, the Lady Elizabeth's Men.

*Portrait of actor/playwright Nathan Field
(1587–1619/20); the date is thought to be
c 1610–15, but the hairstyle and dress appear
c 15 years earlier, suggesting this might be the
first British portrait to show an actor in costume*

Phoenix, Drury Lane, 1616

The Phoenix, located just behind Drury Lane, was the first theatre in what we now know as the 'west end' home of theatres. As only the second indoor theatre, it was probably conceived as a competitor to the Blackfriars. Drury Lane has its origins in the medieval period, as a roadway running south-east from the line of High Holborn to the Strand. The area north-east of Drury Lane was a large field known as Aldwych Close, which had been part of the lands of St Giles Hospital. After the Dissolution it passed through various hands until bought by the Holford family in 1567. Development of the area was slow but by the beginning of the 17th century such roads as (the modern) Great Queen Street to the west and Kemble Street to the east had begun to be formed, and on 28 April 1607 one Walter Burton leased a three-acre triangular plot between the two roads, with the north and south bounded by what became Wild Street and Drury Lane (Walk 5, location **9**). Two days later, however, Burton sub-leased part of this area to John Best, Cockmaster to the Prince of Wales, who then (according to a 1647 lawsuit) 'erected or caused to be erected seven or eight houses or dwelling houses with their appurtenances as namely one messuage house or tenement called a Cockpitt and afterwards used for a play house and now called the Phoenix with divers buildings thereto belonging and one other messuage howse or tenement'.

Christopher Beeston, an actor since at least 1598 and now leader of the Queen's Men, further sub-leased the property on 9 August 1616. It was then described as 'all that edifices or building called the Cockpittes and the cock-houses and shedds thereunto adjoining ... Togeather alsoe with one tenement or house and a little Garden thereunto belonging next adjoining to the said Cockpittes ... and one part or parcell of ground behind the said Cockpittes Cockhouses three tenements and garden devided as in the said indenture'. Acquisition of this property was clearly with the intention of providing a new home for his company, hitherto at the Red Bull. It was an affluent area and richer patrons were obviously anticipated, though the benchers of Lincoln's Inn, about 550yd (500m) north-east, complained in October about 'the converting of the Cock Pytte in the feildes into a playe house'. However, nothing further was heard of this and the Queen's Men had moved in by at least the end of February 1617.

Analysis of the architectural form of the Phoenix has been problematic because of its relationship to the original 'cockpit'. The notion that the original cockpit was only slightly modified or converted was given credence because two drawings from the studio of Inigo Jones were thought to represent such a modification. These show a U-shaped, or elongated semi-circular, structure with a domed roof. Certainly Shakespeare could refer to a playhouse (the Curtain) as a 'cockpit' large enough to 'hold the vasty fields of France' (in the Prologue to *Henry V*), but this is clearly rhetoric. The dates of Jones's drawings are still debated, and it is uncertain that Jones, the Surveyor-General of the King's Works, would be employed on such a project without some record of it. Wright's *Historia histrionica* of 1699 noted that the Phoenix was similar to the other theatres, the Blackfriars and the Salisbury Court – 'for they were all three built almost exactly alike for form and bigness' – which suggests that they were all rectangular, though the Blackfriars was actually larger than the other two. The only other clue to its construction is a rude quip by John Middleton, indicating that it was made of brick. Analysis of plays performed at the Phoenix suggests that its stage had three openings with a balcony over it. As we will see, the theatre must have been entered on the north with a stage, probably, in the south.

Luckily, the Phoenix actually appears in a 1556 drawing by Wenceslaus Hollar as a three-storeyed, three-gabled building (p 130), located exactly where modern research established it in 1988. The original 1609 cockpit was most likely a small wooden structure, whereas research suggests that the new building appears to have been a 40ft (12.2m) square brick one. Indeed, it has been suggested that the name Phoenix related to a new building arising from the (metaphorical) ashes of the previous building. Careful analysis of property leases by Graham Barlow, lawsuits and plans drawn up by the Metropolitan Board of Works in 1877, have pinpointed its location adjacent to Cockpit Alley that formerly ran between Drury Lane and Wild Street.

Hardly had the Queen's Men arrived at their new site than it was wrecked by the London apprentices during their annual Shrove Tuesday spree, which fell on 4 March in 1617. 'Many disordered persons of sundry kinds, amongst whom were very many young boys and lads, that assembled themselves in Lincolns Inn Field, Finsbury Field, in Ratcliffe, and Stepney Field, where in riotous manner they did beat down the walls and windows of many victualling houses and of all other houses which they suspected to be bawdy houses. And that afternoon they spoiled a new playhouse, and did likewise more hurt in diverse other places.' Another account records the loss of the company's most valuable assets: the rioters cut 'the players apparell all to pieces, and all other theyre furniture, and burnt theyre play bookes'. Other accounts note death and destruction, but it is clear that at the Phoenix it was the interior that was wrecked. Nevertheless, the Queen's Men had to return to the Red Bull before reoccupying the repaired Phoenix in June, by which time they would have had to find new costumes and a new repertoire.

The company stayed at the Phoenix until they were dissolved at the Queen's death in March 1619. They were followed by the Prince Charles [I] Men and then the reconstituted Lady Elizabeth's Men. They in turn became the (new) Queen Henrietta Maria's Men in 1625 until another serious outbreak of plague in 1636, after which Beeston formed a new company, called the King and Queen's Young Company, who stayed there until the closure of the theatres in 1642. Beeston had died in 1638 and was succeeded as manager by his son William. The Phoenix was one of the most successful and popular of Caroline theatres, with a string of works by the likes of Thomas Heywood, James Shirley, Richard Brome and Sir William Davenant; the latter was also briefly involved in its management. There are occasional illegal performances during the Interregnum but, in clear anticipation of the Restoration, it hosted operas by Davenant in 1658–9.

The Phoenix fell out of use in *c* 1663 and was probably converted into tenements. It was demolished in a widescale redevelopment of 1721 which lasted until the 1870s, by which time

Detail from Hollar's 'Great map' of west-central London, showing the Phoenix theatre

the area had become a slum and was compulsorily purchased to make way for the new Wild Street Peabody Estate (Walk 5, location **9**). In December 1991, an archaeological excavation was located immediately to the south-east of the Phoenix. This revealed 17th-century brick foundations to a rectangular cellared structure that was probably contemporary with the Phoenix.

Salisbury Court, 1629

The Salisbury Court playhouse was the last theatre, or playhouse, built before Parliament closed them down in 1642. It was also the only one built with explicit authority, since the owners were William Blagrave, Deputy Master of the Revels, and Richard Gunnell, who had been involved as an actor, sharer and manager at the first and second Fortune. Moreover, the Master of the Revels himself, Sir Henry Herbert, had some sort of stake in it, and the landlord, the Earl of Dorset, was not only the Queen's Chamberlain but an ardent supporter of the theatre. Nevertheless, it was probably fairly small and was never very successful.

Blagrave and Gunnell took a lease from Lord Dorset on 6 July 1629 for a piece of land on the east side of Water Lane measuring 42ft (12.8m) north–south by 140ft (42.7m) eastwards to the garden wall of Dorset House (Walk 5, location **2**). Somewhere in the northern part of this land was a barn where Blagrave and Gunnell 'should at their costs and charges erect a playhouse and other buildings'. According to a 1658 lawsuit, they spent *c* £1000 later converting the barn into a theatre and in building a separate dwelling house. Its exact location is uncertain, though it was probably within the corner bound by Whitefriars Street on the west and Tudor Street on the south.

There was plague in London for much of 1630 and it appears that the new venture finally opened on 12 November 1630, with the first performance of Thomas Randolph's *The muses' looking glass*. The players were the newly-formed King's Revels, but they were succeeded after about a year by another new company, the Prince Charles's [II] Men. The King's Revels returned in 1634, but became dissolved in the great plague of 1636–7 and subsequently merged with the Queen Henrietta Maria's Men until the final closure in 1642. The playwright Richard Brome was for a while the 'writer in residence', but among the successes of the Salisbury was Shackerley Marmion's *Hollands leaguer*, which was premiered in 1631 and ran for six consecutive days – a record second only to the nine-day run of *A game of chess* at the Globe in 1624. The only sour note there was the killing, in March 1634, of one George Watson 'at the playhouse in Salisbury Court'. After the deaths of Blagrave and Gunnell in the mid 1630s, there was a succession of managers culminating in Christopher Beeston and his son William, who were both involved in the Phoenix.

The little that is known of the size and layout of the Salisbury Court playhouse comes from later documents, mostly relating to its re-emergence after the Restoration in 1660. In fact it was

Title page of Hollands leaguer *by Shackerley Marmion, published 1632*

the anticipation of a reopening of the theatres that prompted renovation and rebuilding. A lawsuit of 1666 mentions that already before 1660 the external walls were of brick. In 1660 two carpenters were engaged to 'build and erect on the said theatre [that is, over it as an added upper storey] a large room or chamber for a dancing school 40 feet square' (12.2m²), which suggests that the theatre itself was of these dimensions. Furthermore, the carpenters were to 'repaire and amend the said theatre and the seates and boxes and viewing rooms thereto belonging', which would have been part of the original fixtures. A masque put on in 1637 required a proscenium and mechanisms for moving spheres and the like around the stage.

The theatre was used illegally during the Commonwealth and, as we have seen, restored and reopened in 1660. It was burnt down in the Great Fire of 1666 and not rebuilt thereafter. The nearest archaeological excavation, just to the north-east, between Salisbury Square and Hutton Street, revealed complete truncation, with no 17th-century, or any other, remains present.

As a postscript we might note that the last planned, but never started, theatre of the 'Shakespearean period' was a proposal of 1639 by Sir William Davenant for a theatre in Fleet Street. Davenant gained a licence dated 16 March 1639, which granted him permission to build 'a Theatre or Playhouse, with necesary tireing and retiring Rooms and other places convenient, containing in the whole forty yards square at the most, wherein Plays, musical entertainments, Scenes or other like Presentments, may be presented'. It is unlikely that this project ever got off the ground, unlike our earlier abortive projects, the George, Wapping and Porter's Hall, and it was clearly banned by a royal 'indenture' of 2 October of the same year.

OTHER VENUES:

THE ROYAL PALACES AND THE INNS OF COURT

The royal palaces

Introduction

The production of entertainments at royal courts is as old as time. The Tudors, particularly under Henry VIII, provided a series of lavish spectacles. The court functioned at whichever 'house' the monarch happened to be living at the time. Within the London area the original royal residence and place of business was Westminster, but other palaces around were acquired or new built, virtually all of them on the river. In our period, the royal and aristocratic patronage of the professional playing companies included 'invitations' for command performances. These provided up-to-date drama for the court and enhanced the reputation of the playing companies, who were also handsomely rewarded. In the last 20 years of Queen Elizabeth's reign, there was a vast increase and improvement in court performance. Details of such performances are provided in the court records. In one of the few documentary references to Shakespeare, we find an account from the Treasurer of the Queen's Chamber for 'William Kempe, William Shakespeare & Richarde Burbage servants to the Lord Chamberleyne', for performances in Greenwich on 26 and 27 of December 1594. There is no indication of what play(s) they were performing, but many of Shakespeare's named plays were put on at other occasions, noted below. Because the calendar at the time was based on religious festivals, court performances were usually required only at specific times: mostly at Christmas and Shrovetide (the week before Lent). Such commercial drama is distinct from the 'masques', which can be defined as the socially exclusive 'amateur theatricals of royal and noble enthusiasts' that were increasingly popular in the Jacobean and Caroline periods.

For royal performances, the players would often append a prayer, in the form of an epilogue, for the Queen. One such example was discovered 30 years ago and dated to *c* 1598–9. Its authorship has been disputed, but contenders include both Shakespeare and Jonson. As such, the former's *As you like it* has been associated with the play performed, probably on a Shrove Tuesday, possibly at Richmond in 1599.

> *To the Queen by the players*
> As the dial hand tells o'er
> The same hours it had before,
> Still beginning in the ending,
> Circular account still lending,
> So, most mighty Queen we pray,
> Like the dial day by day
> You may lead the sessions on,
> That the babe which now is young
> And hath yet no use of tongue
> Many a Shrovetide here may bow
> To that empress I do now,

> That the children of these lords,
> Sitting at your council boards,
> May be grave and aged seen
> Of her that was their fathers' queen
> Once I wish this wish again,
> Heaven subscribe it with
> 'Amen'.

The (great) hall was usually the largest, albeit solemn, gathering place in a medieval mansion or palace and an obvious place for court performance in those palaces that still had them. The last one built was added to Hampton Court by Henry VIII in 1535, but most later palaces had a more intimate 'great chamber' (deriving from a 'watching' or 'guard chamber') usually on an upper floor. The records are not always clear which room was used for various performances, but it was increasingly the latter. The 'banqueting house' was generally a later development, though the history of this venue at Whitehall Palace, in particular, ranged from the 1530s to the 1620s.

Hampton Court

This riverside palace, out to the south-west of the city, was built by Cardinal Wolsey from 1514–5. After Wolsey's fall, it was appropriated by Henry VIII, who greatly enlarged it and built a great hall on the first floor there in 1532–5, forming the north side of the inner court (Walk 7, location **1**). It is a large cavernous space measuring c 108 x 40ft (33 x 12.2m), with a very high roof. It survives, today, very much as it was first built; it was the largest court theatre space before the Restoration, being fitted up for plays in 1625–6 and 1631–2. The great chamber (Walk 7, location **2**) is also on the first floor immediately east of the hall. This measures 55 x 27ft (16.8 x 8.2m) and was certainly fitted up for plays in 1627–8. Plays, and masques, were certainly performed at Hampton Court before this; we know that Shakespeare's *A midsummer night's dream* was performed there on 1 January 1603, though it is uncertain which room was used.

Whitehall

Whitehall, then known as York Place, started as an offshoot of the palace of Westminster. By the 1520s it was in the hands of Cardinal Wolsey. Subsequently it too was taken over by Henry VIII, and it replaced Westminster as the main London residence for the English monarch for 200 years. Henry VIII died there in 1547, as later did Charles I in less happy circumstances. By 1698, when most of it burned down, it covered an immense area.

The main part of Henry VIII's palace was on the riverfront; the original hall, or great hall, was a north–south building forming as usual, one side (the west) of the chapel court, measuring 75 x 40ft (23 x 12.2m). The hall and the chapel on the east side were parallel to the river. The

Hampton Court great hall

Painting of Whitehall Palace from St James's Park, Hendrick Danckerts, c 1674–75; the octagonal theatre is visible on the right and the 1619 banqueting hall on the left

great chamber, added later in Henry VIII's reign, formed the west side of the inner court, but on the first floor; it measured *c* 65 x 35ft (19.8 x 10.7m).

Masques were performed in the hall in the 1570s, though by the 1580s the professional companies, such as Lords Sussex's, Howard's and Leicester's Men, were performing in both the hall and the chamber, though it is sometimes not recorded which venue was used (mostly the latter according to the accounts). Shakespeare's *Comedy of errors* was played in one of them on 28 December 1604.

Inigo Jones provided a (temporary) 'stage and diverse tymber woorks for a seane with several mocions and devices' in the great hall in 1635, for which drawings survive. It was not, however, permanently transformed into a theatre until after the Restoration, by Charles II.

Queen Elizabeth built a temporary wooden banqueting hall some 200ft (60m) west of the earlier buildings. Although this hosted a masque in 1571, it was replaced by a much more magnificent structure, with carved timbers, painted canvas and hundreds of lights, in 1581 that took 300 workmen only three weeks to complete. In 1584 the banqueting hall was given a semi-permanent U-shaped auditorium and was henceforth the principal Whitehall venue for a variety of entertainments.

Shakespeare's *Othello* and *The merry wives of Windsor* were performed in this banqueting hall in early November 1604, but by 1606 it was showing its age. In that year King James I 'puld downe the old rotten sleight builded banquetting house at whitehall, and new builded the same yeare very strong and stately, being every way larger than the first'. It was built by the carpenters of the Office of Works and measured 120 x 53ft (36.6 x 16m). The masque was popularised by Queen Anne, and Ben Jonson provided the first such pieces for the new building. We get an idea of how the building was set up for these occasions from the pen of the Venetian Orazio Busoni, who in 1618 described it as 'a large hall fitted up like a theatre, with well secured boxes all round. The stage is at one end and his Majesty's chair in front under a canopy. Near him are stools for the foreign ambassadors.' Nevertheless, the professional companies occasionally performed there and Shakespeare's *The tempest* was put on there on 1 November 1611, having been premiered at the Blackfriars the year before.

This building burned down in 1619 and was replaced by the magnificent stone banqueting hall of Inigo Jones, which still survives as the only remnant of the great palace (Walk 5, location **11**). It was slightly larger than its predecessors and the earlier hall and chamber, but it was used almost exclusively for masques until the installation of the famous Rubens ceiling paintings curtailed the use of smoke-polluting candles. Instead, another temporary 'masquing house' was built in the court just to the east.

Further west of the main palace, the chronicler John Stow recorded that there were 'diverse fair tennis courts, bowling alleys, and a Cockpit, all built by King Henry the Eight' and representing the recreation areas of the palace. The famous octagonal cockpit was indeed mostly used for cock fighting, though references to temporary stage playing emerge in the early Jacobean period (Walk 5, location **12**).

The main proponent for using the place as a temporary venue for staging plays was the young Prince of Wales, Henry Frederick (who died in 1612 aged 18), and many of the costs are from his household accounts. The first mention of such a use is from December 1607: 'Making ready the Cockpitt at Whitehall for the plaies there three severall times'. A further payment for playing there in the following January 'for one play presented by the Children of the blackfriers before his highnes in the Cockpitt at Whitehall' notes that the boys' company that had just moved to the Whitefriars. There are further references for 1611 and 1618, but they are all interspersed with records of cockfighting.

The building was finally fully transformed into a permanent theatre, albeit mostly for court masques, in 1629–30 by Inigo Jones. The building accounts included reference to the stage, the *scenae frons* ('back') balconies and galleries: 'finishinge a backe wrought wth crooked tymber behinde them wth five Doores in the first Story, and in the second story one open Dore & iiijer neeches in the same upper Storye. … Framinge and setting up the Deegres in the galleryes over the Cockpitt, Cuttinge fyttinge and naylinge Bracketts uppon the same, woorkinge and setting of upright postes to the Ceelinge for the better strenthninge therof, and bourdinge the same Degrees three bourds in highte wth a bourde to stay theire feet'. External staircases were also added at this time.

The new theatre is generally referred to as the Cockpit-in-Court to distinguish it from the Drury Lane cockpit that was rebuilt as the Phoenix. At the opening of the new theatre, the playwright Thomas Heywood delivered 'A Speech Spoken to Their Two Excellent Majesties at the First Play Play'd by the Queen's Servants in the New Theatre at Whitehall', recounting the glories of ancient Greek and Roman theatres, though concluding that 'may this structure last, and you be seen Here a spectator, with your princely Queen, In your old age, as in your flourishing prime, To outstrip Augustus both in fame and time'. The new venue was mostly used for masques, though stage plays were occasionally performed there after the Restoration.

Greenwich

Downstream from central London, royal occupation at Greenwich began in the early 15th century when Henry V's brother, Humphrey, Duke of Gloucester, built a modest palace there. It grew over the next 80 years and the future Henry VIII was born there in 1491. However, his father, Henry VII, completely razed it and built a magnificent new palace, which Henry VIII added to and where he spent the first 20 years of his reign. His daughters, Mary and Elizabeth, were born there and his son, Edward VI, died there.

There was a fairly small hall, measuring 68 x 30ft (20.7 x 9.1m), on the east side of the great court (Walk 6, location **1**), and a great chamber on the upper floor just to the north of it; both of these are known to have hosted performances. The great chamber had hangings and lights installed for performances in 1586–7. In 1588 there was an amateur performance of *The misfortunes of Arthur*, at either the hall or the chamber, for which the Office of Works had to build 'degrees

View of the palace at Greenwich c 1617

[tiered seating] and partitions'. The stage directions for this piece specified the need for a trapdoor and for at least three entrances onto the stage.

As part of the tiltyard range to the south, Henry VIII built a banqueting house (Walk 6, location 2) and a 'disguising house'. In 1527 the latter was equipped with a stage and seating for a performance of a comedy by the Roman writer, Plautus. Both of these buildings appear to have been suitable for performances, though there is no specific evidence that they were so used. Elizabeth kept the old banqueting house in good repair, but also built a new, temporary one for a festivity in July 1559.

Companies including the Queen's Men, the Admiral's, Leicester's, Strange's and the Chamberlain's Men, with Shakespeare in 1594, played at Greenwich throughout the 1580s and 90s, when the Queen spent much time there. There was not so much playing at Greenwich in the Jacobean period, but *Cardenio*, generally thought to be by Shakespeare, was performed there for the Ambassador of Savoy in June 1613.

Richmond

Richmond was not far from Hampton Court and there had been a medieval manor here; like Greenwich, it was completely rebuilt by Henry VII. The hall here, measuring 100 x 40ft (30.5 x 12.2m), was a free-standing building forming the west side of the inner court (Walk 8, location **2**) and was probably the model for Henry VIII's later halls at Whitehall, Hampton Court and Greenwich. There was also a great chamber, just to the south-west, within the 'privy lodgings' overlooking the great orchard to the west (Walk 8, location **3**). In 1588–9 the Office of Works had to erect a 14ft (4.3m) square stage, 'for the plaiers to playe on' and for 'posts, rails, degrees [tiered seating] and boardes' for a court audience. Like Greenwich, companies such as the Queen's Men, the Admiral's, Leicester's, Strange's and the Chamberlain's Men played there throughout the 1580s and 90s. Dekker's *Shoemaker's holiday* was amongst the few named plays performed at Richmond by the Admiral's Men on 1 January 1600. Queen Elizabeth died at Richmond Palace in March 1603 and there was no playing thereafter, except for a brief revival in the 1630s.

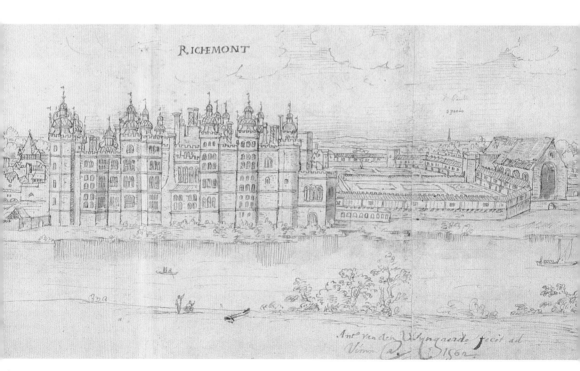

A sketch of Richmond Palace by Anthonis van den Wyngaerde in 1555; the remains of the old palace of Sheen can be seen to the right

View of St James's Palace (right) from the north side of Pall Mall, in 1660

St James's

St James's Palace was built anew by Henry VIII on the site of an old hospital (Walk 5, location **13**). It remains the senior royal palace in England and was the only London palace not on the Thames. Although the monarch no longer lives there, it remains today a working building with surviving Tudor elements amongst 19th-century remodelling. As befitting its smaller size, there was no hall, but a great chamber survives on the first floor in the north-west corner of the inner court as the 'armoury room', measuring 19 x 40ft (5.8 x 12.2m). Theatrically, the space was only used in the Stuart period, when works by Jonson, Shirley and Beaumont were performed in the 1630s, alongside older favourites by Shakespeare and others.

Somerset House

The Strand, the riverside route linking the city to Westminster, had become a populated and fashionable area by the 16th century. Edward VI's protector, the Duke of Somerset, cleared a large area to build the Renaissance-inspired Somerset House on the riverbank in 1549 (Walk 5, location **10**). On Somerset's fall a few years later, it reverted to the Crown. It was then used by a succession of queens and princesses, particularly in the later period, and was briefly known as Denmark House during the residence of James I's queen, Anne of Denmark. It was very occasionally refurbished, but finally demolished and replaced with the present masterpiece by Sir William Chambers in 1775.

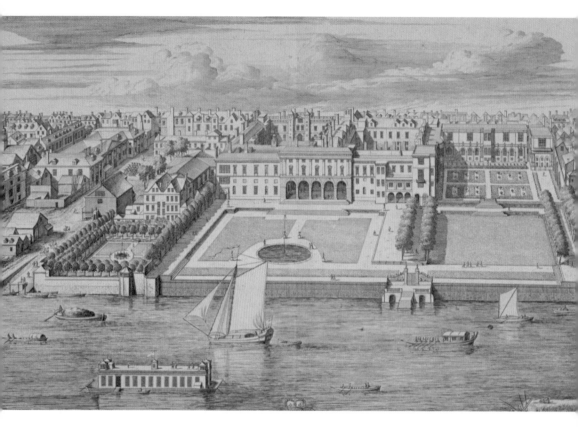

Old Somerset House, shown here in a drawing by Jan Kip published in 1722, was a sprawling and irregular complex with wings from different periods in a mixture of styles; the buildings behind all four square gardens belong to Somerset House

Until the 17th century, there was only intermittent use of Somerset House for dramatic performance, though the Queen's Men played there in 1585. There was a hall along the southern, riverside, end of the great court measuring 60 x 31ft (18.3 x 9.5m). Payments in 1626 were made for 'makeing a lardge theatre at the upper end of the hall' which, Simon Thurley writes, resulted in it being 'the first royal palace in England to be permanently equipped with a modern theatre'. The first performance in the new hall was by a visiting French troupe, in which Queen Henrietta Maria participated. A temporary wooden theatre was built in the courtyard in 1632–3. This was the Paved Court theatre measuring 76 x 36ft (23.1 x 11m), which saw Montagu's *The shepherd's paradise*, also performed by the Queen and her ladies. Professional performances at Somerset House appear to be rare, though the (new) Queen's Company put on Heywood's *Love's mistress*, and some old revivals were also performed.

Queen Henrietta Maria, Charles I's consort, who acted in many court masques; Anthony Van Dyck, London, 1632

145

The Inns of Court

Introduction

Although the professional playing companies could not ignore invitations to play at court, there were plenty of other venues available for private performances. Certainly plays were put on at country houses and at the colleges of Oxford and Cambridge, but within London other corporate bodies were eager for seasonal entertainment.

The Inns of Court – Inner Temple, Middle Temple, Gray's Inn and Lincoln's Inn – were where lawyers were trained and, collectively, they were regarded as England's third university. During the Elizabethan period, Gray's was the largest, followed by the Inner Temple. They are situated just to the west of the city, with the Inner and Middle Temples near the river, and Gray's and Lincoln's in Holborn just to the north. There were a further eight smaller Inns of Chancery, such as the surviving Staple Inn on High Holborn, most of which disappeared by the 19th century, as did many of the courts in this area.

The 'students' were varied and ranged from would-be lawyers and country gentlemen learning about estate management, to young aristocrats, spending a year or two in London, often preparatory to becoming courtiers. Gray's had the reputation of being the most aristocratic, whereas Lincoln's became the most puritan. They had their own amateur actors, who themselves performed elsewhere, even occasionally at Court. There seems to have been some jealousy shown by the professional actors – miscreants from Lord Oxford's company were jailed for 'commiting of disorders and afrays upon the gentlemen of the Innes of Court', possibly at the Theatre.

The four Inns of Court provided the right sort of venue and the companies were steadily performing there, again at beginning of November and beginning of February, and occasionally at Christmas. Professional companies appeared at the Inns from the 1580s; not many are identified, though the main companies are listed every now and again. From c 1605 on, most were listed as 'visiting players', though after 1614 it was usually the King's Men – with other 'visiting players' – though the Palgrave's company appeared in 1615. In the Caroline period, the King's and the (new) Queen's Players often appeared. The Inns could mount lavish productions, far more extravagant than anything that a public playhouse could produce, often at great cost. The halls were used for meetings and dinners, and temporary stages with suitable decoration would be set up at one end, probably the screen end, allowing use of 'stage' doors and possible balconies above.

There were certainly performances at the Inner Temple and at Lincoln's Inn, but few details are known. At the Inner Temple there was much rebuilding and adornment in the 16th century, and it became the second largest of the Inns. In 1561 great revels were held in honour of Robert Dudley, Earl of Leicester. The hall, which probably measured c 70 x 29ft (21.3 x 9m), and the library were both rebuilt in the 19th century.

The original hall of Lincoln's Inn was one of the oldest in the area and measured c 81ft 2in x

Middle Temple hall

Gray's Inn hall, painted in 1886

32ft 10in (24.75 x 10m). It was extensively remodelled in the 18th century but, after restoration, still survives today. A new, larger, adjacent hall was also constructed in the 1840s.

Middle Temple

Middle Temple hall is perhaps the finest example of an Elizabethan hall in the country. It measures 88ft 10in x 40ft 3in (27.1 x 12.3m) and is spanned by a magnificent, double hammer-beam roof (Walk 5, location **7**). It was begun in 1562 when Edmund Plowden, the famous law reporter, was Treasurer of the Inn. It has remained virtually unaltered to the present day and represents one of the very few venues which saw the premiere of a play by William Shakespeare. John Manningham attended a feast at Middle Temple hall on 2 February 1602, when they were treated to *Twelfth night*, which reminded him of Italian comedies and was a great success.

Gray's Inn

Gray's Inn was the largest of the four Inns, where the young gentry delighted in entertainments (Walk 5, location **8**). Among its students were the future playwrights George Chapman, Thomas Middleton and James Shirley. Shakespeare's *Comedy of errors* was performed at Gray's for its Christmas revels on 28 December 1594. A contemporary account of the evening records: 'So that night was begun, and continued to the end, in nothing but Confusion and Errors; whereupon, it was ever afterwards called *The night of errors*'. Later on the Inn's 'entertainment committee' was jovially maligned for having 'foisted a Company of base and common Fellows, to make up our Disorders with a Play of Errors and Confusions, and that night had gained to us Discredit, and itself a Nickname of Errors'.

The performance would almost certainly have been on a dais at the west, upper end of the hall, which measured 59ft 8in x 31ft 10in (18.2 x 19.7m). It was badly damaged during the Second World War, but faithfully reconstructed afterwards.

ANIMAL-BAITING ARENAS

The Banck

The bolle bayting

The Beare bayting

Introduction

The cruel sport of animal baiting would not seem to belong in a book on the more sedate delights of the theatre. However, there are a number of reasons why they are included here. Firstly, whatever our modern sensibilities, they were regarded as entertainment almost equal to the theatre; King James I was a great fan and kept a menagerie of wild and exotic animals at the Tower of London. Individual bears became celebrities known to all Londoners, and one, Sackerson, is mentioned in Shakespeare's *The merry wives of Windsor*. Slender, when trying to impress a girl, boasts 'I have seen Sackerson loose twenty times, and have taken him by the chain'. However, the records of animal baiting mostly come from the later 16th century, when it was finally included in restrictions of crowded events.

It must be stressed that there is no evidence whatsoever that animal baiting in any form occurred in the outdoor playhouses except, as we have seen, at the Hope, where there was an unsuccessful cohabitation between baiting and drama. Nevertheless, of importance to our studies is the fact that the bear gardens, as they were known, were *constructionally* similar to the playhouses and our excavations of parts of three of them (including the Hope) provide interesting comparative analysis, though as we shall see, they did not in fact provide the architectural origins of the playhouse form.

From the second half of the 16th century, the manor of Paris Garden became the usual venue for public animal baiting and, though it later extended into Bankside on the east, the name stuck. It was believed to be necessary to bait bulls in order to tenderise their meat, in other words baiting as 'entertainment' was not the original purpose. Nevertheless, bear baiting was regarded as a royal monopoly, and the Master of the Game was a royal appointee and responsible for the Yeoman of the Bears. In September 1546 Thomas Fluddie, the Yeoman of the King's Bears, was given a licence for baiting on Bankside. The following December John Allen, the Yeoman of the Prince's Bears, was given a similar licence to bait in Southwark. The keeping of mastiffs, let alone bears, was an expensive operation. But it could be a lucrative business and thus, just like the theatres, subject of much litigation.

In contrast to the inns and playhouses, the bear-baiting rings were specifically licensed to operate on Sundays. This seems to have been traditional since at least 1550, when the poet Robert Crowley wrote:

At Paris Gardens each Sunday, a man shall not fail

To find two or three hundred for the bearward's vale.

Many of the descriptions of bear baiting note that it was on a Sunday until James I banned it on the Sabbath in 1603, opening up available weekdays.

Detail from the Agas map of c 1562 showing two animal-baiting rings on Bankside, labelled The bolle bayting *and* The Beare bayting

In his 1923 book on the Globe, W W Braines provided an appendix on the Bankside bear gardens – or animal-baiting rings. Here, he followed the testimony of John Taylor, who in 1620 remembered 'that the game of beare bayting hath been kept in four several places'. As we will see, one of them was so completely rebuilt that it should be designated separately, and Braines added a later one built long after Taylor had passed on.

Bear garden no. 1, near Mason's Stairs

We presume that no. 1 was the earliest, therefore dating to the 1540s. Taylor said it was at 'Mason Stairs on the Bankside', which was one of the river steps used by the ferrymen. From old maps it can be easily located just north of the Tate Modern (Walk 4, location **7**).

Bear garden no. 2, by the corner of the Pike Garden

The second was 'neer Maid Lane by thr corner of Pyke Garden'. Maid Lane was, as we have seen, modern Park Street. There were a number of pike gardens, or ponds, in the area, but Braines suggested that it was probably within the angle formed by Moss Alley (a former alley just east of the Tate Modern) and Park Street (Walk 4, location **10**). Excavations on this site in 1988 did not reveal any structure that might be identified with a bear-baiting ring, but did find many dog bones, possibly associated with mastiffs from a nearby ring.

The map by Agas of *c* 1562 (and other similar maps) shows two animal-baiting rings on Bankside, labelled *The bolle bayting* and *The Beare bayting*. The map is not very accurate, and may represent bear gardens no. 1 and no. 2 or even no. 2 and no. 3 operating simultaneously. It is a pity that we do not know much about the first two rings, because it would have been interesting to know about their form and size, and if they were similar to the later one. All we can tell, from the map evidence, is that they were circuits of single-storeyed roofed galleries.

It may have been the second or third ring that was described by the Venetian visitor Alessandro Magno in 1562, when he noted various animal pens then 'In the midst of these is an open circular space surrounded by stands with their awnings for the sun and the rain, where every Sunday in the training of these dogs people find great entertainment. To enter below one pays a penny and two to go up into the stands. The amusement lasts from the vesper hour until evening, and they put on very fine baitings. First they lead into this space, which is closed about, and there is no way out unless they open certain doors'; after this he describes the baiting itself.

Bear garden no. 3, 'Payne's standings'

The third ring was 'at the beare garden wch was parcel of the possession of William Payne', which can be located nearer the river just south of the Bell inn (Walk 4, location **13**). Quite a lot is

Bear and bull baiting in Nuremburg, 1685

Street sign

known about the third ring because it was the ultimate predecessor of the Hope and figures in a lengthy land dispute. William Payne, who leased the Bell as well as the adjacent Cock and the Barge pubs (later renamed the Dancing Bears), assumedly built these 'low scaffolds or standings'. Payne's ring cannot have been very large, perhaps only 50 or 60 feet (15–18m) in diameter, but there were nearby houses or huts for bears and kennels for dogs, as well as a pond to wash the bears.

It was this bear garden, perhaps nearly 40 years old, which collapsed in 1583. This prompted the Reverend John Field to describe it as a manifestation of God's wrath. The descriptive passages are worth quoting at length for the details of the building therein and their invective.

That upon the last Lords day being the thirteenth day of the first month, that cruell and lothsome exercise of bayting beares being kept at *Parrisgarden*, in the afternoone, in the time of common praiers, ... Beeing thus ungodly assembled, to so unholy a spectacle ... the yeard, standings, and galleries being ful fraught, being now amidest their joilty, when the dogs and Bear were in the chiefest Battel, Lo the mighty hand of God uppon them. This gallery that was double, and compassed the yeard round about, was so shaken at the foundation, that it fell (as it were in a moment) flat to the ground, without post or peere, that was left standing, so high as the stake whereunto the Beare was tied. Although some wil say (and as it may be truly) that it was very old and rotten and therefore a great waight of people, being planted upon it then was wont that it as no marvaile that it fayled: and would make it but a light matter. Yet surely if this be considered that no peece of post, boord, or stake was left standing. In the fal of it, there were slaine five men and two women ... Of all the multitude there, which must needed be farre above a thousande, it is thought by the judgement of most people, that not the third personne escaped unhurt ... They say also that at first, when the Scaffolde cracked (as it did once or twice) there was a cry of *fire fire*, which set them in such a maze ... But it shoulde appere that they were most hurt and in danger, which stood under the Galleries on the ground, upon whom both the waight of Timbre and people fel ... For surely it is to be feared, beesides the distruction bothe of bodye and soule, that many are brought unto, by frequenting the *Theater*, the *Curtin* and such like ...

From this account, there were clearly two tiers of spectators – a standing room over which a gallery, that collapsed, was built. Alessandro Magno had already noted that it cost a penny 'to enter below ... and two to go up into the stands'. How the lower area was sufficiently protected from the animals is not clear; perhaps it was slightly raised or the arena floor itself was lower.

Although the bears would have been fastened by ropes or chains, they are known to have broken loose on occasion. Henry Machyn recorded that, in 1554, a great blind bear broke loose and mauled a man so much that he died a few days later. Bulls, even tethered, provided another danger. There are numerous records of them tossing dogs high up into the galleries. A loosened bull could jump great heights and anyone who has visited a Spanish bullring will see two sets of very high walls around the arena.

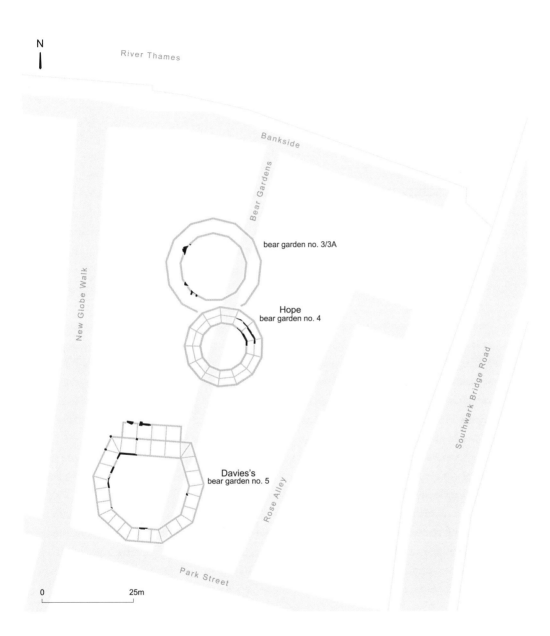

Plan showing bear gardens nos 3A and 4 (excavated remains in black)

As noted above, there is a convention to follow Braines's list of five bear-baiting arenas. However, this does not take account of the building that replaced the third ring that collapsed in 1583. It is far too late to renumber Braines's and, ultimately, Taylor's listing, but henceforth this 1583 bear garden should really be identified as no. 3A.

Bear garden no. 3A, 1583

This replacement, presumably on the same site (Walk 4, location **13**), was swiftly put up and opened by June of the same year. Crucially, it was described as being 'larger in circuit and compasse'. Two descriptions by German visitors to London make it clear that this was a very different kind of building. Lupold von Wedel, in August 1584, described it as a 'round building three stories high', while in 1598 Samuel Kiechel emphatically described it as being built 'in the form of a theatre'. It would appear then, that the new 1583 ring marked a break with its predecessors and was based on the northern playhouses, the Theatre and the Curtain. It should be noted that the bear garden shown on Norden's maps (p 71, p 75) as the *Beare howse* (1593) and the *Bearegarde[n]* (1600) is the same size as the playhouses shown. A 1590 description of its 'stock' included three bulls and nine bears – comprising five great bears, one bear, one she bear, one young bear and one old bear – as well as a horse and an ape. In 1611 two white (?polar) bears were listed, along with a lion. After changing hands a number of times, the lease of the bear garden was finally bought by Edward Alleyn in December 1594 for £450, and was then licenced to hold games. Alleyn and his stepfather-in-law, Philip Henslowe, finally managed to buy the office of Master of the Game in 1604 and no longer had to pay fees to bait beasts, being confirmed as Joint Masters in 1608.

This building, or a small part of it, has been archaeologically excavated. A series of three timber piles supported polygonal wall foundations with an internal diameter of *c* 52ft (16m), which is indeed larger than the postulated size of no. 3 (above). Whether the bear garden was ever renovated or repaired is not known, but in 1606 Henslowe had employed Peter Street to build a gatehouse entrance on the northern side of it; the gatehouse was later known as the Dancing Bears. This included a tenement for the bear keeper, a tap house for the audience members and an office for Henslowe and Alleyn. In 1614 the 30-year-old building was finally pulled down to make way for the Hope, just to the south, otherwise listed as bear garden no. 4.

Bear garden no. 4, the Hope

The fourth in Taylor's list was 'the place where they are now kept', in other words the Hope of 1613 (Walk 4, location **12**). It was a dual-purpose venue for playing and gaming, but its life as a playhouse was limited and it soon became a full-time animal-baiting arena. Its history and archaeology are discussed above.

Dog skull and tibia of adult brown bear from bear garden no. 4, the Hope

Left-hand side of horse's lower jaw found in pond near bear garden no. 4; shows chop mark through midline at the chin indicating butchering for feeding the dogs

Excavations in 2008 on the site of bear garden no. 5, Davies's, in Park Street, with part of the polygonal brick foundation shown left (dotted outline)

Bear garden no. 5, Davies's

The fifth such baiting arena listed by Braines was built by James Davies, 'Master of his Majesty's Game', in 1662 and, strictly speaking, falls outside our period. Since it has also been subject to archaeological excavation, however, it is included here, not least to complete descriptions of this still polygonal form of 'entertainment' building.

This bear garden was situated just south of the Hope, which had been demolished only six years earlier. Fragments of its inner and outer wall foundations have been uncovered at the southern end of (the modern) Bear Gardens (street) (Walk 4, location **11**). Preliminary analysis, however, suggests that although it was a polygonal building, its northern side was a long straight wall that was probably the entrance building containing the ale house that Samuel Pepys visited – much like the 1606 gateway building for the earlier bear garden no. 3A. The external east–west diameter of this ring may have been as much as 98ft (30m). This is slightly larger than the Swan, Globe and Hope, and would make it, appropriately for this final Bankside arena, the largest of them all.

The last keeper, or manager at Davies's arena in the 1680s was Henry Bayley and it was with excitement, therefore, that two London stoneware tankards inscribed to him were found in 2008 excavations in Holland Street, just to the west, where he might have retired to. It might finally be noted that another area of bear baiting in the later 17th and early 18th century was located at Hockley in the Hole (see map p 105), in Clerkenwell.

London stoneware tankard inscribed with 'Henry Bayle at ye Paul Head in St Lawrence Lane'; dated to c 1702–4 and found in Holland Street, 2008

PLAYERS, PLAYHOUSES AND PLAYGOERS

The players

The fascinating array of personalities involved in the development of the Shakespearean theatre is as exciting as the great drama itself. London's theatreland was a small place and most of the players – the entrepreneurs, builders, carpenters, actors and other people associated with the playhouses – knew each other through various links and many were at loggerheads.

The first playhouse 'builder' that we know of was John Brayne, a grocer by trade, though we may call him, like so many others, a 'businessman' in modern parlance. Brayne became easy prey for unscrupulous rivals – the most prominent being his own brother-in-law, James Burbage. For the construction of the Red Lion in 1567, he hired two carpenters: William Sylvester to build the galleries and John Reynolds to build the stage of his playhouse. The ensuing lawsuits, however, reveal that he was particularly finicky over a number of details, which would indicate that he had a very clear idea of what kind of 'playhouse' he wanted. It has, of course, been suggested that Burbage, a joiner turned actor, may have made suggestions on the playing space required, but Brayne's subsequent theatrical 'career' should perhaps place him as the father of Shakespearean theatre.

We know very little about the playhouse at Newington Butts, but it seems that it was a 'converted' house or tenement. Jerome Savage, only known to us as an actor with the Earl of Warwick's company, took a sub-lease on the property before 1576 and presumably also employed carpenters to do the work. As his playhouse was probably square or rectangular, it is not certain where his inspiration came from, though his experience of touring in the provinces may have provided some background. Nevertheless, he was engineered out of Newington by his landlord, Peter Hicks, who described him as a 'lewd player' only, hypocritically because he wanted control of the building himself – which suggests that it had some success.

Like Savage, Burbage will have been concerned to find a home for his playing company in building the Theatre. Financial advice came from Brayne, but the origin of the polygonal form is, again, far from certain. The actual builders are unknown, though Burbage's younger brother Robert was a carpenter. It has also been speculated that the young Peter Street and, more certainly, John Griggs had a hand in it too. Despite the claim for Burbage's precedence in playhouse construction and development, and his family's Shakespearean connections, he was not financially successful and personally quite unscrupulous.

We know nothing about who built, let alone who commissioned, the Curtain, but its proximity and probable similarity to the Theatre might suggest an origin there in form and experience. Whoever built the Curtain was not ultimately successful and the playhouse was probably taken over by the Burbages. However, the venue itself turned out to be the longest lived.

Philip Henslowe was probably the most successful theatrical entrepreneur of the period; he owned three playhouse venues and had an interest in three more. He made a lot of money and, though he supported actors and playwrights (and a host of tenants) financially, there is no need to ascribe this to altruism. By the time that he embarked on the Rose project, there were two standing precedents: he probably employed Griggs precisely because of his knowledge of these earlier playhouses. Griggs was involved in the original construction in 1587 and the alterations of 1592, as well as in work on other properties belonging to Henslowe. They clearly knew each other well and Henslowe apprenticed his niece to Mrs Griggs to learn sewing. Griggs's daughter married Robert Shaw, one of the leading actors at the Rose.

As we have seen, Peter Street was employed to dismantle the Theatre and the inference is that he was contracted to build the Globe immediately afterwards. In December 1599, Henslowe's accounts included a payment 'pd vnto Mr grimes at the apoyntment of strette'. Grimes had been noted for unspecified work on one of Henslowe's houses in 1595, but this 'appointment' suggests that Grimes introduced Henslowe to Peter Street. His friend Griggs had died early in that year and he will have needed a master carpenter for new projects. Street's most important commission from Henslowe was the construction of the Fortune playhouse in 1600, but he was further employed in 1606 to build the new gateway into bear garden no. 3A. Street died in 1609 and Henslowe then employed Gilbert Katherens to build the Hope playhouse in 1613.

From Henslowe's papers we learn that many of his tenants were part of the large and varied theatre 'family' that will have been necessary and available for these great enterprises. Despite any local or official opposition to the theatres, they were certainly beneficial to local economy and employment. Rental accounts for 1602 include 'ower tireman', who would look after the costumes in the tiring house. Elsewhere, 'steven the tyerman' has been identified as Steven Magget, who bought and sold various costumes in the mid 1590s. Apart from the tireman himself, there were many others associated with costuming and other properties, although not all may have been on the premises. There would also have been the gatherers, who, like various other assistants, may also have acted as supernumeraries on the stage. From the legal papers we learn that gatherers at the Theatre included Henry Johnson, who was also a silk weaver, which may indicate a relationship with the all-important costume business. Stephen Haward in 1604 and one Richwell the next year were both doorkeepers at the Rose. They were probably also gatherers but, since the end of playing at the Rose, they may have been caretakers to the empty building. Many women are known to have been gatherers, although Margaret Brayne, who succeeded Johnson at the Theatre, will have had a more proprietary interest. There were two women gatherers at the Red Bull in 1607 and Alleyn was asked if he could procure a 'gathering place' at the Fortune for a petitioner's wife. It is possible that these women were also connected with costume. On another occasion the Fortune company complained to Alleyn about a dishonest gatherer and did not want him to 'take the box'.

Francis Langley was also an entrepreneur and theatrical investor, with 'interests' in a number of playhouses, though most of what he touched turned to dross. His main interests were money lending, probable usury and an unending stream of litigation, accompanied by threats and cajolery. He died in July 1602, probably unloved, leaving a widow and six children with horrendous debts. Shady characters such as Martin Slater, Robert Keysar and Thomas Woodford abounded in the later period, vying for control of various premises and mostly working with the more exploitable children's companies.

To emphasise the commercial nature of the theatre, hundreds of money box fragments have been found at the Theatre, Rose and Globe sites. They were made like modern 'piggy banks' with a coin slot and so cheaply produced that they were smashed to obtain the collected monies. Not surprisingly, little money has been found at the theatre sites as it either went into the money boxes or was retrieved at the end of the day; some, however, escaped the cleaners and was left for later archaeologists. A few silver pennies and twopences were found at the Rose below the galleries, where they had presumably fallen between the floorboards. As there was no copper 'small change' in the Elizabethan period, thousands of imported brass jettons are found throughout Britain and a goodly number have come from the playhouses too. Most, at the Rose and Theatre, were found in the stage area and in the yard.

Complete pottery money box with fragments of similar ones found at the Rose

Two Elizabeth I silver pennies and an
Elizabeth I silver twopence from the Rose;
and two brass Nuremburg jettons (one
from the Rose and one from the Globe)

The playhouses

This section largely discusses building details from the outdoor playhouses. The indoor theatres were virtually all situated within existing buildings and most of them were on the 1st floor of these buildings. Thus there is no archaeological potential for them, though the documentary sources often pinpoint the locations and provide a record of their dimensions. Their theatrical alterations will have been undertaken by carpenters, joiners and specialist set designers, like Inigo Jones. The only theatre probably built *de novo*, the Phoenix, is fairly precisely located (Walk 5, location 9) and the nearest archaeological examination was only a few yards away.

There are no surviving building contracts for any of the earlier playhouses – from the Theatre to the Globe – but those for the Fortune and the Hope survive amongst the Henslowe papers and have provided historians with a wealth of detail on clients, builders and buildings. It is clear that these (and other such contracts) once included plans, sadly lost today. Details of the first Fortune were 'prefigured in a plot therof drawn' and the carpenters building the 1606 bear garden gatehouse were to use a 'a platt [plan] maide of the said frame subscribed by the saide Peter [Street] and by him delivered to the said Philipp Henslowe and Edward Alleyn'. We know that there was also a plan of the second Fortune because Edward Alleyn showed 'ye fortune plot' to Lord Arundel and the builders worked to 'a plottforme by them allready drawne'. As Shakespeare put into the mouth of Bardolph (*2 Henry IV*):

When we mean to build, We first survey the plot, then draw the model ...

The preparation for most timber buildings started at the beginning of the year, when the seasoned timber was cut; groundwork, however, digging trenches for the stone or brick foundations,

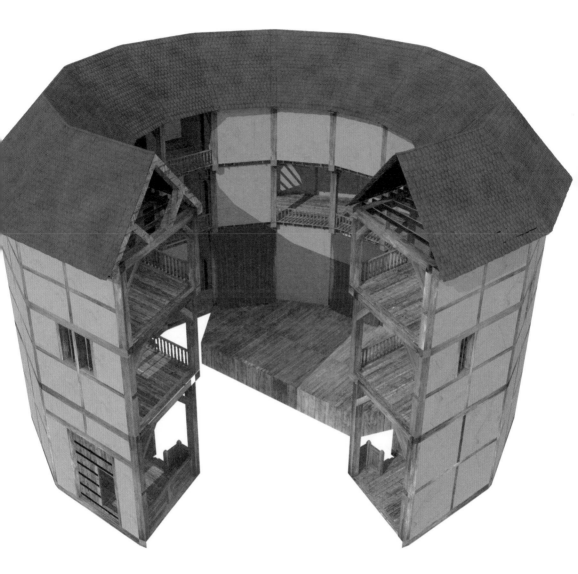

Computer-generated reconstruction of the Theatre with segment cut away to show construction of galleries and interior with its stage

was usually done in the spring when the ground had thawed out a little. From existing documents, it appears that most playhouse construction programmes were completed in about six months. The Red Lion was to be ready by July 1567, and we might note that in 1583, bear garden no. 3A was built on the site of its smaller collapsed predecessor in six months. The Rose and the Globe were probably built within the same timespan, though we know that the Fortune overran its construction period.

There was not always much room on the various playhouse plots and there were often existing properties on them, utilised for associated enterprises, such as for storage or tap houses (below).

According to contemporary accounts, and the Swan drawing (p 84), the ring of galleries around the yard contained three storeys. The inner wall was open, but fronted with a balustrade. A wooden baluster was actually found amongst demolition debris at the Rose excavations. It was subsequently used as a model for the hand-made ones around the galleries of the modern Globe, providing a neat descent from the originals. Seating within the galleries was on benches, as seen in the Swan drawing, though there may have been standing room there too. There were areas of more expensive higher-status seating, or boxes, known variously as lord's rooms, gentlemen's rooms or sixpenny rooms. The earliest examples may have been the partitioned areas in the upper galleries at the Theatre, but in most cases they were in the lower galleries next to the stage, where they are labelled the 'orchestra' on the Swan drawing. They are recorded at the Curtain, Rose, Globe, Fortune and Hope. There were also such boxes at the indoor theatres, such as the Blackfriars.

It used to be thought that all the stages were situated in the southern or south-western part of the open playhouses. This was because that was the area of greatest sunshine in the afternoons, when performances took place. The discovery that the Rose stage was on the north led to a review of these playhouse stages, and it became clear that they were opposite the main entrances and the main entrances were as near the public highway as could be managed, in order to channel people through one paying area. The playhouses and theatres were commercial enterprises, and their builders were quite pragmatic.

There was also a 'back door', recorded at the Rose as the 'tyeringe howsse doore' in 1592. The first Globe had 'but two narrow doors', through which people escaped the fire of 1613; these are interpreted as one 'back' and one 'front' door. The Hope probably had its main entrance from the north, but there was also a back door towards Maiden Lane. The second Fortune is also recorded to have had two doors. In an age where there were no appreciable safety regulations (apart from a concern over fire hazards), two doors were probably sufficient. The 'front' door was the main public entrance, opposite the stage, where entrance fees were collected. The 'back' door was a stage or service door to the rear of the building used by actors, management and perhaps by those provisioning victuals to the playhouse. It was probably also used by the lords or gentlemen to gain access to their private rooms. There would not have been much space in the tiring house, though the 'box office' will have been the management area. It was probably this room that had some heating in the form of a wood-burning stove, for distinctive stove tiles, with the Tudor coat of arms, were found at the Rose amongst the backstage debris and at the Theatre in a similar location.

*Green-glazed heraldic stove
tile from the Rose*

*Wooden baluster from the gallery front at the Rose;
found in the north ditch*

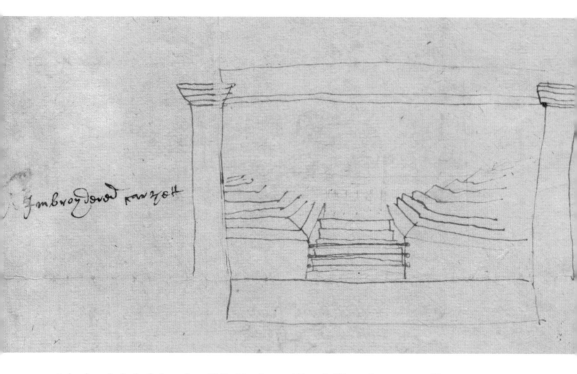

A sketch on the back of a letter from Philip Henslowe to Edward Alleyn, showing a possible ingressus

The Swan drawing (p 84) has a feature on the left labelled *ingressus*, meaning internal entrance, though contemporary English accounts refer to it as another 'door'. This accords well with the system of entry to the earlier playhouses. One entered through the main entrance and then into the galleries via the *ingressus*. Traces of these internal entrances were found in the Theatre, possibly the Curtain, and Rose excavations. There will have been internal stairs here, as at the Theatre, where the gatherers were to 'stand at The door that goeth uppe to the Gallaries of the said Theater to take … money that should be given to come uppe unto the said Gallaries at that door'. There might have been further stairs adjacent to the main entrance (though they will have obstructed the best views) and, more likely, in the separate backstage area.

A new system of entry developed in the early 17th century that allowed the richer playgoers to get to their gallery seats via external stairs, rather than having to go through the crowded yard. This implies a different pricing structure too, as entry directly into the galleries would cost more than entry into the yard. These 'stair towers' were built against the outside walls with entrances at the base, though there may have been passages into the lower galleries from them – perhaps represented by the small walls found at the Globe. From contemporary illustrations it appears that such features were added to many older playhouses such as the Curtain and the Swan. This new feature at the Swan was noted in the Hope contract of 1613, and such towers are clearly seen at the Hope and the second Globe in Hollar's engraving (p 93). Excavations at the Globe revealed the remains of a rectangular brick tower base, measuring *c* 16 x 6ft 6in (5 x 2m), which was distinctly added to the outer gallery wall over the fire debris of 1613. The Fortune contract ambiguously mentions 'steares, conveyances & divisions withoute and within' as at the Globe; but it cannot, therefore, refer to stair turrets at the first Globe of 1599.

Archaeological evidence revealed that the galleries of the Theatre were roofed with tiles, almost certainly spoil from the earlier priory buildings. Thatch was used at the Rose, but the stage cover of 1592 was probably made of wooden shingle tiles, fragments of which were found in the yard. When the first Globe burned down on 29 June 1613, there were many witnesses who testified that it was the thatch that had caught fire. The nature of the building was summed up by Sir Henry Wootton, who wrote that 'nothing did perish but wood and straw' and as we saw the use of tiles for the second Globe was emphasised by Ben Jonson.

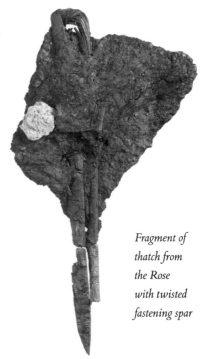

Fragment of thatch from the Rose with twisted fastening spar

A lineage has been provided by the existing building contracts. The new Fortune playhouse of 1600 was specifically to be based on the recently erected Globe, but when Henslowe built a hybrid form of playhouse and animal baiting ring known as the Hope, in 1613, its contract specified details to be based on the Swan. Although the 19-year-old Swan was the only playhouse standing on the south bank at the time, it is probable that it had seen improvements and modifications since its original build. When the Globe was rebuilt in updated opulence in 1614, it was the same size as its predecessor but was probably influenced by the recently completed Hope.

The size of the playhouses and, therefore, estimates of their capacities can provide information on their popularity and thus their importance to the cultural life of the time. There has been much work on Henslowe's income figures for the Rose, but the archaeological remains allowed for an estimate of c 2000–2500 depending on how crowded the building was. As we have seen the next generation of playhouses were larger and the figure given for both the Swan in 1595/6 and the (second) Globe in 1624 is 3000.

Production and staging

The stage

The one essential area of any playhouse was the stage, and the way that actors used it is of great importance. There has been much study of stage directions in surviving play texts of the time in order to gauge the features and conditions of these early stages. There are a number of documentary accounts and illustrations, but it was only with the excavation of the Rose that concrete evidence emerged.

There is a hint that the stage at the Theatre may have been the same shape as that at the Rose in 1587, and we assume that the Curtain had a similar one. The Rose stage was fairly small and covered some 490ft square (47.7m²). There was no trace of any permanent 'cover' or roof over it though there could have been stretched awnings. It was fairly shallow and acting must have been largely directed forwards. In 1592 Henslowe rebuilt the northern half of the Rose with a distinct change of emphasis in the shape of the stage, which was also provided with a permanent roof supported by two columns. The stage itself had the same square footage as the first, but it was now 'thrust' into the yard. The yard was extended outwards on either side in order to maintain sight lines from the upper galleries. The changes of 1592 were probably related to the heroic plays of Kyd and of Marlowe, then in his prime. This innovation in stage shape marked a new development in dramatic potential. Firstly, the shape meant that acting was now in three directions and the addition of a roof meant that people or properties could be let down from it. As we have noted above, Henslowe exploited these developments adding stage machinery in 1595, perhaps in reaction to the new hi-tech Swan.

Computer-generated reconstruction of the Theatre, showing the view from the stage

1592 was clearly a period of competition, for the Theatre in Shoreditch underwent 'further building and Reparacions' costing £40 at precisely the same time as the Rose alterations. It is, therefore, tempting to wonder if there were stage improvements here too, though at less than half the cost of the Rose alterations, anything at the Theatre will not have been as ambitious.

The new Swan was said in 1595/6 to be the most magnificent playhouse, but whatever the size of the Swan stage, it is clear that it also had a roof and was 'thrust' far into the yard, almost certainly following the new trend set at the remodelled Rose. There is no secure evidence for the stage at the Globe, but it was described by James Shirley, in the prologue to *The doubtful heir*, as 'vast' – albeit in comparison with the Blackfriars stage. Hollar's engraving shows that at the rebuilt playhouse of 1614 there was a very large double gabled 'cover', suggesting that the stage itself was rectangular and thrust.

The 'Shakespearean' stages were small by modern standards, but they still had to accommodate a number of people. The acting companies usually comprised 15–20 players and the opening scene of *Titus Andronicus* – first performed at the Rose on 23 January 1594 – calls for 25 parts to be present on stage at the same time.

Within the rectangular playhouse venues, there seems to have been a similar development. The rearranging of the Boar's Head in 1599 added a roof over the new, larger stage. The dimensions given in the Fortune contract reveal that the stage extended into the 'the middle of the' yard (perhaps as at the Swan and the Globe), albeit leaving only 6ft (1.83m) either side, if it was rectangular. The surface of the yard adjacent to the first stage frontage at the Rose was severely

Henry Peacham's drawing of Titus Andronicus, *performed at the Rose in 1595; the stage is indicated in outline*

The stage at the modern Globe

eroded and patched. This might have been because of poor drainage, but was surely enhanced by the crush of the groundlings against the front of the stage, still seen today at the reconstructed Globe. Already in 1580, a puritan diatribe described the 'presse against the scaffolde [stage]' at the Theatre, and this Tudor 'moshing' was one of the facets that attracted today's actors as much as those of the period.

The limited evidence we have for stages at the theatres is slightly contradictory. Two illustrations from title pages, purporting to be indoor stages of the 1630s, show angled fronts like that at the first Rose. Another late engraving, possibly of the Red Bull stage, is rectangular with lighting and seated audience that suggests an indoor venue. Some of the intimacy of the playhouses was lost in the theatres because of the low stage-front rails that separated the actors from the audience with a greater physicality. Nevertheless, the theatres were more socially cohesive and a different dynamic was created by the increasing presence of 'gallants' – rich young dandies-about-town – actually sitting on the stage. The consequent lack of space on these smaller stages made for a different performance style with less movement. Ben Jonson, in his *The devil is an ass* and elsewhere, wanted to 'repossess the stage' from the gallants. The new theatres of the Restoration and the development of the proscenium produced a flat front and it was only in the 20th century that the 'thrust' stage made a come back.

We saw that the temporary stage at the Bell Savage Inn was regarded as dangerously high and Thomas Platter in 1599 recorded that playing elsewhere was on a 'raised stage'; but the only record for the height of any stage was that at the Red Lion, which was 5ft (1.52m) high, presumably above yard or ground level. We assume that the first Rose stage was at the same height as the gallery and back stage floor level, but the alterations of 1592 suggest that the northern stage area was separated from the main galleries and may thus have been higher.

The stage back, or *scenae frons*, at the Rose appears to have been angled, following the polygonal shape of the building. There could have been any number of doors or entrances here for the movement of people on and off the stage, as well as the transport of varying properties. The Swan drawing suggests that part of the new stage development involved the creation of a more forward flat-planed *scenae frons*. This may have created slightly more room backstage, where the cramped space also explains why Henslowe had to add a shed at the tiring house door after his 1592 alterations. The balcony shown on the Swan drawing (p 84) would have been used for all the 'above' scenes such as Juliet's balcony, in many of the dramas of the time. The 'turret' at the Red Lion may have been used for a similar purpose.

At the Red Lion 'a certayne space or voyde part of the same stage [was] left unboarded'; this probably implies a trapdoor. The area below was often described as Hell, due to the preponderance of devil characters to emerge from below. Although the actual boards of the stage had long disappeared, hard floor surfaces were found within both stage areas at the Rose, which indicates that the 'below' space was certainly used and entrance must have been via a trap. Under the first Rose stage, discarded items such as shoes and props were found, and when the stage of the Boar's

Indoor stage, from the title page of Roxana, *1632*

Head was being rebuilt in 1599, the builders found 'rubbish' there. The playbill for *England's joy* at the Swan in 1602 noted that the intended delights included from 'beaneath under the Stage set forth with strange fireworks, divers black and damned souls ...' presumably via a trapdoor that had probably been an original feature.

Stage properties

Special effects at the playhouses were clearly as important as those in today's cinema. Apart from the various hoisting mechanisms, there are references to fireworks, while a cannon ball found at the Rose would have been rolled along to replicate the sound of thunder. On another level, many plays included directions for music, and the jigs and dances often performed at the end of a play would be accompanied by music. There is evidence that there were 'music rooms' at many of the playhouses and indoor theatres. Henslowe's accounts list a number of instruments, while a tuning peg probably from a harp was found at the Rose.

Apart from items mentioned in the play texts themselves, the Rose accounts include inventories of properties and costumes belonging to the resident Admiral's Men. Given the lack of space on the earlier stages, great stress was laid on the audience's power of imagination, much emphasis being on the rich language of the delivered words. There was little room for large elaborate properties and those listed included a cauldron, a cage, a rock, a mossy bank and a Hell's mouth, which are likely to have been easily removable items. Further accounts include payments for extra properties, such as a scaffold, a bear, a table and a coffin. William White, who was paid for making 'crowns and other things' in 1601 may have been the resident property maker at the Rose, although the next year payment was also made 'unto the painter of the properties'. The Rose excavations found few artefacts with specific theatrical associations, though there was a possible make-up brush and fragments of what might be mirrors.

Arms and armour were some of the most prominent stage props, typical of the heroic drama of the 1590s. Displays of swordsmanship were often presented at some of the inns and playhouses, and swords were also probably the most common weapon used dramatically. Henslowe's accounts record many pieces being bought and probably made locally, including lances and 'targets' (small

Cannon ball used for sound effects at the Rose

*Bone tuning peg and
?makeup brush handle*

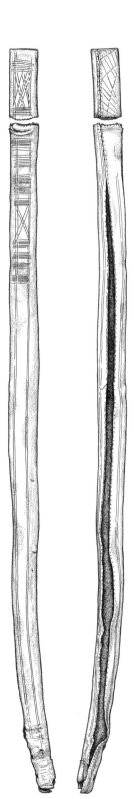

*Decorated leather sword scabbard
and Italian iron dagger guard
from the stage area at the Rose*

shields), whilst the props inventories include a 'longe sorde'.

Amongst the many pieces found at the Rose excavations in the debris associated with the first stage were a long leather sword scabbard and a fragmentary shield which had iron strengthening, suggesting that it had been constantly used and repaired until finally discarded. From the second stage was the hilt guard from a very fancy Italian dagger, as well as a fragmentary rapier blade and metal scabbard chapes – also found at the Theatre excavations.

Costumes and clothing

Anyone conjuring up an image of an actor on the Elizabethan stage will clothe him in gorgeous costume; their rich dress has almost become proverbial. Amongst the many descriptions, that by the excellent witness Thomas Platter reveals how he saw the actors:

> The comedians are most expensively and elegantly apparelled, since it is customary in England, when distinguished gentlemen or knights die, for nearly the finest of their clothes to be made over and given to their servants, and as it is not proper for them to wear such clothes but only to imitate them, they give them to the comedians for a small sum.

One of the largest areas of expenditure noted in Henslowe's *Diary* was on 'theatrical' costumes. There are constant references in the accounts to the purchase of materials or finished costumes, as well as to their alteration or embellishment, often associated with named plays. The expense of stage costume was a concern to all the playhouse managers and Francis Langley, owner of the nearby Swan, complained in 1598 about the £300 he had just spent on 'apparel and rich attire', and 'making ready' his playhouse. Costumes listed in one of the famous Rose inventories was headed 'all the apparell ... leaft above in the tier-house in the cheast' – no doubt in the care of the tireman. However, they were not enough for a full company and this list may just represent the expensive or 'special' costumes.

Like modern theatres, the playhouses of the 16th and 17th centuries will have had a network of tailors, costumiers and prop makers. There are references in Henslowe's *Diary* to 'Radford the littell taylor', and the 'tailor in the borough' is probably 'Dover the tayller'. Radford and Dover, the two regular tailors, were sometimes employed together, sometimes separately, and it would seem that they made the high-quality costumes, whilst the tiremen, acting as wardrobe keepers, made the cheaper ones; there is also a note of a payment to one John Rossel for mending garments. Most costume was contemporary, with only minor modifications for stock characters such as Romans, Orientals and the like. It was not always 'gorgeous' and the description of Petruchio in Shakespeare's *Taming of the shrew* reveal what may be made of more humble attire:

> Why, Petruchio is coming, in a new hat and an old jerkin, a pair of old breeches thrice turned; a pair of boots that have been candle-cases, one buckled another laced; an old rusty sword ta'en out of the town armoury, with a broken hilt, and chapless; with two broken points ...

Costumes at the modern Globe

Costume is a relatively rare commodity in archaeology, but the few pieces found at the Rose are quite revealing; be they worn by actors or audience. Fragments of high-quality clothing textiles from the Rose excavations included recycled garment trimmings of silk and patterned velvet. Some are elaborately patterned, but all of them would have been applied to clothing, worn by both men and women, as decoration. A fragment of velvet lace once had an edging of metal thread and was a luxury item stitched to a stylish garment as decoration, probably imported from Italy or Spain.

Among the many fragments of leather found at the Rose were parts of a plain cowhide jerkin, worn by men and women. Two were pieces of the skirting below the waist line, and another larger but fragmentary piece may be a front panel from a jerkin or doublet.

Much more common from archaeological sites, including the playhouses, are 'dress accessories'. There were a number of wire fragments probably from the ubiquitous frames that were used to hold up or stiffen various areas of dress, such as collars, ruffs and cuffs and, more commonly, head tiers, supporting the elaborate headdresses worn by Elizabethan women. Henslowe certainly paid for their manufacture by local women including the 12 shillings to Mrs Gossen for 'headtyers' in December 1601. The Mountjoy family of Silver Street (Walk 1, location **9**), with whom Shakespeare was lodging in 1604, were head tire makers.

Some of the most common finds on many sites of this date are copper-alloy dress pins, used to support and fasten the myriad layers of clothes worn at the time. The smaller ones would not have taken much strain and could be used only for attaching decorations or holding delicate linens. Indeed, the most obvious use for such a size was for securing ruffs, coifs, cuffs or bands worn by both men and women of some status, although it is possible that smaller items of women's dress could be held together with these pins. The larger ones would also be associated with women, to secure the flounces on wheel farthingales or for attaching bodices to stomachers and corsets. The bustle of clothes, particularly in a crowd, would certainly result in great numbers being lost. The hundreds found at the Rose, and slightly less at the Theatre and Globe, would suggest the uniformity of dress amongst actors and yard audience, as well as general domestic rubbish in fills, but not perhaps amongst the 'higher' audience in the galleries. Aiglets, or lace chapes, were used to bind the ends of laces that tied together larger pieces of dress. The utilitarian aspect of these aiglets may be seen in the fact that none were decorated.

There were two categories of find that might have come from higher-status clothing: embroidery and attached glass beads. Thin metal thread, particularly of gold or silver, was often embroidered on richer clothing. It is thought that such embroidery was added to stage costumes to embellish and enhance their appearance. Henslowe recorded payments to the 'copper lace man' and for some productions, copper lace was the only thing purchased. This addition of *faux* gold was clearly enough to enhance a production costume. Most fragments of 'costume wire' found at the Rose are indeed of copper alloy, although often quite fine. There was also a fragment of silver-wrapped copper alloy, which is reminiscent of the 'copper lace of sylver' bought for a

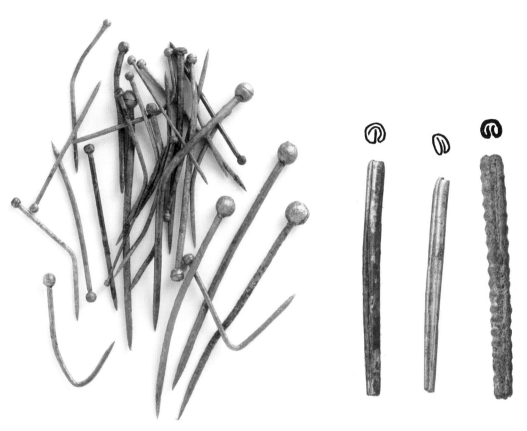

Dress pins (2:1, left) and 'aiglets' or lace ends (2:1, right), from the Rose and the Globe

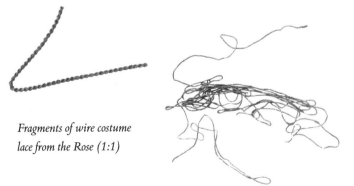

Fragments of wire costume lace from the Rose (1:1)

costume in 1597. Rich attire was, indeed, constantly altered to cater for new fashion. As such it might confirm the idea that aristocratic cast-offs were given to acting companies, who might have wanted similarly to enhance them.

The small glass beads recovered from the Rose excavations are some of the earliest found in London. They would have been sewn onto costumes or other items as decorative motifs. The beads from the Rose were not of the highest quality and they may be English rather than imported, but there were also two made from seed pearls (unique amongst the archaeological repertoire but known in contemporary dress) and a single example of amber. Most of the glass beads found at the Rose site came from below the galleries, which might indicate an audience with richer clothing, though a number came from the stage area. Many of these small items – pins, beads and pearls – would have been easily detached from clothing, particularly in a crowd. At the socially superior indoor theatres, the wearing of bejewelled costumes, by actors and audiences, would have created a greater visual impact through the sparkling effects of candlelight.

Small glass costume beads from the Rose (5:1)

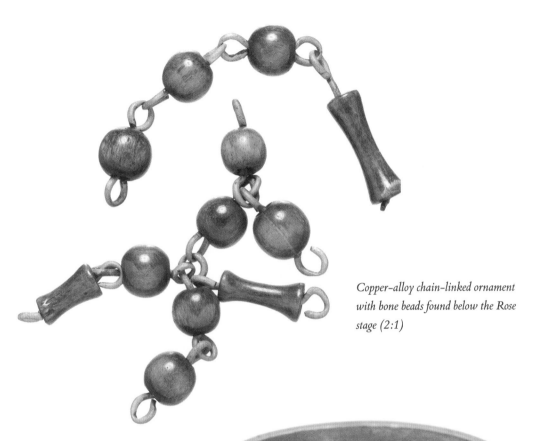

Copper-alloy chain-linked ornament with bone beads found below the Rose stage (2:1)

Mid 16th-century gold finger ring (4:1) from the second phase yard floor; the French inscription translates as 'think of me, God willing'

The majority of leatherwork recovered from the Rose excavations relates to footwear, most of which was very worn. The most interesting items, in our theatrical context, are the pieces from two separate boots, which are extremely unusual amongst archaeological finds of comparable date. The earliest fragment, from behind the stage, is from a calf-length boot or 'buskin'. The 16th-century perception of buskins was particularly associated with classical drama. George Puttenham in his *Arte of English poesie* of 1589 described ancient drama as:

> These matters of great princes [which] were played upon lofty stages, & the actors thereof ware upon their legges buskins of leather called Cothurni, and other solemne habits, & for a speciall preheminence did walke upon those high corked shoes …

He further notes that these 'buskins and high shoes were commonly made of 'goats skinnes very finely tanned, and dyed into colours' and that the word tragedy may thus derive from the Greek word for goat – *tragos*. The second boot, taller and more complete came from demolition deposits over the stage area.

Although the wearing of boots on stage was used to signify travellers, the Rose boots are fairly plain and, were it not for their archaeological provenance, might have been worn by anyone. A spur recovered from a ditch just to the north of the building is of slightly higher status, although it may have been associated with a worldlier theatregoer as much as with an actor on the stage. Fragments of a 'high corked shoe' were also found. The best-quality shoes would be covered with textile, the more ordinary ones with leather, although they could be decorated. Those found at the Rose are generally uniform in style with no differentiation in style between genders, though there were also children's shoes. Interestingly, a number of shoes were found in the stage area, including the only pair found. Some shoes have 'pinked', or slashed, decoration, particularly on the quarters (heels), which made the leather suppler. This decoration was clearly so common at the time that it was remarked on in Shakespeare's *Taming of the shrew* where Grumio, defending the apparel of Petruchio's servants comments that

> Nathaniel's coat sir, was not fully made,
> and Gabriel's pumps were all unpink'd i' the heel.

The playgoers

Andrew Gurr has collected many accounts of the individuals attending plays at most of the venues discussed here. His playgoers include men, women and children – nobles and high-ranking foreign visitors, gentry, students, tradesmen, artisans and servants. We have noted various descriptions of performances by playgoers, above, but Simon Forman, the astrologer and doctor, clearly well known to the Henslowe circle at least, including Jonson and probably Shakespeare, made detailed notes of the performances he attended in his diary. Amongst his documented visits were those to

Leather upper and insole of square-toed high boot (1:3),
with reconstruction drawing, from the Rose

Copper-alloy spur (c 1:2) found in the north boundary ditch at the Rose

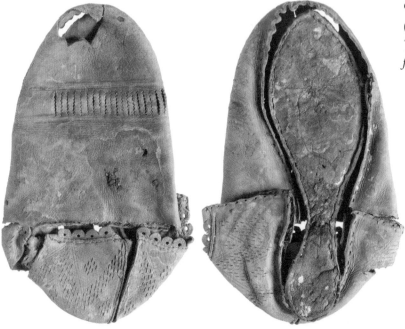

Complete leather shoe (length 213mm) with 'pinking' at the heel found at the Rose

the Rose and the Curtain in 1600. The Curtain visits were actually for assignation with a lady, Sarah Archdall, but he went to the Globe on numerous occasions in 1611, and wrote summaries of the plots of Shakespeare's *The winter's tale* and *Macbeth* amongst others, sometimes pointing out moral lessons to be learned from the characters.

The presence of men, women and children at the playhouses and theatres appears to be borne out by the few archaeological finds that can be defined by age or gender. In terms of social status there were very few items that can be described as high quality and the overwhelming bulk of personal items were mundane.

The audience at the modern Globe

Eating and drinking

The association of the playhouses with eating and drinking was made clear in 1599 by Thomas Platter, who recorded that 'during the performance food and drink are carried around the audience, so that for what one cares to pay one may also have refreshment'. Indeed, this association was a cause for concern to the authorities and the church.

Neither the playhouses nor the theatres had any room for internal services – a bar or a foyer, let alone conveniences – in the modern sense. Provision, therefore, was largely made through the dedicated 'tap houses', attached to most of them; these must have played an important part in theatre economy.

Although there were other buildings on the Theatre plot that could have been used as a tap house, Burbage is known to have kept a 'tippling house' for theatregoers in nearby Holywell Street. He was constantly fined for keeping such a house – which testifies to its success. It is possible that it catered to the Curtain audience too. The earliest document to give details of the building of the Rose, the so-called 'partnership agreement' of January 1587, between Henslowe and John Cholmley, is in fact what would be called a 'catering franchise' today. The agreement notes that Cholmley's house at the south-west corner of the plot, was 'to keepe victualinge in' and that he was to have the exclusive right to the catering and victualling of the enterprise. Part of this house was found in the excavations, though there was no hint of its function.

A plan of 1627 shows a small building at the back of the Swan (p 82) which was probably a tap house. A similarly located building seen next to the Globe on Hollar's view (p 93) must have been the tap house built by John Hemminges, one of the sharers. It was also lost in the 1613 fire, but built again the next year. The Fortune had an adjacent tap house occupied by one Mark Brigham in 1618, though probably extant since 1600 when the playhouse was built. It was probably one of the tenements on the Golden Lane frontage that came with the land. In 1606 Henslowe had built a new gatehouse for bear garden no. 3A and its contract suggests that it also served as a tap house for that building; it was later a tavern under the name of the Dancing Bears. These buildings were mostly too small for in-house brewing or cooking, and it is more probable that they were used for storage and dissemination around the theatre or playhouse.

Cholmley's agreement states that he had 'any breade or drinke' for sale at the Rose. Paul Hentzner, visiting London in 1598, recorded that at the playhouses 'fruits, such as apples, pears and nuts, according to the season, are carried about to be sold, as well as wine and ale'. A lot of fruit was imported into London in the 16th century and dried fruits, such as raisins, currants, prunes, figs, dates and almonds, were popular at the time. Apart from 'a Water-bearer on the floore of a play-house', the only clear reference to what was actually being drunk at the playhouses is to 'bottle[d] ale'. This liquid was used to extinguish the burning breeches of the unfortunate man caught up in the Globe fire in June 1613 and the sound of bottled ale being opened at the theatre or playhouse appears to have been a common distraction. From the plays themselves, bowls, dishes and cups were the most common props referred to in the numerous 'banqueting scenes'.

Joris Hoefnagel's c 1566 painting Marriage feast at Bermondsey, *showing Elizabethans at their leisure, with food being prepared in the open-ended timber-framed buildings (centre right)*

The archaeological findings from the Theatre, Rose and Globe have provided much associated evidence for the vessels and foodstuffs themselves. Serving and drinking vessels were the most common ceramic finds, though most glass drinking vessels were high-status items, storage bottles were basic domestic items. A number of spoons were excavated at the playhouses, but a very high-quality fork found at the Rose is probably the earliest fork found in London and may reflect ostentatious consumption at the playhouse.

Animal bones found at the Rose and other contemporary sites largely relate to post-playhouse dumps of waste rather than *in situ* consumption waste. However, a turtle carapace (undershell) found in a ditch at the Rose represents exotic foodstuff which probably graced a richer table than one in the playhouse.

By far the greatest quantity of shellfish food waste found in the playhouses – and on most other archaeological sites – is from the common oyster. These were supplemented by cockle, mussel, periwinkles and whelk. However, fragments of edible crab were found below the galleries at the Rose. Although apples are mentioned in contemporary accounts, their seeds were not as common within the botanical assemblage at the Rose as grape, fig, elder, plum and blackberry/raspberry, along with pear, cherry and peach. Also at the Rose there were many cucurbit (marrow/pumpkin, squash/gourd) seeds which represent relatively early evidence of contact with the New World. Walnut and hazel shells were common at most sites too.

Food waste in the form of fruit seeds and nutshells from the Rose

Black-glazed ware pottery tyg
or goblet from the Rose and a
green-glazed one from the Theatre

Part of the carapace (undershell) of a turtle found at the Rose

Brass-topped iron fork
(length 221mm) from
the Rose

Cucurbit (?pumpkin) seeds (1:1) from the Rose

Smoking and gambling

Tobacco pipes are first noted in England in the 1570s and were made fashionable at court by Sir Walter Raleigh. King James I, however, was virulently anti-smoking and attacked the practice in his celebrated *Counterblaste to tobacco*. There are many references to smoking in contemporary dramas and diaries. Thomas Platter recorded that 'tobacco was obtainable in ale houses, it is lit in a small pipe, the habit is so common that they always carry the instrument on them, and light up on all occasions, at the play, the taverns or elsewhere'. Nevertheless, there were clearly specialist tobacconists such as Abel Drugger, a 'Tobacco-man' in his 'corner shop', in Ben Jonson's *The alchemist*, which was performed in and set around the smart Blackfriars area in 1610. Complaints about smoking at the Blackfriars theatre a few years later suggest that it was a fairly widespread activity – to the extent that it was banned in a Cambridge theatre in 1632.

Clay tobacco pipe fragments, dating to between the 1570s and *c* 1610, have been found at all the playhouse excavations. These are likely to have been relatively expensive items and were not as common as later tobacco pipe finds, suggesting that the practice was not as widespread as indicated by the documentary sources.

Gambling was not far from everyday life in the Shakespearean period and frowned upon by the authorities, almost equally with theatregoing. However, leisure activities within the playhouses, possibly even on the stage, might be represented by numbers of dice found at the Rose.

Conclusions

The end of playing

It is often stated that the growth of Puritanism was responsible for the eventual closure of playing venues, but, as we saw above, it was the fear of unrest as well as infection caused by theatrical crowds that caused more concern to the authorities than moral outrage. The playhouses and theatres were periodically shut down because of plague outbreaks, though by at least the 1620s closure orders were increasingly flouted, often with an official blind eye turned. The perception of 'seditious' plays, as well as misbehaviour by the audiences, was common to both the outdoor playhouses and the indoor theatres, despite the social superiority of the latter audience.

By 1642, there was unrest in the air and impending national strife in Ireland as well as in England. As Martin Butler pointed out, this was of much greater concern to Parliament than the theatres. When, however, the future of public playing was eventually debated, it was probably influenced by fears about public order, rather than by moral disapproval of the stage, and a number of 'puritan' members of Parliament voted against closure. The wording of the final prohibition order of September 1642 almost reflects sadness that the closure was a victim of the increasingly deteriorating national situation:

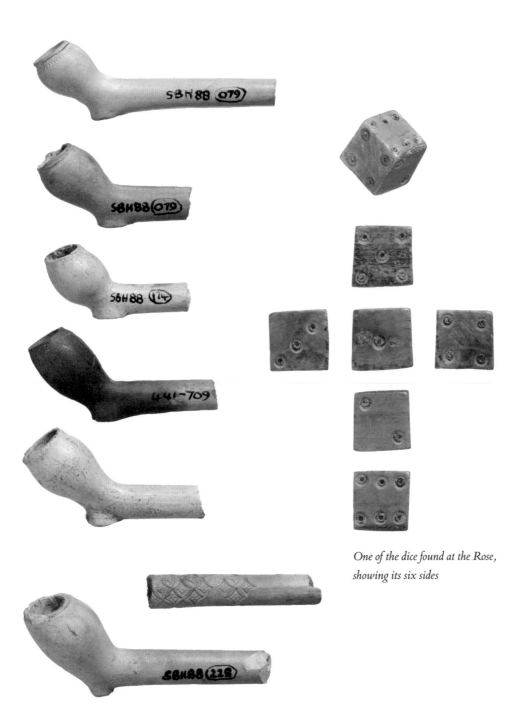

*One of the dice found at the Rose,
showing its six sides*

Late 16th- and early 17th-century clay tobacco pipes from the Rose

Whereas the distressed Estate of Ireland, steeped in her own Blood and the distracted state of England, threatened with a Cloud of Blood, by a Civill Warre ... Whereas publike sports doe not well agree with publike Calamities, nor publike Stage-playes with the seasons of Humiliation, ... it is therefore thought fit ... and ordeined ... in this Parliament Assembled, that while these sad causes and set times of Humiliation doe continue, publike stage-playes shall cease, and bee foreborne.

The legacy of Shakespeare's London theatreland

This order was not entirely successful and, as some of the venues continued to host illegal performances, further closure orders followed in 1647 and 1648, by which time 'puritan' attitudes had indeed hardened. Butler mused on how different the history and development of the English theatre might have been, had Parliament and the King settled their differences more amicably. Given the capacity of the playhouses and theatres during the period 1567–1642, there will have been hundreds of thousands of Londoners who saw and experienced this great period of dramatic production.

As it was, our 76-year Shakespearean theatrical era ended; but as we noted in the Introduction, its legacy is everlasting. Throughout the great theatrical periods of the succeeding Restoration, 18th century, Victorian and modern times these 'classics', the plays of Shakespeare and his contemporaries, have been performed ever since, both in their original form, but also as inspiration to new dramatic development. The influence of Shakespeare lies not just with new creative writers, directors and actors, but also in performance spaces: the intimacy enjoyed between Elizabethan actors and audience was revived with 'theatre in the round'.

Today, there is a healthy world-wide appetite for all things Shakespearean, even beyond the performances of the plays. There is an historical excitement and a biographical one – as his birthplace in Stratford-upon-Avon testifies. New documents are discovered, old ones are reanalysed, discussed and published every year to cater for this hunger. Archaeological discoveries have added a new dimension, with the immense impact of 'touching' Shakespeare. It is not just with the excavation of his home in Stratford, but in the actual buildings in London where he worked, where the resonance of those plays can be heard and where today's actors can feel the presence. And archaeology has the potential to discover so much more.

The Sanders portrait of Shakespeare

WALKS

Introduction

These walks are designed for those keen to visit the actual sites of Shakespeare's theatrical London. They include the sites of all the inns, playhouses, theatres, palaces and Inns of Court as well as the animal-baiting rings described above. However, these walks also contain wider geographical adventures and include the sites of the churches, houses, inns, brothels and fields known to 'Shakespearean' Londoners. The areas cover the city, and its eastern, northern, southern and western fringes as well as some areas of Greater London, each accompanied by short descriptions and histories.

There are accompanying maps show all the sites noted below with discrete numbers – though that does not force the walker to adopt any particular route. Nevertheless, local stations are noted and for those with GPS facilities, a National Grid reference figure is provided for each site. It should be recognised that at most 'sites' there is little or nothing to see and your own imagination, helped by our text, is required.

Two important factors must be borne in mind, however. Many long-disappeared sites of historical interest are now in private or institutional hands and are *not* open to the public. A few sites are inaccessible and some are situated in particularly *dangerous* locations – such as the middle of a road.

Walk 1 – the city

Centre

The main north–south axis of the city of London was originally the Roman Ermine Street and later known as the Great North Way. It links the southern- and northernmost of our theatrical areas: the Elephant and Castle with Shoreditch. Within the city it is known, from the south, as Gracechurch (once Gracious) Street and, north of Cornhill, as Bishopsgate. Further north it becomes Norton Folgate and then Shoreditch High Street, discussed below (Walk 3). Within its passage through the city proper were three of the inns that hosted playing.

The southern end, Gracechurch Street, was diverted a little westwards in the 1830s with the rebuilding, on a slightly different alignment, of London bridge. This realignment resulted in the razing of much of old Eastcheap (street) in this area including the **Boar's Head tavern (1)**. This was where Shakespeare famously set two scenes in *Henry IV*. In part I, act 2, Falstaff and characters from London's low life entertain the young Prince Hal. In part 2, act 2, it is the scene of Hal's introduction to such delightful 'bawdies' as Doll Tearsheet and Mistress Quickly.

The tavern was originally built in the 15th or early 16th century, but was burnt down in the Great Fire of 1666. It was rebuilt soon afterwards and its 'sign', with the date 1668, is in the collections of Museum of London (location **10**, below). Even this rebuilt tavern was famous until the late 18th century for hosting

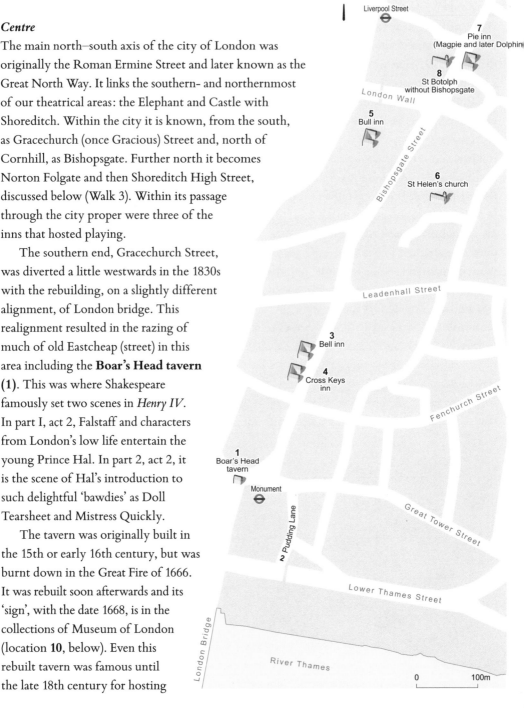

'Shakespearean dinners'. The exact site would be just south of the House of Fraser store, where the traffic island is at the beginning of the bridge (NGR 532875 180832).

A little to the south-east brings you to **Pudding Lane (2)**, later famous as where the Great Fire started in 1666. In the 16th century it was largely occupied by butchers, and their waste gave the area a filthy reputation. But it was also here that two of the carpenters of our story lived: John Grigg, who built the Rose, and John Mago, who converted the Boar's Head inn into a playhouse.

Painted stone tavern sign from the Boar's Head tavern, Eastcheap, dated 1668

Our walk through this central area is described northwards and five minutes will bring you to the junction of Lombard Street on the west (where the comic actor Richard Tarlton ran a pub) and Fenchurch Street on the east, with Gracechurch Street running north. Just north of this junction, past clothes shops on the west side you would come to the modern Cross Keys bar. Although this commemorates the famous medieval and Tudor inn, it is on the north side of Bell Inn Yard which lies on the site of where the **Bell inn (3)** was, at NGR 532993 181033. Confusingly, however, the plaque at its entrance notes that it is the site of the original **Cross Keys inn (4)** but

*Gracechurch Street looking north-west towards the Cross Keys and Bell inn sites, with detail of plaque on the entrance commemorating the Cross Keys inn, location **4***

this was actually some 25 yards (23m) further south
(NGR 532983 181007). If you were here on 23 June
1579, you would have seen James Burbage being
arrested for debt as he was strolling down from
Shoreditch towards the Cross Keys.

Continuing five minutes further north, along
the left, west side, across Cornhill and just past
Threadneedle Street, you come to a large office
block being no. 55 Bishopsgate; behind this was a
maze of alleyways and yards that comprised the
Bull inn (5). This area was unscathed by the Great
Fire and the inn actually survived until 1866, though
regrettably there are no surviving illustrations of it.
The yard used for playing, see on the 1676 map
(p 45), would be at *c* NGR 533093 181379.

The parish **church of St Helen's (6)** is almost
opposite, through an alley on the east side of
Bishopsgate at NGR 533202 181283. It was
originally built in the 1480s and is one of the few
city churches that escaped the Great Fire of 1666 –
though it was damaged in the blitz of the Second
World War. Shakespeare was recorded as living in

*The area of the Bull inn site, location **5***

this parish in 1596 and would have worshipped in this church; there is a Victorian stained glass
window depicting him in the north wall. His fellow actor Thomas Pope was married here in
1584.

Continuing northwards on the eastern side of Bishopsgate a little further north brings you to
the original city boundary, now marked by Wormwood Street (west) and Camomile Street (east).
Just beyond, somewhere between the modern Devonshire Lane on the north and Houndsditch on
the south, was the inn, owned by Edward Alleyn (senior), 'Porter to the Queen', known variously
as the **Pie (7)**, the Magpie and later the Dolphin (*c* NGR 533258 181502). Here, his actor sons
John and, most famously, Edward (or Ned) were born, though excavations in this area in 2003
failed to locate any early remains. Edward, at least, was baptised in the parish church almost
opposite on the west side of the road on 2 September 1566.

St Botolph, a Saxon saint, was the patron saint of travellers, so his churches are always found
just beyond city gateways. **St Botolph without Bishopsgate (8)**, just south of Liverpool Street
Station (built on the original site of St Mary of Bethlehem – or Bedlam Hospital), was certainly
of Saxon origin, though rebuilt in 1572 and the present church dates to 1725. The prolific
anti-theatrical writer Stephen Gosson was rector here from 1600 until his death in 1624.

*The ancient parish church of St Helen's Bishopsgate, location **6***

Western city

Returning south, there are a few other sites famous for Shakespearean associations on the way to the other theatrical area of the city further west, at St Pauls and beyond. As noted above (p 20), Shakespeare lodged in a house in **Silver Street (9)** in 1604 – and possibly for a few years either side. A fellow lodger was the innkeeper and playwright George Wilkins, who collaborated with Shakespeare on the play *Pericles* of 1608. Their landlords were the Huguenot Mountjoy family, for whom they appeared as witnesses in a lawsuit against their son-in-law eight years later. The house, at the corner of Silver Street and Muggle or Monkswell Street, can be clearly seen on Faithorne and Newcourt's map of 1658. The area was engulfed by the Great Fire and rebuilt, but destroyed for good in the Second World War after which the whole streetscape was rebuilt on a new pattern. Nevertheless, by comparing earlier maps we can clearly see that this corner house was situated on the southern side of London Wall, just west of the large bridge building that is 125 London Wall, at *c* NGR 532290 181547. The site is only *c* 150 yards (137m) east of **Museum of London (10)** (NGR 532174 181627), which has a very comprehensive exhibition of Elizabethan London, displaying many of the archaeological finds of that date.

Detail from Faithorne and Newcourt's map of 1658 showing the house in Silver Street where Shakespeare lodged in 1604

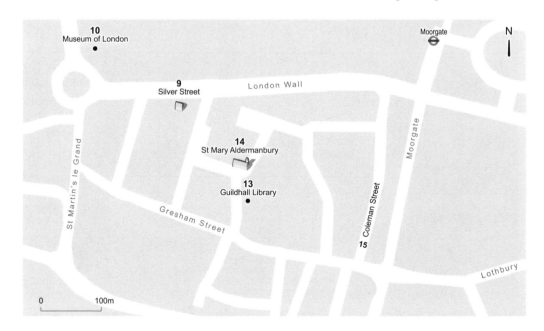

If you walk westwards along Cannon Street, which was Kissing Lane in Elizabethan times, you will find a short stretch of Bread Street on your left. On the east/right side was the **church of St Mildred (11)** (NGR 532284 181003), which was the parish church that owned the Little

Rose Estate on Bankside where Henslowe built his playhouse. Just further along, at the junction of Bread Street, Friday Street and Queen Victoria Street, roughly where the Sea Horse Bar is now (NGR 532250 180966), was the famous **Mermaid tavern (12)**. This is certainly where a number of actors and writers met, though the Victorian painting (p 23) is almost certainly a fictional gathering that may not have taken place. Philip Henslowe spent nine shillings on supper at the Mermaid on 21 August 1602, whilst arranging terms for

Site of the Mermaid tavern, location 12

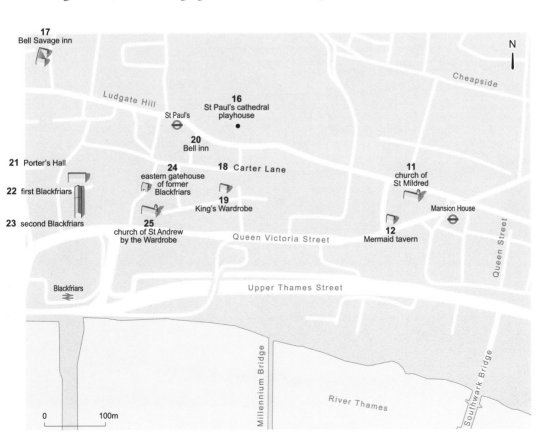

Bust of Shakespeare on site of former St Mary Aldermanbury, location **14**

Worcester's Men to play at the Rose. Shakespeare certainly knew the landlord, William Johnson, as he was a witness to Shakespeare's purchase of the Blackfriars gatehouse in 1613.

Going north, Bread Street turns into Milk Street and, beyond Cheapside and over Gresham Street, it turns into Aldermanbury Street. Just beyond the **Guildhall Library (13)** (NGR 532426 181385), which housed many of London's historical records, on your right/east, there is a little garden marking the site of the former **St Mary Aldermanbury (14)** (NGR 532413 181442), where there is a fine bust of Shakespeare which is actually a memorial to his two fellows, Henry Condell and John Hemmings, who put together the 'First folio' publication of Shakespeare's plays. Condell and Hemmings lived in the parish of St Mary Aldermanbury most of their lives and were churchwardens there. The church itself survived the Great Fire only to succumb to the blitz of the Second World War, after which its stones were transported to Fulton, Missouri, where it was rebuilt as a memorial to Sir Winston Churchill.

Just west of the Guildhall, and parallel to the lower end of Moorgate, is **Coleman Street (15)**. It lay within the parish of St Stephen's Coleman Street which was actually a long parish stretching northwards. Somewhere within the parish lived a number of families in our story. James Burbage lived here, his sons Cuthbert (1565) and Richard (1568) were born here, before they moved to Shoreditch in 1576. His brother-in-law, John Brayne, also lived here, as did the Street family whose carpenter son Peter was to dismantle the Theatre and then build the Globe and the Fortune. By the early 17th century, however, the church and the area were a favourite haunt of the puritans – preachers and politicians – like Oliver Cromwell.

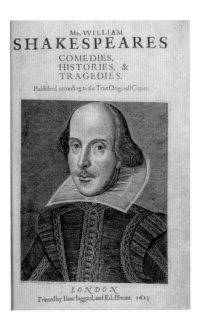

Engraved portrait of William Shakespeare on the title page of the 'First folio' of 1623, by Martin Droeshout

St Paul's

Christopher Wren's masterpiece, **St Paul's cathedral (16)**, stands almost exactly on the site of the original, destroyed in the Great Fire, though the steeple collapsed in a storm in 1561. The small **playhouse** used by the choir boys was situated near the doorway into the south nave, which in the Wren building would be roughly in the side chapel at the west end of the south aisle (*c* NGR 531999 181124). Running along the south side of the cathedral was the roadway known then and now as St Paul's Churchyard, which was the centre of the publishing and printing trade in Shakespeare's time.

Continue westwards and the road becomes Ludgate Hill. On the north side, opposite City Thameslink railway station, is a large modern development (which is being redeveloped as this is being written) that covers the site of the **Bell Savage inn (17)** where performances were held in one of its yards, at *c* NGR 531686 181225. Just to the west of the inn was the Fleet prison, built in 1197 and in use until 1844. The poet John Donne, later the father-in-law of Edward Alleyn, was briefly incarcerated there in 1601. At the close of Shakespeare's play, *Henry IV*, part 2, Falstaff is surprised when, instead of being promoted by the new king, the Chief Justice tells his officers to 'Go, carry Sir John Falstaff to the Fleet;/Take all his company along with him'.

Blackfriars

The southern side of Ludgate Hill was, in medieval times, dominated by the priory of the Dominican Black Friars (p 119), suppressed in 1538. Sir Thomas Cawarden, first Master of the King's Revels under Henry VIII, lived there afterwards and by Shakespeare's time it had become a very fashionable area. It was formally incorporated into the City of London in 1608 and (in 1619) thus 'scituated in the bosome of the Cittie,' which made it attractive to theatre development.

Walk down Blackfriars Lane and on your left, running eastwards, you will see **Carter Lane (18)** – an ancient street retaining some of its old world character. On the south side, just past the junction with St Andrew's Hill, is the discrete entrance into the delightful Wardrobe Place (NGR 531882 181034), which covers the area occupied since 1361 by the **King's Wardrobe (19)** until it was destroyed in the Great Fire. A plaque on no. 5 serves as a memorial.

Further east along Carter Lane, on the south side, was the site of the 16th-century **Bell inn (20)** (NGR 531933 181051). A plaque on a pilaster of its modern successor commemorates

*Carter Lane, off Blackfriars Lane, location **18***

*Site of the King's Wardrobe, location **19***

Richard Quiney who stayed there in October 1598. Quiney was a neighbour of Shakespeare's from Stratford; his son Thomas married Shakespeare's daughter Judith in 1616. On 25 October 1598 he wrote from there to 'his 'loveinge good frend & contreyman Mr William Shackespere' asking for a loan of £30; but in the event the letter was never sent. The plaque notes that this is the only known letter sent *to* Shakespeare. Other residents in the Blackfriars area included Richard Field, the printer who was a boyhood friend of Shakespeare's from Stratford, and his fellow playwright, Ben Jonson.

Return westwards until you get to the junction of Blackfriars Lane again and continue southwards, beyond the plaque marking the site of the Blackfriars Priory and past the Apothecaries' Hall – which saw rehearsed performances of Sir William Davenant's *The siege of Rhodes* – probably the first English opera – in the 1650s. The short-lived **Porter's Hall theatre (21)** was probably on this site (NGR 531741 181057). South and east of the Apothecaries, is Playhouse Yard, created after the Great Fire of 1666 (centered at NGR 531731 181016), where the two **Blackfriars theatres** were located, the first **(22)** straddling the Yard (NGR 531741 181017) and the second **(23)** just to the south (NGR 531736 180993). We might note that a very good modern reconstruction of the second Blackfriars (p 121) has been built by the American Shakespeare Center at Staunton, Virginia, USA.

If you go through Playhouse Yard and along

Playhouse Yard, view looking east

UPON THIS SITE FORMERLY STOOD "THE BELL" CARTER LANE. FROM WHENCE RICHARD QUINEY WROTE THE LETTER TO WILLIAM SHAKESPEARE DATED THE 25TH OCTOBER 1598. THIS IS THE ONLY LETTER EXTANT ADDRESSED TO SHAKESPEARE AND THE ORIGINAL IS PRESERVED IN THE MUSEUM AT HIS BIRTHPLACE. STRATFORD UPON AVON.

THIS TABLET WAS PLACED UPON THE PRESENT BUILDING BY LEAVE OF THE POSTMASTER GENERAL 1899.

*Site of the Bell inn, Carter Lane, location **20***

*The Cockpit public house, on the site of the Blackfriars gatehouse, location **24***

Ireland Yard, you will come to the Cockpit pub (NGR 531848 181019), which stands almost on the site of the eastern **gatehouse (24)** of the former priory. Shakespeare bought the gatehouse on 10 March 1613 for £140. The site comprised a dwelling house or tenement, part of which was built over 'a greate gate', as well as some land just to the west – that is, within the former priory lands. It is not certain that he lived there himself, as he had retired back to Stratford the year before, and it may have been simply bought as an investment. For some reason he had three trustees, which may have been a legal detail, who were John Hemmings, his co-player, William Johnson, the landlord of the Mermaid tavern, and John Jackson whose identity is not certain.

Turn right out of Ireland Yard down St Andrew's Hill (formerly Puddle Dock) and a short distance from the Cockpit you will find the west door of the church of **St Andrew by the Wardrobe (25)**, the main south door is on Queen Victoria Street (NGR 531855 180980). The medieval church was burned down in the Great Fire, but rebuilt by Christopher Wren afterwards. It will have been well known to Shakespeare and others in the neighbouring parish of St Ann Blackfriars. There are two fine carved monuments in the west gallery to Shakespeare and to his contemporary, John Dowland, the most famous musician of his age.

Church of St Andrew by the Wardrobe, location **25**

Walk 2 – the east

Whitechapel

An area of some theatrical concentration lay just beyond the eastern border of the city in Whitechapel. A ten minute walk from the junction of Lombard Street and Fenchurch Street brings you to the eastern border of the city at **Aldgate (1)** and beyond to Whitechapel High Street, which was the main route out to Essex. The gate itself was on the site of the Roman one, but the medieval structure, in which Geoffrey Chaucer lived for a while, was rebuilt in 1606 and finally demolished in 1761 (NGR 533550 181152). The line of the city wall on the north side is marked by Duke's Place, which is named after the Duke of Norfolk's mansion, where fencing bouts were held in the 1580s and 90s. The line of the wall immediately to the south is represented by modern Jewry Street.

    St Botolph without Aldgate (2) lies just outside the walls (NGR 533578 181211), presently in the modern traffic island. The medieval church was greatly rebuilt in the 16th century, though the present building dates to the 1740s. St Botolph was the patron saint of travellers and his churches

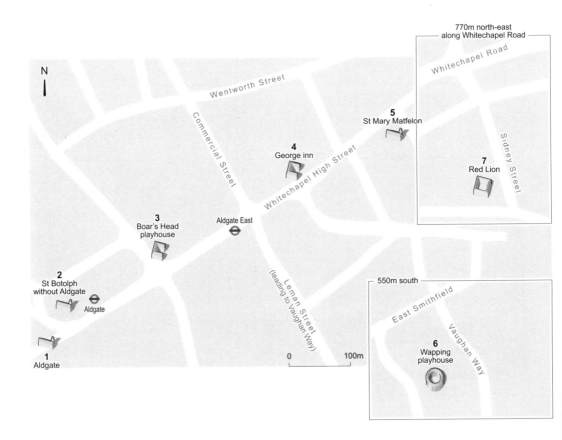

are usually next to city gates – see also St Botolph without Bishopsgate (Walk 1, location **8**). The church records reveal quite a theatrical community, with the births, marriages, such as Martin Slater's in 1594, and deaths of many players and their families. Probably the best known is Robert Armin, one of Shakespeare's best comic actors, who was buried here in 1615.

The site of the **Boar's Head playhouse (3)** lies 190m east of the church, just beyond the modern Aldgate island. It is presently (2012) an open rectangle of undeveloped land bounded by Middlesex Street on the west and Whitechapel High Street on the south (NGR 533737 181297), much as it has been since the archaeological excavations of 1998. Middlesex Street was increasingly developed in the late 16th century and became known as Peticote (Petticoat) Lane – the centre of a flourishing clothes market – only becoming Middlesex Street in the 19th century.

A further five minute walk along Whitechapel High Street brings you to the modern White Hart pub (NGR 533961 181422), almost next door to the Whitechapel Art Gallery. The passageway running through the pub to become Gunthorpe Street is the only clue to the layout of the original early inn, much like the city ones described above. For this was the site of the **George inn (4)** that John Brayne, latterly with Robert Miles, intended to transform into a playhouse. As we

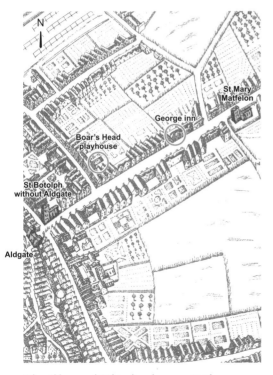

The Aldgate and Whitechapel area on Faithorne and Newcourt's map of 1658

Derelict site of the Boar's Head playhouse looking north-west, location 3

know, it remained an inn and was the last home of the Braynes, John dying there in 1586 and his wife Margaret in 1592.

Continuing 100 yards (91m) eastwards, turn right into White Church Lane and you will see a large open space now known as Altab Ali Park. In fact it is the site of the ancient **St Mary Matfelon church (5)** (NGR 534123 181480). This was originally built by *c* 1280 and its white stone exterior (common to most churches of the time) led to it, and the whole surrounding area, being known as Whitechapel. As the population in the area grew, the church was enlarged and

The modern White Hart, on the site of the George, location **4**

Site of St Mary Matfelon, Whitechapel, location **5**

its burial ground extended in 1591. Its importance to us, however, is that here is buried John Brayne (and his wife), who can really be called the father of the London playhouses. Oliver Woodliffe, who started the Boar's Head playhouse, and Robert Browne of the Queen's Men, who later 'managed' it, both died in the plague of 1603 and are buried here. The church was rebuilt in the 17th and 19th centuries, but demolished after bomb damage in the Second World War. Excavations in the 1870s for the latest building revealed a little of the medieval structure, but recent limited archaeological work has not penetrated very deep in order the preserve what may lie below.

Wapping

Two excursions further south and east bring us to the sites of two further playhouses, though nothing remains to be seen within these heavily built-up areas.

If you head down towards the Tower of London and turn right into East Smithfield, where the poet Edmund Spenser was thought to have been born in 1552, past the old dock walls and then turn left, you will be in Thomas More Street. This was Nightingale Lane, which only changed its name in 1936; it was an ancient way down to the small settlement on the Thames. It was still rural enough in 1629 for Charles I to have hunted stags in the locality. Somewhere along here, quite possibly on the east side near the massive Trinity Tower building (NGR 534189 180537), John Wolf started building a **playhouse (6)** in 1600. However far he got, there's not much likelihood of archaeological remains surviving in this area.

Stepney

The second excursion, only for those concerned with going back to the **Red Lion (7)** of 1567, is a much longer journey eastwards. You can take a bus along Whitechapel High Street to just beyond the Royal London Hospital, although the nearest tube is Whitechapel underground station.

The medieval manor of 'Mile End', which straddled Whitechapel High Street just north of the site, had developed into a small settlement, which included the prestigious house known as Ashwyes, with another known as Philpots just to the east; the origins of the Blind Beggar pub, on the north side of the highway, go back to this period. It was also where the trained bands of the City militia went every May to muster and drill. The area was far from being 'in the middle of nowhere'; it even had an earlier theatrical history, as an entry in the account book of the King's Chamber of 1501 was for payment 'to the players at Mile End, 3s 4d'.

The Red Lion was described as a farm, but may have been part of the Ashwyes property. As such, it is difficult to provide a precise location for the site of the playhouse, but it will have been within the block bound by Cavell Street on the west, Sydney Street on the east and Stepney Way on the south, at c NGR 534986 181690.

Walk 3 – the north

Shoreditch

The presence of the Augustinian priory of Holywell had made Shoreditch into a well-known settlement by the medieval period. From the later 16th century, however, it is best known as the home of what were thought to be the two earliest 'Shakespearean playhouses', and in this case they were associated with Shakespeare himself. Like many other areas of London, Shoreditch has an older theatrical history: in 1541 John Foxe recorded that the keeper of the Carpenter's Hall was indicted for 'procuring an interlude to be openly played' in 'Shoreditch, London'. Shoreditch was an easy walk from the city, passing along Bishopsgate then through Norton Folgate and into Shoreditch High Street.

The **Theatre (1)** was situated within the grounds of Holywell Priory, just to the west, at NGR 533322 182392, though only a small area has been excavated. On the east side of Curtain Road, behind the site, are two plaques recording the building of the Theatre. Excavations near this corner in 2002 also found the priory 'curtain' or wall, itself, as well as a part of the 'great barne'.

By the late 16th century, Shoreditch was just as dissolute, if not more, as the Bankside (Walk 4, below) and the association of theatre and immorality was often remarked on. Everard Guilpin refers to one

> Who comming from the Curtaine sneaketh in
> To somme odd garden noted house of sinne …

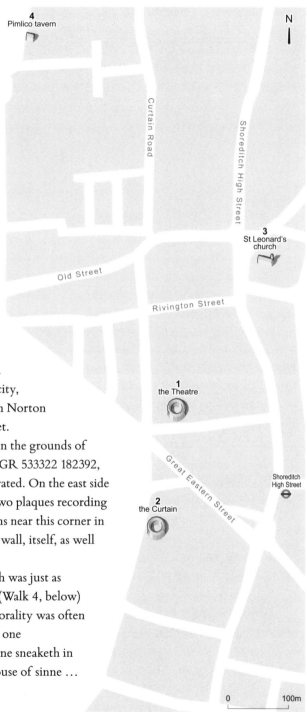

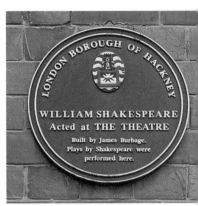

Appropriately decorated hoarding around the Theatre excavations at the New Inn Broadway site, location 1

Commemorative plaques to the Theatre on Curtain Road

The **Curtain (2)** playhouse was outside the priory precincts to the south, beyond Holywell Lane and fronting onto Curtain Road at NGR 533284 182288. The commemorative plaque is situated just to the north-east, in Hewett Street, a later 18th-century street. It is particularly emotive to stand by the site that first heard, in 1598, some of the most famous lines in the history of English drama:

> O for a Muse of fire, that would ascend
> The brightest heaven of invention,
> A kingdom for a stage, princes to act
> And monarchs to behold the swelling scene!
> Then should the warlike Harry, like himself,
> Assume the port of Mars; and at his heels,
> Leash'd in like hounds, should famine, sword and fire
> Crouch for employment. But pardon, and gentles all,
> The flat unraised spirits that have dared
> On this unworthy scaffold to bring forth
> So great an object: can this cockpit hold
> The vasty fields of France? or may we cram
> Within this wooden O the very casques
> That did affright the air at Agincourt?

Plaque commemorating the Curtain in Hewett Street, location 2

View along Curtain Road; the playhouse was situated behind the older buildings, centre right

Largely because of the playhouses, Shoreditch became an early home to many actors and playwrights. Christopher Marlowe is recorded as living in the area in Norton Folgate in 1589. Although his exact address cannot, of course, be known, excavations along this roadway have uncovered a number of houses dating from this period. Running west from the north end of Norton Folgate is Worship Street, then known as Hog Lane, where, in September of the same year, Marlowe's friend, the poet Thomas Watson, killed William Bradley, who had been brawling with Marlowe. He was in the same area in 1592 when he was sharing lodgings with Thomas Kyd and was arrested in Holywell Lane after an 'affray'. There was a further death there in December 1596 when the Rose actor Gabriel Spencer killed James Freake in a duel. Shakespeare may have

lived here or in Holywell Lane in his early years and a number of other actors are known to have lived there too. James Burbage kept an illegal 'tippling house' there to quench the thirst of playgoers. His sons later had two adjoining houses there and in February 1618 they were both burgled on the same night, losing expensive costumes.

Holywell Lane, looking west from Shoreditch High Street

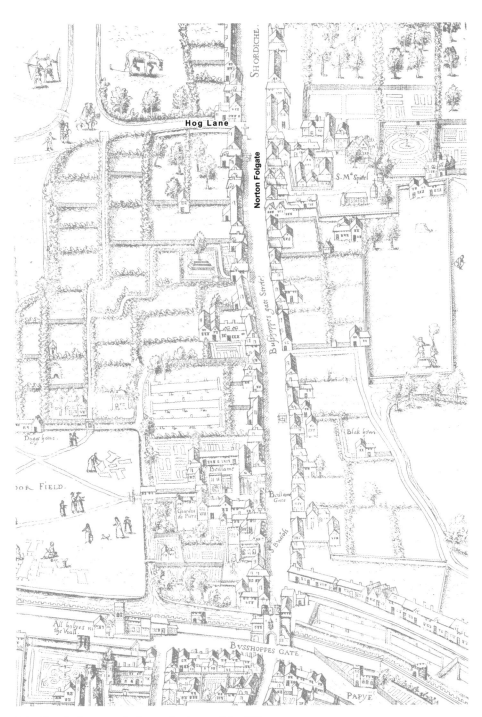

The Shoreditch area on the 'copperplate' map of the 1550s

Towards the northern end of Shoreditch High Street is **St Leonard's church (3)** (NGR 533464 182632), often known as the actors' church on account of the many who were baptised, married and buried there. A plaque inside records many of them.

It is interesting to note that, even after the theatrical area of London had shifted southwards, many of the actors were still living here and commuting to the Bankside. West of Curtain Road were the Holywell Fields, across which many playgoers tramped. It was also an occasional execution site and on 18 August 1588, William Gunter, a Welsh Catholic priest, was 'conveyed into Hollywell fieldes near to the Theator or Playhouse' and hung, drawn and quartered. A similar fate befell another catholic priest, William Hartley, in the same place on 5 October the same year. It is thought by some that the lines in Shakespeare's *Comedy of errors* (act 5, scene 1) referred to these local executions:

> By this, I think, the dial points at five:
> Anon, I'm sure, the duke himself in person
> Comes this way to the melancholy vale,
> The place of death and sorry execution,
> Behind the ditches of the abbey here.

To the north-west of Shoreditch was the village of Hoxton, famous for the **Pimlico tavern (4)**, which had a 1609 play written about it and was popular with theatregoers from Shoreditch, as well as Cripplegate. A plaque on the east end of Arden House, just east of St John's church at *c* NGR 533083 182986, commemorates the approximate site of the tavern and the nearby Hoxton Fields, where in September 1598 Ben Jonson killed his fellow actor, Gabriel Spencer. The two had known each other for many years, even sharing a cell in Marshalsea prison (Walk 4, location **20**) three years earlier. As noted above, Spencer had already killed another man and Jonson would later complain that his own sword was the shorter one, making him literally 'fight for his life'.

This stone is placed here to the glory of God and in ac knowledgement of the work done for English drama by the players musicians and other men of the theatre who are bu ried within the precincts of this church and in particular to the memory of those who are named below James Burbage, died 1597· a joiner by trade and the head of Lord Leicester's Players who in 1576 built in Shoreditch the first English playhouse – this he called the Theatre. Cuthbert Burbage, died 1636· his son who in 1599 built in Southwark the famous Globe playhouse. Richard Burbage, died 1619· also his son the great tragedian· The first actor to play the parts of Richard III and Hamlet· William Somers, died 1560· Court jester to Henry VIII. Richard Tarlton, died 1588· One of Queen Elizabeth's players and the foremost comic actor of his time. Gabriel Spencer, died 1598· A player at the Rose theatre· William Sly, died 1608 and Richard Cowley, died 1619· Players at the Globe theatre

Text of plaque from St Leonard's church (erected 1910)

Medieval St Leonard's church, location 3 (engraving)

Modern St Leonard's church, location 3

Cripplegate

Golden Lane, once Golding or Goulding Lane, ran north from Cripplegate, the northernmost gate of the walled city. It lay in the ancient parish of St Giles Cripplegate, which church is just outside the walls, and was a major route already quite developed by the beginning of the 17th century. It was a plot of land between Golden Lane and Whitecross Street parallel to the east that Edward Alleyn leased in late 1599 to build the **Fortune playhouse (5)**. There were certainly houses on the street front and the playhouse must have been set back a little, at *c* NGR 532321 182091. After its disappearance, Playhouse Yard, now Fortune Street, was built through what must have been its centre. Many actors from the resident Palgrave's Men were recorded as living in Golden Lane in the 1620s. Much of this area was destroyed during the Second World War and is now dominated by 1950s housing estates, but the southern half of the Fortune plot is now an open parkland. The plaque commemorating 'Edward Alleyn's Fortune Theatre' at the north-east end of Fortune Street is a little beyond the actual site.

Clerkenwell

Clerkenwell was the north-westernmost theatrical area in London; as far west from the Fortune as that was from the Curtain. The area, however, had a long dramatic history. Skinner's Well or [the] Clerk's Well, in what is now Farringdon Lane, was the location for a series of 14th- and 15th-century mystery plays performed for the clerks of the City of London. Wells in the area still have theatrical associations, as Saddlers music-house (Saddlers Wells), established some time

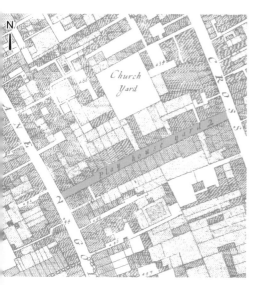

Detail from Ogilby and Morgan 1676 showing Playhouse Yard, site of the Fortune, location 5

Site of the Fortune on Golden Lane, location 5

before 1683 *c* 650 yards (600m) to the north-west, testifies today. We might note that the Saracen's Head tavern in Islington, which hosted an illegal play in 1657, lay just further north somewhere near the junction of St John's Street and Goswell Street.

The buildings might have changed, but the entrance way to Heywood Place (probably named after Thomas Heywood, one of the best known of 'local' playwrights), is still reminiscent of an inn, as is the space inside representative of the **Red Bull (6)** playhouse, at NGR 531668 182289.

*Entrance to the site of the Red Bull looking south-west (left); interior of Red Bull yard looking east (right), location **6***

Medieval St James's church, location 7 (engraving)

*The present St James's
church, location 7*

Further west, the ancient open area
of Clerkenwell Green is dominated by **St
James's church (7)** (NGR 531519 182047),
in which many of the players of the period
were baptised, married and buried.

Just to the north-west of the church stood **Newcastle House (8)** (NGR *c* 531487 182223), the
town house of the Earl (later Duke) of Newcastle, who was a minor poet, playwright (two of his
plays were put on at the second Blackfriars) and patron of the arts. His circle included the
playwrights Ben Jonson, James Shirley and William Davenant, as well as the philosopher Thomas
Hobbes and the 'theatre historian' Richard Flecknoe – all of whom probably knew this house.

Some 150 yards (137m) to the south was the priory and hospital of the Order of St John of
Jerusalem, which was probably associated with the medieval mystery plays. The site was largely
demolished after the Dissolution but the surviving **St John's gatehouse (9)** (NGR 531724
182047) was home to the Revels Office between 1560 and 1608.

Turnmill Street to the south-west was a notorious area of prostitution, so much so that the
street itself was referred to as Turnbull Street and its northern part as Codpiece Row.

*St John's gatehouse, location **9**, view looking north–north–west*

Walk 4 – the south

Bankside

The strip of river frontage running westwards from London Bridge is one of the most famous entertainment areas of old London: the home of bawdy houses, bear-baiting rings and playhouses including the Rose and Globe, 'the glory of the Banke'. You could start at the west end by coming over the pedestrian Millennium Bridge but our description begins at the eastern end with Southwark cathedral, just beyond London Bridge railway and underground station.

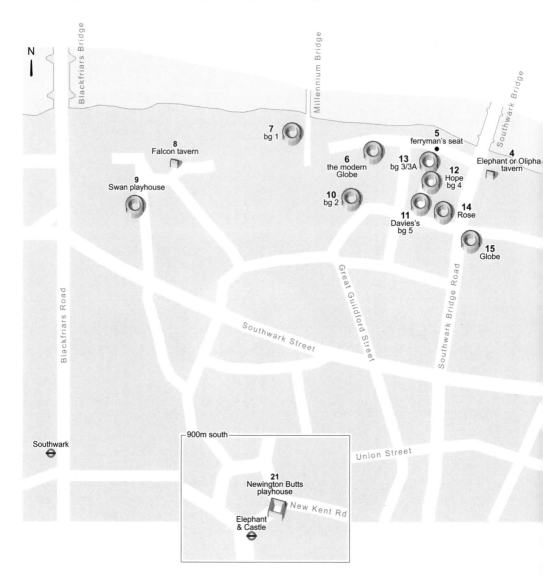

The original St Mary Overie (meaning 'over the water') became **St Saviour's church (1)** after the Dissolution and was only converted into a cathedral in 1905. It dates back to the 13th century and was one of the largest churches in and around London (NGR 532680 180313).

As the local parish church to London's south bank theatreland, it has associations with many of the personalities described above. Shakespeare himself lived locally for a short period: there is a stained glass window depicting scenes from his plays with a fine monument showing Shakespeare set against a background of early Bankside. A more direct association is the burial within the church itself of his actor brother Edmond in 1607, paid for by William, though the commemorative stone in the choir is a modern addition. Due to overcrowding, the parish acquired a new burial ground in 1583 further east, at **Potter's Ground (2)**, near Tower Bridge (NGR 533354 180056), in which most of our community will have been buried: Francis Langley in 1602, Philip Henslowe in 1616, John Fletcher in 1625 and Philip Massinger in 1640.

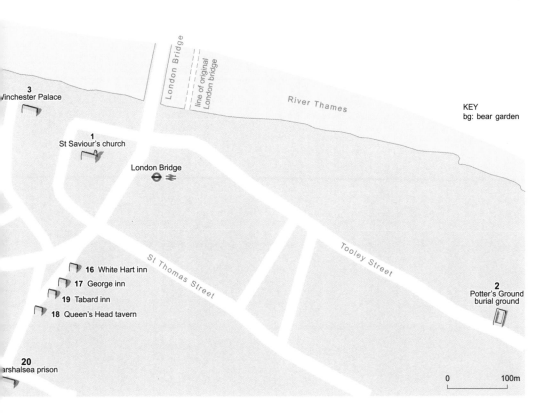

*The east front of St Saviour's church (now Southwark cathedral), location **1***

East of the cathedral is Clink Street, which is where part of **Winchester Palace (3)** (NGR 532582 180387), the London home of the Bishop of Winchester, the lord of the manor there; its name commemorates the manorial lock-up. At its western end, just by the Anchor pub (an 18th-century building) is Bankside proper, a highway since the 13th century. Along here were the 'stews', originally the Bankside brothels but mostly taverns by Shakespeare's day. Excavations on riverside developments have uncovered traces of medieval buildings that may have been some of these stews. Just before Southwark Bridge, probably under the north-west corner of the Financial Times building, was the **Elephant (4)**, or Oliphant, tavern (*c* NGR 532351 180483) noted in Shakespeare's *Twelfth night*:

> In the south suburbs, at the Elephant,
>
> Is best to lodge: I will bespeak our diet …

There were a series of river 'stairs', where the small ferries seen in the early maps would tie up; next to the bridge was Horseshoe Stairs leading into Horseshoe Alley, which led down to Maiden Lane and was the nearest access point for the Globe. About 30 yards (27m) beyond Southwark

Shakespeare memorial (built in 1912) in Southwark cathedral

Bridge would have been Rose Alley, which was originally only a few metres long, but later extended down to Maiden Lane. Beyond this was the Rose stewhouse, after which the playhouse was ultimately named. A little further along you will come to the roadway now known as Bear Gardens, which is actually only as old as the 18th century. However, its northern end marks the sites of the Barge, Bell and Cock taverns, and the later Dancing Bears and just north of bear gardens nos 3 and 3A. On the corner of Bear Gardens and Bankside, set into the wall by the *Real Greek* Bankside restaurant, is the last surviving **ferryman's seat (5)** (NGR 532262 180523), although not on its original site which was probably near one of the 'stairs' noted above. Somewhere a little further on westwards was the Unicorn, another well-known tavern; just beyond New Globe Walk, another 18th-century creation, is the modern **Globe (6)** (NGR 532159 180514) built in 1997. Because of commercial considerations and modern safety regulations, it is larger than (and *c* 300 yards (274m) north-west of) the original, but it gives a wonderful sense of atmosphere and the closest experience we can have of the original performance venues.

The last surviving ferryman's seat, location 5

The modern Globe theatre, location 6, with view along the riverbank

Before retracing our steps southwards to explore Maiden Lane, it is worth going further west to note where other bygone venues were situated. Just beyond the Millennium Bridge, in front of Tate Modern, was Mason's Stairs (*c* NGR 532026 180546), another riverside ferry access, near which was **bear garden no. 1 (7)**. From Tate Modern, turn south-west along Hopton Street (this stretch of which was known as Willow Street) and just north of the junction with Holland Street (at *c* NGR 531834 180500) was the famous **Falcon tavern (8)**, which was also supposedly a well-known players' drinking den of the Shakespearean period. Continue just a little westwards, where Hopton Street turns south, and here, on your right (west) is the monstrous Sampson House which has swallowed up the site of the **Swan playhouse (9)** (NGR 531770 180430). Archaeological work just to the east, at the apex of Hopton and Holland Streets, found much evidence for buildings and other features dating back to the 16th century. There was very little riverside development further west until one reached Lambeth, though the royal barge house was situated some 450 yards (411m) along from the site of the Swan.

*Samson House, on the site of the Swan playhouse, location **9***

Return a little and either back to the modern Globe or, keeping with traces of the original street pattern, go down Holland Street. Turn left (east) into Sumner Street and then into Park Street on your left, going north-east. This is the medieval Maid or Maiden Lane (so-named after the stews) and just by this turn, somewhere on your left (north) side, was **bear garden no. 2 (10)** (*c* NGR 532123 180441). Continue past New Globe Walk and pause at the southern end of Bear Gardens (street), where a plaque commemorates **Davies's bear garden (11)** (NGR 532230 180440), the fifth and last one on Bankside. Half way up Bear Gardens you would be standing in the middle of the **Hope (12)** (NGR 532246 180474) and just to the north-west was the site of **bear gardens nos 3 and 3A (13)** (NGR 532244 180497). Back at the corner of Park Street, continue past the Globe Education Centre and the building on your left (north) side carries a plaque to note the site of the **Rose playhouse (14)** (NGR 532274 180421). Only 50 yards (46m) further along, on the south side of the street, is a fine large bronze plaque placed on a wall in the 1920s to mark the site of the **Globe (15)**. After the excavations of 1989 found the actual remains, the

View along Park Street at the junction with Bear Garden

Rose plaque

*Bronze plaque marking site of the Globe, location **15**, in Park Street*

outline of the walls was laid out in the paving in the small open area of ground to show the actual site, the centre of which is at NGR 532319 180375. Continue back westwards to London Bridge.

At London Bridge you are at the top, northern end of historic Borough High Street, and it is worthwhile walking down the eastern side where many plaques testify to famous sites.

Just opposite the junction with Southwark Street is the **White Hart inn (16)** (NGR 532656 180135), which was of medieval origin. Shakespeare made it the headquarters of Jack Cade, who led a revolt from Kent to London in 1450, in *Henry VI*, part 2, originally performed at the Rose. The **George inn (17)** (NGR 532641 180110) actually dates from the 1670s, but its one remaining galleried courtyard side is typical of the inns of the Shakespearean period.

*The George inn, location **17**, which dates from the 1670s*

A rectangular plaque at 103 Borough High Street (NGR 532596 180068) marks the site of the **Queen's Head tavern (18)** which was owned by the family of John Harvard, founder of America's oldest university. He was born in Southwark in 1607, possibly on this site, and baptised in St Saviour's. Just to the south was the **Tabard (19)**, later Talbot (NGR 532620 180094), which was the inn from which Chaucer's Canterbury pilgrims set off. Between Newcomen Street and Mermaid Way was the original **Marshalsea prison (20)** (NGR 532546 179952), where Jonson, Spenser and Shaa were imprisoned for their part in the *Isle of Dogs* affair at the Swan (the prison was rebuilt 130 yards (119m) further south in 1811).

North-east view of Marshalsea prison, location 20, off Borough High Street, Southwark

Elephant and Castle

The little village of **Newington Butts** is only a 25 minute walk from London Bridge on the main route southwards. The village was so named after the butts, as in a triangle of land, rather than anything to do with archery targets. It was where the roads to Camberwell and Clapham joined that going north into London. Most of the land in this area had been owned by Canterbury Cathedral since the Norman Conquest and it was regarded as quite well-to-do and a popular spot for outings.

There were two little triangles forming the centre of this junction with a tavern on the northern one known as the White Hart. In the 18th century it was renamed the Elephant and Castle, and the name has been extended throughout the area. It was rebuilt in the 19th century, though the present Elephant and Castle pub, at the junction of New Kent Road and Newington Causeway, was part of the comprehensive 1960s redevelopment.

The unnamed **playhouse (21)** lay just to the east of the former junction and is now in the middle of the roadway at *c* NGR 532003 179049. Although it is not a great distance from the city, the 'tediousnes of the waie' was cited by players wanting to return to the Bankside theatreland in 1594.

Walk 5 – the west

We are defining west here as the area just west of the Fleet River, which was at one time the eastern extent of the city. Today it follows the line of New Bridge Street and, north of Ludgate Circus, Farringdon Street. This area encompasses indoor theatres and the Inns of Court halls, though there are other sites of interest further along. The western side of New Bridge Street, which follows the line of the Fleet, was dominated by **Bridewell prison (1)**, centred on NGR 531595 181062. It was originally a palace built by Henry VIII but it was later given to the City as a hospital for homeless children and destitute women. By Shakespeare's time it was a notorious prison and unofficial brothel.

The exact location of the **Salisbury Court theatre (2)** is not known for certain, though it was on the east side of Water Lane (now Whitefriars Street to the north and Carmelite Street to the south). It was once thought to occupy the area now defined by Salisbury Square, where Bulstrode Whitelock, who helped organise the drama at the Inns of Court, and the young Samuel Pepys once lived. Nowadays it is thought that the theatre was further south, just beyond Tudor Street and east of Carmelite Street at NGR 531486 180975.

The original Carmelite friary of the White Friars occupied a large area between Water Lane (modern Whitefriars Street) on the east and Temple Lane on the west. Fragments survived after the Dissolution and substantial areas were discovered in excavations in the 1920s. A **medieval crypt (3)** belonging to the friary was moved in major redevelopments in the 1980s and can still be seen behind a glass in Magpie Alley (NGR 531418 181053). The **Whitefriars theatre (4)** was on the west side of the friary precinct and currently lies below the block defined as 11/12 Bouverie Street (NGR 531370 181063), bound by Bouverie Street on the east and by both angles of Temple Lane on the north and west. In the Jacobean period playgoers would have walked down

View looking south from Lombard Lane towards the site of the Whitefriars theatre in Temple Lane, location 4

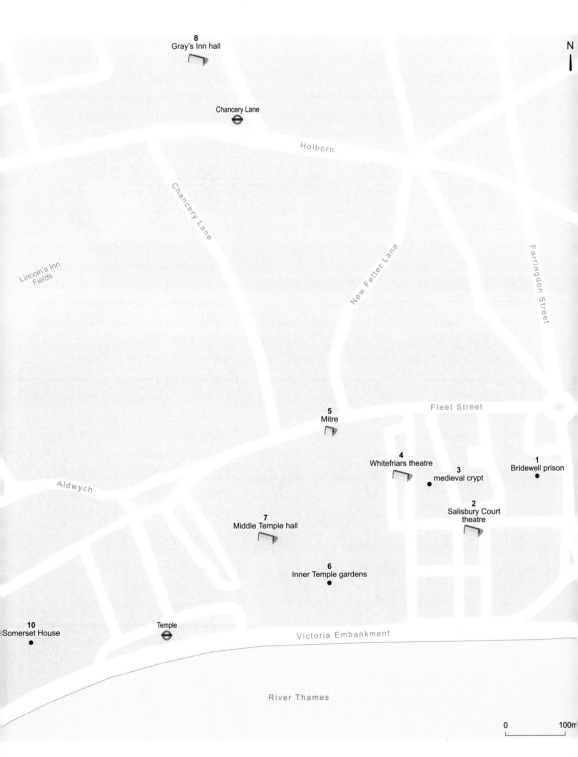

N

8
Gray's Inn hall

Chancery Lane

Holborn

Chancery Lane

Lincoln's Inn
Fields

New Fetter Lane

Farringdon Street

Fleet Street

5
Mitre

4
Whitefriars theatre

3
medieval crypt

1
Bridewell prison

Aldwych

2
Salisbury Court
theatre

7
Middle Temple hall

6
Inner Temple gardens

10
Somerset House

Temple

Victoria Embankment

River Thames

0   100m

from Fleet Street through what are now Pleydell Street and Lombard Lane. Although this area began as a reputable one, the increase in low taverns in places such as Ram Alley led to a poor reputation throughout the 17th century. A tavern, said to be patronised by the local theatrical community, was the **Mitre (5)** on Fleet Street, at *c* NGR 531253 181141. There was a great scandal in 1612 when Lord Sanquhar hired two ruffians to murder one John Turner, a fencing master who had accidently wounded him a few years before. Turner was shot by the ruffians and, after a sensational trial, Sanquhar was hanged outside Westminster Hall. The sordid side of the Whitefriars area was later described by Sir Walter Scott in his 1822 novel *The fortunes of Nigel*.

Continuing down Temple Lane until it meets Tudor Street you will find yourself at the gateway into the two Temple Inns of Court, though it must be stated that the buildings themselves are private and *not* accessible to the public. With Paper Buildings on your left walk around to Crown Office Row, which forms the northern side of **Inner Temple gardens (6)**, an ancient three-acre garden with its centre at NGR 531253 180897. This is where Shakespeare set the meeting between Plantagenet and Beaufort that sparked off the Wars of the Roses, and where they picked their red and white emblems in *Henry VI*, part 1.

Henry Payne's 1908 painting, Choosing the red and white roses, *showing the scene from Shakespeare set in the Inner Temple gardens, location 6*

Continue along under the archway and turn right into Middle Temple Lane then left into a court, which has the magnificent **Middle Temple hall (7)** on your right (NGR 531149 180965) where Shakespeare's *Twelfth night* was performed in 1602. Return to Middle Temple Lane and Fleet Street to the north.

Gray's Inn hall (8) lies considerably to the north, off Holborn (NGR 531040 181726), and is a reconstruction of the original building, which was largely destroyed in the Second World War. Shakespeare's *Comedy of errors* was performed here in 1594.

Middle Temple hall, location 7

Drury Lane

This roadway was of medieval origin and took its name from Sir Thomas Drury, who had a house there in the later 16th century in which John Donne later lodged. However, it was not unknown as an area of 'entertainment', for Aaron Holland, later builder of the Red Bull, managed a 'common bowling alley' there in 1594 that also hosted 'dicing, tabling and carding'. After the Restoration and later, it became the centre of a new 'theatrical' area, though the original Theatre Royal Drury Lane was actually in Catherine Street around the corner. The area has a long history of Shakespearean performance by the likes of Nell Gwynne, David Garrick and Mrs Siddons, as well as of plays by the new playwrights of the 18th and 19th centuries – Sheridan, Kemble and Kean.

By the later 19th century the area had become a crowded slum and the new Peabody Estate was built in the 1870s. From Wild Street you can see into the private carpark which covers the site of the **Phoenix theatre (9)** but is not accessible to the public (NGR 530512 181156).

Peabody Estate, Drury Lane – site of the Phoenix theatre, location 9

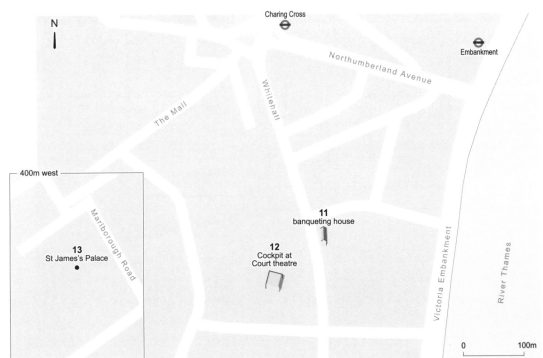

N

Charing Cross

Embankment

Northumberland Avenue

Whitehall

The Mall

400m west

Marlborough Road

13
St James's Palace

12
Cockpit at
Court theatre

11
banqueting house

Victoria Embankment

River Thames

0   100m

A very long walk following the line of the river would bring you to Westminster and Whitehall, though a bus journey is probably preferable. In the Strand, however, one might note **Somerset House (10)** (NGR 530765 180804) which is the 18th-century successor to the earlier Tudor palace with its court theatres. The architect and stage designer Inigo Jones died here in 1651.

Whitehall

Whitehall Palace burned down in 1698 and little remains; most of the area is now covered by government buildings. Three hundred yards (274m) south of Trafalgar Square on your left, at the corner of Horse Guards Avenue, is the magnificent **banqueting house (11)** built by Inigo Jones in 1619 (NGR 530165 180067), and which survived the fire. Cross over the road into Horse Guards Parade and near the Cabinet Office, at its southern end, was the site of the **Cockpit at Court theatre (12)** (NGR 530074 179989).

The site of the Cockpit at Court theatre, location 12

Inigo Jones's banqueting house, location 11, at Whitehall Palace

St James's Palace

This palace is still very much a working royal building and not accessible to the public. However, its original north gate and facade of **St James's Palace (13)** can be seen at the junction of Pall Mall and St James's Street (NGR 529348 180099). The original 'great chamber', now the armoury room, redecorated by William Morris in the 1860s, lies beyond.

Walk 6 – Greenwich

Downstream from the city, nearly four miles (6km) as the crow flies, lies Greenwich. You can get there by ferry or railway (Greenwich Station) or Docklands Light Railway (Maritime Greenwich). Within the grounds of the Old Royal Naval College was the magnificent Greenwich Palace, built by Henry VII. It was greatly enhanced under Henry VIII and was still a favourite residence of Queen Elizabeth – both of whom were born there. There have been numerous excavations here, revealing much of the Tudor palace.

There are records of playing in Greenwich Palace from the reign of Henry VIII. For our period the most famous account was that of 15 March 1595, when the Treasurer of the Queen's Chamber paid 'William Kempe, William Shakespeare & Richarde Burbage servants to the Lord Chamberleyne' for performances at court in Greenwich on 26 and 27 December of the previous year.

Although the main layout of the palace is known, it is not certain where plays were performed. The **great hall (1)** of the palace was on the eastern side of the great court, under the site of the present Queen Anne Quarter (NGR 538607 177981). However, a **banqueting house (2)**, also known as the disguising house, and a temporary theatre were built for a grand reception next to the tiltyard in 1527. Queen Elizabeth built a new one in 1559 and refurbished and strengthened it in 1583; it is possible that performances were played here, though the building was wooden and some way from the royal apartments. The tiltyard was situated just to the south, largely in the front lawns of the National Maritime Museum; the banqueting house, on the west side of the tilt, would have been at *c* NGR 538695 177805.

Greenwich is not that far from Deptford, where Christopher Marlowe was killed in a tavern brawl on 30 May 1593. He is buried in the grounds of St Nicholas church (NGR 537398 177745).

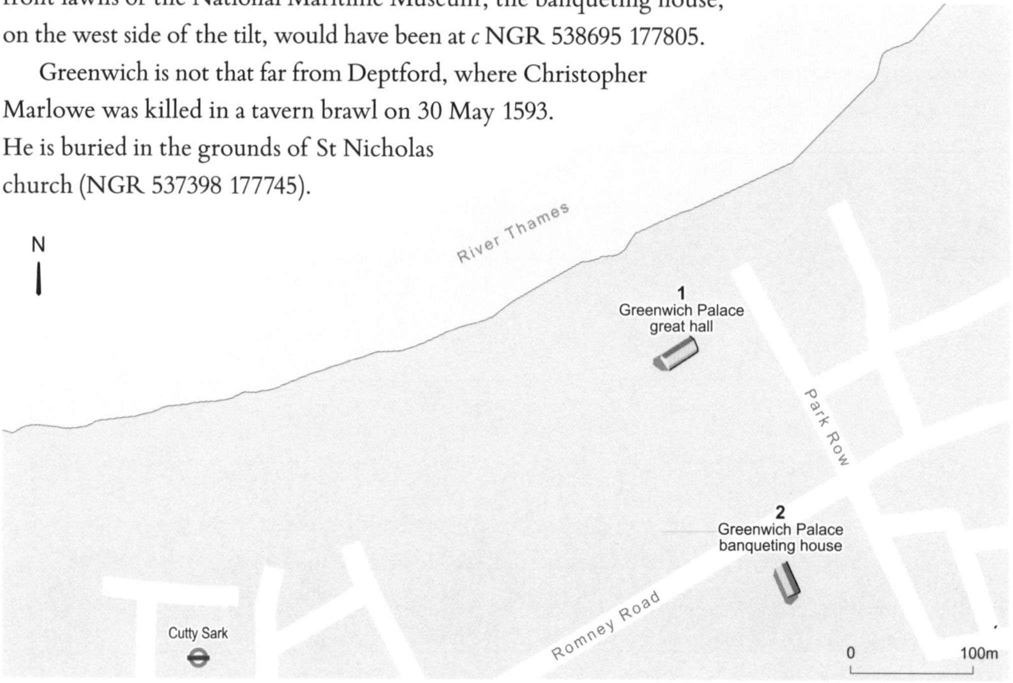

N

River Thames

1
Greenwich Palace
great hall

Park Row

2
Greenwich Palace
banqueting house

Cutty Sark

Romney Road

0   100m

Walk 7 – Hampton Court

Hampton Court is further upstream from Richmond, but trains from Waterloo run to Hampton Court station. From the station, the site is a short walk over the bridge. Local buses from Richmond and elsewhere in the south-west also pass by the site. Hampton Court is a magificent evocation of Tudor power and magnificence, and is open to the public, being managed by Historic Royal Palaces.

Hampton Court, Surrey, view from the east (anon, c 1663–70)

Along with Middle Temple hall, Hampton Court Palace is the only other surviving venue where it is almost certain that Shakespeare played and where his plays were definitely performed; both venues, of course, being for private court entertainment. Enter through the main great gatehouse and walk through the base court into the clock court. On your left is the **great hall (1)** (NGR 515715 168485) and the **great chamber (2)** (NGR 515738 168480), both of which were used for performances.

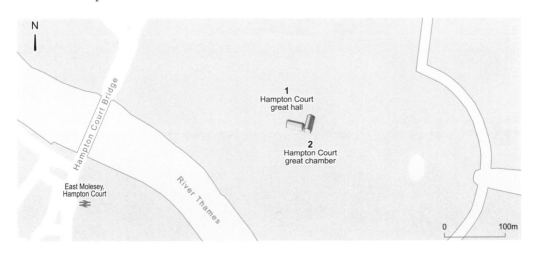

Walk 8 – Richmond

There was a medieval priory at Sheen, but it was pulled down by Henry VII, who then built a luxurious palace there and named it after his earldom of Richmond in Yorkshire. Our Richmond is about 15 miles (24km) south-west of central London, but is at the end of the District Line on the underground or a quicker journey on overland railway from Waterloo station.

A 10-minute walk from Richmond station towards the river, then veering right/west will bring you to the area of the palace, though very little remains. The main **gatehouse (1)** survives, as two private houses off Maids of Honour Row (NGR 517571 174941) and there are a couple of stretches of walling. An early plan of the site and archaeological excavations there have helped to refine the layout of the palace, though it should be stressed that most areas are now in private hands. The site of the **great hall (2)** was at NGR 517514 174890 and the **great chamber (3)** in gardens to the south-west at c NGR 517479 174846.

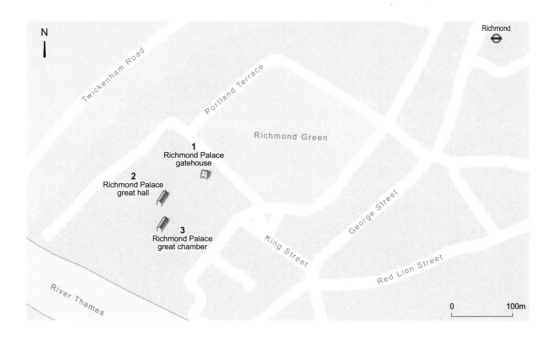

12

Kemps nine daies vvonder.

Performed in a daunce from
London to Norwich.

Containing the pleasure, paines and kinde entertainment
of *William Kemp* betweene *London* and that Citty
in his late Morrice.

Wherein is somewhat set downe worth note; to reprooue
the slaunders spred of him: many things merry,
nothing hurtfull.

Written by himselfe to satisfie his friends.

LONDON
Printed by *E. A.* for *Nicholas Ling*, and are to be
solde at his shop at the west doore of Saint
Paules Church. 1600.

SOURCES USED AND FURTHER READING

Introduction

J Bate and D Thornton 2012 *Shakespeare: staging the world*, London

Bob Dylan 1966 Stuck inside of Mobile with the Memphis blues again, in *Blonde on blonde* album, Nashville

Tudor London

Administrative, social and economic life

R Ashton, 1983 Popular entertainment and social control in later Elizabethan and early Stuart London, *London Journal* 9, 3–19

F C Chalfont, 1978 *Ben Jonson's London: a Jacobean placename dictionary*, Athens

M Eccles, 1982 Tudor and Stuart authors, *Studies in Philology* 79(4), 1–135

M C Erler (ed), 2008 Ecclesiastical London, *Records of Early English Drama*, London and Toronto, 206

M Hattaway, 2009 Dating *As you like it*, epilogues and prayers, and the problems of 'As the dial hand tells o'er', *Shakespeare Quarterly* 60(2), 154–67

I H Jeayes (ed), 1906 *The Letters of Philip Gawdy of West Harling, Norfolk, and of London to various members of his family, 1579–1616*, London

L Picard, 2003 *Elizabeth's London: everyday life in Elizabethan London*, London

S Porter, 2009 *Shakespeare's London: everyday life in London 1580-1616*, Stroud

A Saunders and J Schofield (eds), 2001 *Tudor London: a map and a view*, London Topographical Society Publication no. 159, London

E H Sugden, 1925 *A topographical dictionary to the works of Shakespeare and his fellow dramatists*, Manchester

Shakespeare in London

T Cooper (ed), 2006 *Searching for Shakespeare*, National Portrait Gallery, London

N MacGregor, 2012 *Shakespeare's restless world*, Harmondsworth

C Nichol, 2007 *The lodger: Shakespeare on Silver Street*, London

S Schoenbaum, 1975 *William Shakespeare: a documentary life*, Oxford

M Wood, 2004 *In search of Shakespeare*, London

Theatre in London

History and development

J Quincy Adams, 1917 *Shakespearean playhouses: a history of English theatres from the beginnings to the Restoration*, New York

J H Astington, 1991 The origins of the Roxana and Messalina illustrations, *Shakespeare Survey* 43, 149–69

J Bate and D Thornton, 2012 *Shakespeare: staging the world*, London

H Berry, 1991 *The noble science: a study and transcription of Sloane MS 2530, papers of the Masters of Defence of London, temp Henry VIII to 1590*, Newark, Delaware, and London

H Berry, 1998 Folger MS V.b.275 and the deaths of Shakespearean playhouses, in *Medieval and Renaissance drama in England* 10 (ed J Pitcher), 262–93

H Berry, 1987   *Shakespeare's playhouses*, New York

G E Bentley, 1941–68   *The Jacobean and Caroline Stage* (7 vols), Oxford

L Boynton, 1967   *The Elizabethan militia, 1558–1638*, London

J Bowlton, 1987 *Neighbourhood and society: a London suburb in the seventeenth century*, Cambridge

M Butler, 1984   Two playgoers, and the closing of the London theatres, 1642, *Theatre Research International* 9(2), 93–8

L B Campbell, 1941   Richard Tarlton and the earthquake of 1580, *Huntingdon Library Quarterly* 4(3), 293–301

F C Chalfont, 1978   *Ben Jonson's London: a Jacobean placename dictionary*, Athens

E K Chambers, 1923   *The Elizabethan stage* (4 vols), Oxford

C G Cruickshank, 1966   *Elizabeth's army*, Oxford

D Crystal and B Crystal, 2002   *Shakespeare's words*, London

M Eccles, 1982   Tudor and Stuart authors, *Studies in Philology* 79(4), 1–135

M Eccles, 1991   Elizabethan actors I: A–D, *Notes and Queries* 236(1), 38–49

M Eccles, 1991   Elizabethan actors II: E–J, *Notes and Queries* 236(4), 454–61

M Eccles, 1992   Elizabethan actors III: K–R, *Notes and Queries* 237(3), 293–303

M Eccles, 1993   Elizabethan actors IV: S–Z, *Notes and Queries* 238(2), 165–76

G Egan, 2003   Theatre in London, in *Shakespeare: an Oxford guide* (eds S Wells and L Cowen Orlin), 22–33, Oxford

A Feuillerat, 1908   *Documents relating to the Office of the Revels in the time of Queen Elizabeth*, Louvain

R A Foakes, 1985   *Illustrations of the English stage, 1580–1642*, London

R A Foakes, 2000   *Henslowe's diary*, Cambridge

I H Jeayes (ed), 1906   *The letters of Philip Gawdy of West Harling, Norfolk, and of London to various members of his family,*
    1579–1616, 120–1, London

A Gurr, 2009   *The Shakespearean stage 1574–1642*, 4 edn, Cambridge

A Gurr, 2004   *Playgoing in Shakespeare's London*, chapter 5, Cambridge

E A J Honigman and S Brock, 1993   *Playhouse wills 1558–1641*, Manchester

W Ingram, 1992   *The business of playing*, chapter 6, Ithaca, New York

A Lancashire, 2002   *London civic theatre*, Cambridge

K Melnikoff, 2005   Jones's pen and Marlowe's socks: Richard Jones, print culture, and the beginnings of English
    dramatic literature, *Studies in Philology* 102(2), 184–209

T F Ordish, 1904   *Shakespeare's London, a commentary on Shakespeare's life and work in London: a new edition with a chapter on*
    Westminster and an itinerary of sites and reliques, London

B D Palmer, 2005   Early modern mobility: players, payments and patrons, *Shakespeare Quarterly* 56, 259–305

S Porter, 2009   *Shakespeare's London: everyday life in London 1580–1616*, Stroud

E Nungezer, 1929   *A dictionary of actors and other persons associated with the public representation of plays in England before 1642*,
    New York

A Saunders and J Schofield, 2001   *Tudor London: a map and a view*, London Topographical Society Publication no. 159,
    London

T Stern, 2009   *Documents of performance in early modern England*, Cambridge

E H Sugden, 1925   *A topographical dictionary to the works of Shakespeare and his fellow dramatists*, Manchester

B Traister, 2001   *The notorious astrological physician of London: works and days of Simon Foreman*, Chicago

K Tyler, 2000   The 'western stream' reconsidered: excavations at the medieval Great Wardrobe, Wardrobe Place, City
    of London, *Transactions London Middlesex Archaeological Society* 51, 21–44

G Wickham, 1959–72 *Early English stages, 1300–1660* (3 vols), London

G Wickham, H Berry and W Ingram, 2000   *English professional theatre, 1530–1660*, Cambridge

J Wilson, 1997   *The archaeology of Shakespeare: material legacy of Shakespeare's theatre*, Stroud

J Wright, 1699   *Historia histrionica: an historical account of the English stage shewing the ancient use, improvement, and perfection of dramatick representations in this nation: in a dialogue of plays and players*, printed by G Groom for the bookseller William Hawes (his shop was at the sign of the Rose, in Ludgate Street)

The playing companies

A Gurr, 1996   *The Shakespearian playing companies*, Oxford

S Keenan, 2002   *Travelling players in Shakespeare's England*, Basingstoke

L Munro, 2005   *Children of the Queen's Revels: a Jacobean theatre repertory*, Cambridge

H Ostovich, H Schott Syme and A Griffin (eds), 2009   *Locating the Queen's Men, 1583–1603: material practices and conditions of playing*, Farnham

T Schoone-Jongen, 2008   *Shakespeare's companies: William Shakespeare's early career and the acting companies, 1577–94*, Farnham

G Wickham, H Berry and W Ingram, 2000   *English professional theatre, 1530–1660*, Cambridge

The city inns

H Berry, 1991   *The noble science: a study and transcription of Sloane MS 2530, papers of the Masters of Defence of London, temp Henry VIII to 1590,* Newark, Delaware, and London

H Berry, 2000   The Bell Savage inn and playhouse in London, *Medieval & Renaissance Drama in England* 19, 121–43

O Brownstein, 1971   A record of London inn-playhouses from *c* 1565–90, *Shakespeare Quarterly* 22(1), 17–24

M Carlin, 1996   *Medieval Southwark*, London (see esp chapter 8, Inns and alehouses, hucksters and victuallers)

E K Chambers, 1923   *The Elizabethan stage* (4 vols), vol 2, 380–3, Oxford

D Kathman, 2009   Alice Layston and the Cross Keys, *Medieval and Renaissance Drama in England* 22, 144–78

R Dutton (ed), 2009   *The Oxford handbook of early modern theatre*, Oxford

D Mateer, 2006   New light on the early history of the Theater in Shoreditch, *English Literary Renaissance* 36(3), 335–75

L Manley, 2008   Why did London inns function as theaters? *Huntington Library Quarterly* 71(1), 181–97

D F Rowan, 1981   Inns, inn-yards and other playing places, *Elizabethan Theatre* 9, 1–20

D Salkend, 2004   The Bell and the Bel Savage inns, 1576–7, *Notes and Queries* 51, 242–3

G Wickham, H Berry and W Ingram, 2000   *English professional theatre, 1530–1660*, chapters 17–20, 295–305, Cambridge

The playhouses

Introduction

J M C Bowsher, 2011   Twenty years on: the archaeology of 'Shakespeare's' London playhouses, *Shakespeare, Journal of the British Shakespeare Association* 7(4), 452–66

J Bowsher and P Miller, 2009   *The Rose and the Globe – playhouses of Shakespeare's Bankside, Southwark: excavations 1988–90*, MOLA Monograph Series 48, London

R A Foakes, 1985   *Illustrations of the English stage, 1580–1642*, London

R A Foakes, 2000   *Henslowe's diary*, Cambridge

The Red Lion, Whitechapel

W Ingram, 1992   *The business of playing*, chapter 4, 92–114, Ithaca, New York

G Wickham, H Berry and W Ingram, 2000   *English professional theatre, 1530–1660*, chapter 16, 290–4, Cambridge

Newington Butts 1576

E K Chambers, 1923   *The Elizabethan stage* (4 vols), vol 2, 404–5, Oxford

W Ingram, 1992   *The business of playing*, chapter 6, 150–81, Ithaca, New York

G Wickham, H Berry and W Ingram, 2000   *English professional theatre, 1530–1660*, chapter 22, 320–9, Cambridge

The Theatre, Shoreditch, 1576

J M C Bowsher, 2007   Holywell Priory and the Theatre in Shoreditch, *London Archaeologist* 11(9), 231–4

H Berry (ed), 1979   *The first public playhouse: the Theatre in Shoreditch 1576–98*, Montreal

J Bird and P Norman (eds), 1922   *The parish of St Leonard, Shoreditch*, Survey of London 8, London

W H Braines, 1917   The site of the Theatre, Shoreditch, *Records London Topographical Society* 11, 1–27

E K Chambers, 1923   *The Elizabethan stage* (4 vols), vol 2, 383–400, Oxford

W Ingram, 1992   *The business of playing*, chapter 7, 182–218, Ithaca, New York

H Knight, 2009   Shakespeare's Theatre? Excavations at 4–6 New Inn Broadway, London EC2, *Post-Medieval Archaeology* 43(2), 347–9

D Mateer, 2006   New light on the early history of the Theater in Shoreditch, *English Literary Renaissance* 36(3), 335–75

C W Wallace, 1913   *The first London theatre: materials for a history*, Lincoln, Nebraska

G Wickham, H Berry and W Ingram, 2000   *English professional theatre, 1530–1660*, chapter 23, 330–87, Cambridge

The Curtain, Shoreditch, 1577

G E Bentley, 1941–68   *The Jacobean and Caroline stage* (7 vols), vol 6, 131–9, Oxford

H Berry, 2000   The view of London from the north and the playhouses in Holywell, *Shakespeare Survey* 53, 196–212

J Bird and P Norman (eds), 1922   *The parish of St Leonard, Shoreditch*, Survey of London 8, London

E K Chambers, 1923   *The Elizabethan stage* (4 vols), vol 2, 400–4, Oxford

G Egan, 2000   Thomas Platter's account of an unknown play at the Curtain or the Boar's Head, *Notes and Queries* 245, 53–6

R A Foakes, 1985   *Illustrations of the English stage, 1580–1642*, London

W Ingram, 1992   *The business of playing*, chapter 8, 219–38, Ithaca, New York

R Linnell, 1977   *The Curtain playhouse*, London

A Saunders and J Schofield (eds), 2001   *Tudor London: a map and a view*, London Topographical Society Publication no. 159, London

C W Wallace, 1913   *The first London theatre: materials for a history*, Lincoln, Nebraska

G Wickham, H Berry and W Ingram, 2000   *English professional theatre, 1530–1660*, chapter 25, 404–18, Cambridge

The George, Whitechapel, 1580

W Ingram, 1992   *The business of playing*, chapter 7, 182–218, Ithaca, New York

C J Sisson, 1972   *The Boar's Head theatre – an inn yard theatre of the Elizabethan age*, London

G Wickham, H Berry and W Ingram, 2000   *English professional theatre, 1530–1660*, Cambridge

The Rose, Bankside, 1587

J Bowsher and P Miller, 2009   *The Rose and the Globe – playhouses of Shakespeare's Bankside, Southwark: excavations 1988–90*, MOLA Monograph Series 48, London

E K Chambers, 1923   *The Elizabethan stage* (4 vols), vol 2, 405–10, Oxford

G Wickham, H Berry and W Ingram, 2000   *English professional theatre, 1530–1660*, chapter 26, 419–36, Cambridge

The Swan, Bankside

H Berry, 2001   Richard Vennar, England's joy, *English Literary Renaissance* 31(2), 240–65

E K Chambers, 1923   *The Elizabethan stage* (4 vols), vol 2, 411–14, Oxford

B J Corrigan, 2001   Of dogges and gulls: sharp dealing at the Swan (1597) ... and again at St Paul's (1606), *Theatre Notebook* 55(3), 119–29

T S Graves, 1912   A note on the Swan theatre, *Modern Philology* 9(3), 431–4

W Ingram, 1978   *A London life in the brazen age: Francis Langley, 1548–1602*, Harvard

C W Wallace, 1911   The Swan theatre and the Earl of Pembroke's servants, *Englische Studien* 43, 340–95

G Wickham, H Berry and W Ingram, 2000 *English professional theatre, 1530–1660*, chapter 27, 437–51, Cambridge

The Boar's Head, Aldgate

H Berry, 1986 *The Boar's Head playhouse*, London and Toronto

G Wickham, H Berry and W Ingram, 2000 *English professional theatre, 1530–1660*, chapter 28, 452–92, Cambridge

The Globe, Bankside

G E Bentley, 1941–68 *The Jacobean and Caroline stage* (7 vols), vol 6, 178–99, Oxford

J Bowsher and P Miller, 2009 *The Rose and the Globe – playhouses of Shakespeare's Bankside, Southwark: excavations 1988–90*, MOLA Monograph Series 48, London

W W Braines, 1924 *The site of the Globe playhouse, Southwark*, 2 edn, London

E K Chambers, 1923 *The Elizabethan stage* (4 vols), vol 2, 414–34, Oxford

W Ingram, 1984 The Globe playhouse and its neighbors in 1600, *Essays in Theatre* 2, 63–72

G Wickham, H Berry and W Ingram, 2000 *English professional theatre, 1530–1660*, Cambridge

The Fortune, Cripplegate, 1600 and 1623

J Astington, 2006 Playing the man: acting at the Red Bull and the Fortune, *Early Theatre* 9(2), 130–43

G E Bentley, 1941–68 *The Jacobean and Caroline stage* (7 vols), vol 6, 139–77, Oxford

E K Chambers, 1923 *The Elizabethan stage* (4 vols), Oxford

G Wickham, H Berry and W Ingram, 2000 *English professional theatre, 1530–1660*, Cambridge

Wapping, 1600

E K Chambers, 1923 *The Elizabethan stage* (4 vols), vol 4, 327, Oxford

J Cox, 1994 *London's east end (life and traditions)*, p 64, London

M B Honeybourne, 1929 Two plans of the precinct and adjoining property of St Mary Graces, *Transactions London Middlesex Archaeological Society* 6, 199–204

The Red Bull, Clerkenwell, 1606

J Astington, 2006 Playing the man: acting at the Red Bull and the Fortune, *Early Theatre* 9(2), 130–43

H Berry, 2005 Building playhouses, the accession of James I and the Red Bull, *Medieval and Rennaissance Drama in England* 18, 61–74

G E Bentley, 1941–68 *The Jacobean and Caroline stage* (7 vols), vol 6, 214–46, Oxford

E K Chambers, 1923 *The Elizabethan stage* (4 vols), Oxford

E Griffith, 2001 New material for a Jacobean playhouse: the Red Bull theatre on the Seckford Estate, *Theatre Notebook* 55, 5–23

E Griffith, 2011 Martin Slatiar and the Red Bull playhouse, *Huntington Library Quarterly* 74(4), 553–74

W Ingram, 2002 Playhouses make strange bedfellows: the case of Aaron and Martin, *Shakespeare Studies* 30, 118–27

G Wickham, H Berry and W Ingram, 2000 *English professional theatre, 1530–1660*, Cambridge

The Hope, Bankside, 1613

W W Braines, 1924 *The site of the Globe playhouse, Southwark*, 2 edn, London

O Brownstein, 1979 'Why didn't Burbage lease the beargarden?': a conjecture in comparative architecture, in *The first public playhouse: the Theatre in Shoreditch 1576–1598* (ed H Berry), 81–96, Montreal

E K Chambers, 1923 *The Elizabethan stage* (4 vols), Oxford

J Lawrence and W H Godfrey, 1920, The bear-garden contract of 1606 and what it implies, *Architectural Review* 47, 152–5

A Mackinder with L Blackmore, J Bowsher and C Phillpotts, in prep *Excavations at Riverside House and New Globe Walk, Bankside, Southwark*, MOLA Studies Series

G Wickham, H Berry and W Ingram, 2000 *English professional theatre, 1530–1660*, Cambridge

The theatres

Introduction

J H Astington, 1991a   The origins of the Roxana and Messalina illustrations, *Shakespeare Survey* 43, 149–69

E K Chambers, 1923   *The Elizabethan stage* (4 vols), Oxford

J Orrell, 1984   The private theatre auditorium, *Theatre Research International* 9, 79–93

St Paul's

H Berry, 2000   Where was the playhouse in which the boy choristers of St Paul's performed plays?, *Medieval and Renaissance Drama in English* 13, 101–16

R Bowers, 2000   The playhouse of the choristers of St Paul's, *c* 1575–1608, *Theatre Notebook* 54(2), 70–85

R Gair, 1982   *The Children of Paul's: the story of a theatre company, 1553–1608*, Cambridge

J Schofield, 2011   *St Paul's Cathedral before Wren*, London

G Wickham, H Berry and W Ingram, 2000   *English professional theatre, 1530–1660*, Cambridge

First and second Blackfriars

G E Bentley, 1941–68   *The Jacobean and Caroline stage* (7 vols), vol 6, 3–43, Oxford

A Feuillerat, 1913   *Blackfriars records*, Malone Society Collections 2(1), Oxford

I Smith, 1966   *Shakespeare's Blackfriars playhouse: its history and its design*, London

G Wickham, H Berry and W Ingram, 2000   *English professional theatre, 1530–1660*, Cambridge

Whitefriars 1606

G E Bentley, 1941–68   *The Jacobean and Caroline stage* (7 vols), vol 6, 115–20, Oxford

A W Clapham, 1910   The topography of the Carmelite priory of London, *Journal British Archaeological Association* ns 17, 15–31

M C Erler (ed), 2008   *Ecclesiastical London*, Records of Early English Drama, 206, London and Toronto

J Greenstreet 1887–92   The Whitefriars theatre in the time of Shakspere, *Transactions of the New Shakspere Society* 13, 269–84

J MacIntyre 1996   Production resources at the Whitefriars playhouse, 1609–12, *Early Modern Literary Studies* 2(3), 1–35

A W Martin, 1927   The excavations at Whitefriars, Fleet Street, 1927–28: report of committee, *Journal British Archaeological Association* ns 30, 293–320

L Munro, 2005   *Children of the Queen's Revels: a Jacobean theatre repertory*, Cambridge

J MacIntyre, 1996   Production resources at the Whitefriars playhouse, 1609–12, *Early Modern Literary Studies* 2(3), 1–35

G Wickham, H Berry and W Ingram, 2000   *English professional theatre, 1530–1660*, Cambridge

Porter's Hall, Blackfriars, 1615

S R Cerasano 1989   Competition for the King's Men?: Alleyn's Blackfriars venture, *Medieval and Renaissance Drama in England* 4, 173–86

G E Bentley, 1941–68   *The Jacobean and Caroline stage* (7 vols), vol 6, 77–86, Oxford

G Wickham, H Berry and W Ingram, 2000   *English professional theatre, 1530–1660*, Cambridge

Phoenix, Drury Lane, 1616

J Quincy Adams, 1917   *Shakespearean playhouses: a history of English theatres from the beginnings to the Restoration*, New York

G E Bentley, 1941–68   *The Jacobean and Caroline stage* (7 vols), vol 6, 47–76, Oxford

G F Barlow, 1988   Wenceslas Hollar and Christopher Beeston's Phoenix theatre in Drury Lane, *Theatre Research International* 13, 30–44

J Harris and G Higgott, 1989   *Inigo Jones, complete architectural drawings*, 266–9, London

G Wickham, H Berry and W Ingram, 2000   *English professional theatre, 1530–1660*, Cambridge

Salsibury Court, 1629

J H Astington, 1991   The Messalina stage and Salisbury Court plays, *Theatre Journal* 43, 141–56

G E Bentley, 1941–68   *The Jacobean and Caroline stage* (7 vols), vol 6, 86–114, Oxford

P Bordinat, 1956   A new site for the Salisbury Court theatre, *Notes and Queries* 201, 51–2

O L Brownstein, 1977   New light on the Salisbury Court playhouse, *Educational Theatre Journal* 29, 231–42

G Wickham, H Berry and W Ingram, 2000   *English professional theatre, 1530–1660*, Cambridge

Other venues: the royal palaces and the Inns of Court

The royal palaces

J H Astington, 1982   The Whitehall Cockpit: the building and the theatre, *English Literary Review* 12, 301–18

J H Astington, 1999   *English court theatre, 1558–1642*, Cambridge

J Bate and E Rasmussen (eds), 2009   *William Shakespeare, the sonnets and other poems*, Stratford

G E Bentley, 1941–68   *The Jacobean and Caroline stage* (7 vols), vol 6, 255–90, Oxford

H M Colvin (ed), 1963–82   *The history of the king's works* (6 vols), London; vol 4, part ii, 1485–1660, is most relevant to our period

J Cloake, 2001   *Richmond Palace: its history and its plan*, Richmond Local History Society, London

R Cowie and J Cloake, 2001   An archaeological survey of Richmond Palace, Surrey, *Post-Medieval Archaeology* 35, 3–52

D DeMarly, 1981   The Cockpit-in-Court, *Theatre Notebook* 35(1), 32

H J M Green and S J Thurley, 1987   Excavations on the west side of Whitehall 1960–2: Part 1, From the building of the Tudor palace to the construction of the modern offices of state, *Transactions London Middlesex Archaeological Society* 38, 59–130

J Harris and G Higgott, 1989   *Inigo Jones, complete architectural drawings*, London, 266–9

M Hattaway, 2009   Dating *As you like it*, epilogues and prayers, and the problems of 'As the dial hand tells o'er', *Shakespeare Quarterly* 60(2), 154–67

S Orgel and R Strong, 1973   *Inigo Jones: the theatre and the Stuart court* (2 vols), London

J Orrell, 1977   The Paved Court theatre at Somerset House, *British Library Journal* 3(1), 13–19

S Thurley, 1999   *Whitehall Palace, an architectural history of the royal apartments 1260–1698*, Yale

S Thurley, 2004   *Hampton Court Palace: a social and architectural history*, Yale

S Thurley, 2008   *Whitehall Palace: the official illustrated history,* London

S Thurley, 2009   *Somerset House, the palace of England's queens 1551–1692*, London Topographical Society Publications no. 168

D Wood and J Munby, 2003   The historical development of Somerset House: an archaeological investigation, *Transactions London Middlesex Archaeological Society* 54, 79–110

The Inns of Court

M Knapp and M Kobialka, 1984   Shakespeare and the Prince of Purpoole: the 1594 production of *The comedy of errors* at Gray's Inn hall, *Theatre History Studies* 4, 70–81

A H Nelson and J R Elliott Jr (eds), 2010   *Inns of Court* (3 vols), Woodbridge

Animal-baiting arenas

C Barron, C Coleman and C Gobbi (eds), 1983   The London journal of Alessandro Magno, 1562, *London Journal* 9, 136–52

W W Braines, 1924   *The site of the Globe playhouse, Southwark*, 2 edn, London

O Brownstein, 1969   The popularity of baiting in England before 1600: a study in social and theatrical history, *Educational Theatre Journal* 21(3), 237–50

O Brownstein, 1979   'Why didn't Burbage lease the Beargarden?': a conjecture in comparative architecture, in *The first public playhouse: the Theatre in Shoreditch 1576–1598* (ed H Berry), 81–96, Montreal

E K Chambers, 1923   *The Elizabethan stage* (4 vols), Oxford

R Crowley, 1550   *One and thyrtye epigrammes, wherein are bryefly touched so many abuses, that maye and ought to be put away*, London

G E Dawson 1964   London's bull-baiting and bear-baiting arena in 1562, *Shakespeare Quarterly* 15(1), 97–101

C L Kingsford, 1920   Paris Garden and the bear baiting, *Archaeologia* 70, 155–78

J Lawrence and W H Godfrey, 1920   The Bear-Garden contract of 1606 and what it implies, *Architectural Review* 47, 152–5

A Mackinder and S Blatherwick, 2000   *Bankside: excavations at Benbow House Southwark, London SE1*, MoLAS Archaeology Studies Series 3, London

A Mackinder, with L Blackmore, J Bowsher, and C Phillpotts, in prep   *Excavations at Riverside House and New Globe Walk, Bankside, Southwark*, MOLA Studies Series

Survey of London, 1950 *Bankside (the parishes of St Saviour and Christchurch Southwark)*, Survey of London 22, London

Players, playhouses and playgoers

The players

M Edmonds, 1992   Peter Street, 1553–1609: builder of playhouses, *Shakespeare Survey* 45, 101–14

The playhouses

See sources cited for Theatre in London and The playhouses, above.

Production and staging

J Bowsher and P Miller, 2009   *The Rose and the Globe – playhouses of Shakespeare's Bankside, Southwark: excavations 1988–90*, MOLA Monograph Series 48, London

S P Cerasano, 1993   Philip Henslowe, Simon Forman, and the theatrical community of the 1590s, *Shakespeare Quarterly* 44(2), 145–58

G Egan, 2005   *Material culture in London in an age of transition: Tudor and Stuart period finds c 1450–c 1700 from excavations at riverside sites in Southwark*, MoLAS Monograph Series 19, London

A Gurr, 2004   *Playgoing in Shakespeare's London*, Cambridge

A Gurr and M Ichikawa, 2000   *Staging in Shakespeare's theatres*, Oxford Shakespeare Topics, Oxford

Conclusions

M Butler, 1984   Two playgoers, and the closing of the London theatres, 1642, *Theatre Research International* 9(2), 93–8

A Gurr, 2004   *Playgoing in Shakespeare's London*, Cambridge

Walks

W Thornbury and E Walford, 1878 *Old and new London*, London

Walk 1 – the city

D Gadd and T Dyson, 1981   Bridewell Palace: excavations at 9–11 Bridewell Place and 1–3 Tudor Street, City of London, 1978, *Post-Medieval Archaeology* 15, 1–79

P Hunting, 1998   *A history of the Society of Apothecaries*, London

P Marsden, T Dyson and M Rhodes, 1975   Excavations on the site of St Mildred's church, Bread Street, London, 1973–4, *Transactions London Middlesex Archaeological Society* 26, 171–208

S Schoenbaum, 1975   *William Shakespeare: a documentary life*, Oxford

K Tyler, 2000   The 'western stream' reconsidered: excavations at the medieval Great Wardrobe, Wardrobe Place, City of London, *Transactions London Middlesex Archaeological Society* 51, 21–44

Walk 2 – the east

J Cox, 1994   *London's east end (life and traditions)*, London

M B Honeybourne, 1929 Two plans of the precinct and adjoining property of St Mary Graces, *Transactions London Middlesex Archaeological Society* 6, 19–23.

Walk 3 – the north

Anon, 1609 *Ancient drolleries (no. 2): Pymlico, or, Runne Red-cap; tis a mad world at Hogsdon* (reproduced 1891 in facsimile with a preface by A H Bullen), Oxford

M Eccles, 1934 *Christopher Marlowe in London*, Cambridge Mass

A Freeman, 1967 *Thomas Kyd, facts and problems*, Oxford

A Lancashire, 2006 Multi-day performance and the London Clerkenwell play, *Early Theatre* 9(2), 114–29

J Dillon, 2008 Clerkenwell and Smithfield as a neglected home of London theatre, *Huntingdon Library Quarterly* 71(1), 115–35

Walk 4 – the south

M Carlin, 1996 *Medieval Southwark, London*, chapter 8 Inns and alehouses, hucksters and victuallers

W Rendle and P Norman, 1888 *The inns of old Southwark and their associations*, London

Survey of London, 1950 *Bankside (the parishes of St Saviour and Christchurch Southwark)*, Survey of London 22, London

Walk 5 –Walk 8

For the West End and palaces, see sources cited for The theatres and Other venues, above.

WEBSITES

http://www.museumoflondonarchaeology.org.uk/ (MOLA)

http://www.museumoflondon.org.uk/london-wall/ (MOL)

http://www.americanshakespearecenter.com/

http://www.bl.uk/ (British Library)

http://www.britishmuseum.org/

http://www.cityoflondon.gov.uk/Corporation/LGNL_Services/Leisure_and_culture/Records_and_archives/ (London Metropolitan Archives)

http://www.emlot.kcl.ac.uk/ (Early Modern London Theatres)

http://www.explorethetheatre.co.uk (Cloak and Dagger Studios)

http://www.henslowe-alleyn.org.uk/index.html

http://www.hrp.org.uk/HamptonCourtPalace/

http://www.middletemple.org.uk/the_inn/History_of_the_Inn/Middle_Temple_Hall.html

http://www.nationalarchives.gov.uk/default.htm

http://www.oldroyalnavalcollege.org/ (Greenwich)

http://www.reed.utoronto.ca/index.html (Records of Early English Drama)

http://www.shakespearesglobe.com/

http://www.shakespeare.org.uk/home.html (Shakespeare Birthplace Trust)

http://www.shalt.org.uk/ (Shakespearean London Theatres)

PICTURE ACKNOWLEDGEMENTS

MOLA would like to thank the copyright holders for granting permission to reproduce the images illustrated. Images not listed below are © MOLA (except maps etc, pages 43, 45, 46, 105, 150, 153, 202, 211, 217, 220).

cover   Museum of London (139485)

page 10   Yale Center for British Art, Paul Mellon Collection (B1977.48.5548)

page 14   Museum of London (204607)

page 17   see p14

page 18   Museum of London (139485)

page 23   Bridgeman Art Library

page 24   The Shakespeare Globe Trust

page 30   National Portrait Gallery, London (NPG 2082)

page 31   Pepys Library, Magdalene College, Cambridge (PL 2980/311b)

page 33   The Masters and Fellows of Corpus Christi College, Cambridge

page 33   National Portrait Gallery, London (NPG 1)

page 35   by permission of the Trustees of Dulwich Picture Gallery

page 44   The British Library Board (C.40.c.29)

page 48   see p18

page 51   The Shakespeare Globe Trust

page 65   with permission of the London Topographical Society and Clive Burden

page 69   Fulgoni Copyrights Ltd 1989–2009

page 71   Guildhall Library, City of London (COLLAGE 30062)

page 75   National Library of Sweden, Stockholm (KB, KoB Delag 89)

page 80   National Library of Sweden, Stockholm (KB, KoB Delag 89)

page 82   City of London, London Metropolitan Archives (M/92/143)

page 84   University Library Utrecht, Netherlands (MS 842, fo 132r)

page 87   by permission of the Folger Shakespeare Library

page 88   by permission of the Trustees of Dulwich Picture Gallery

page 90   see p10

page 93   Guildhall Library, City of London (COLLAGE 31774)

page 97   The British Library Board (C.34.d.38, title page)

page 99   with kind permission of the Governors of Dulwich College (Mun. 22r)

page 100   Tsubouchi Memorial Theatre Museum at Waseda University, Tokyo, Japan

page 102   The British Library Board (162.d.35, title page)

page 103   City of London, London Metropolitan Archives (SC/GL/PR/GP/002)

page 107   The Huntingdon Library, San Marino, California

page 108   The British Library Board (C.71.h.23)

page 111   National Portrait Gallery, London (NPG 2752)

page 114   The British Library Board (238.L.24, title page)

page 117   Guildhall Library, City of London (COLLAGE 5916)

page 121   courtesy of the American Shakespeare Center; photograph by Tommy Thompson

page 122   National Portrait Gallery, London (NPG 6829)

page 125   The British Library Board, Department of Maps (Crace, portfolio 8, no. 104)

page 127   by permission of the Trustees of Dulwich Picture Gallery

page 130   The Trustees of the British Museum

page 132   The British Library Board (G.2382, title page)

page 134   Museum of London (000887)

page 137   Historic Royal Palaces

page 138   Bridgeman Art Library

page 141   see p134

page 142   Ashmolean Museum, University of Oxford

page 143   Guildhall Library, City of London (COLLAGE 21401)

page 144   Guildhall Library, City of London (COLLAGE 29580)

page 145   Ashmolean Museum, University of Oxford

page 147   reproduced by kind permission of the Masters of the Bench of the Honourable Society of the Middle Temple

page 148   Guildhall Library, City of London (COLLAGE 17997)

page 160   Museum of London (204607)

page 165   Cloak and Dagger Studios

page 168   with kind permission of the Governors of Dulwich College (MS 1, fo 20r)

page 171   Cloak and Dagger Studios

page 172   reproduced by permission of the Marquess of Bath, Longleat House, Warminster, Wiltshire

page 173   The Shakespeare Globe Trust

page 175   Cambridge University Library (Y.5.73)

page 179   The Shakespeare Globe Trust

page 187   The Shakespeare Globe Trust

page 189   Marquess of Salisbury

page 195   Bridgeman Art Library

page 199   Museum of London (65609)

page 205   The British Library Board (G.11631, title page)

page 218   Guildhall Library, City of London (COLLAGE 17287)

page 222   Guildhall Library, City of London (COLLAGE 8454)

page 231   Guildhall Library, City of London (COLLAGE 17609)

page 234   Birmingham Museums

page 239   Ashmolean Museum, University of Oxford

page 241   Bodlean Library, University of Oxford

page 242   The Shakespeare Globe Trust

page 253   see p65

page 254   see p65

INDEX